Economy, Society, and Government in Medieval Italy

ESSAYS IN MEMORY OF ROBERT L. REYNOLDS

Edited by
David Herlihy
Robert S. Lopez
and
Vsevolod Slessarev

THE KENT STATE UNIVERSITY PRESS

Economy, Society, and Government in Medieval Italy
originally appeared as Volume 7, Numbers 1 & 2 of
Explorations in Economic History
Copyright © 1969
by The Kent State University Press
Kent, Ohio 44240
Library of Congress Catalog Card Number 76-105545
Standard Book Number 87338-096-7
Printed in the United States of America

TABLE OF CONTENTS

44909

PREFACE

Several years ago, a number of friends and former students of Robert L. Reynolds began, independently of one another, to plan a collection of essays in his honor. With time, they learned of their common intention, combined their efforts, and the result is this present volume. We had hoped to present the collection to Professor Reynolds, but his death in 1966 deprived us of that satisfaction. The work now appears as a memorial, rather than a presentation volume, although Professor Reynolds was told of these plans a few weeks before his death. We hope that the book may still serve as testimony to the high esteem in which he was held, as a scholar and a person, by his students, colleagues, and friends, at home and abroad.

To those who did not meet Professor Reynolds, he is best described as of slim and yet sinuous build, with bushy eyebrows and a reassuring smile that made approaching him easy. Born on January 17, 1902, in Janesville, Wisconsin, he remained forever faithful to his native state. Studies and research took him to Paris, Ghent, and later to Genoa and Oxford; World War II brought him to London at a time when the V-bombs were falling. But these were relatively brief stays, as was his teaching engagement with the University of Nebraska, compared to decades he spent in Bascom Hall of the Madison campus, lecturing, advising students, and sitting on committees. In spite of a worsening heart condition, he insisted on meeting classes and some of the oldtimers will remember him ascending the stairs slowly a step at the time.

Professor Reynolds' forbearance with those who sought his advice equaled his patience in research and writing. The editing of the Genoese notarial cartularies, which constitute a unique source for medieval social and economic history, must have consumed years. A series of articles based in part on the notarial minutes brought him international acclaim. His last passion was for Anglo-Saxon literature, Beowulf in particular. Cautious and at the same time provocative, he shook the foundations of a sister discipline. But this challenging quest was denied completion before its results could be secured and made sufficiently public. A widower for almost a year, Professor Reynolds lost out against the old ailment, and he died in Madison on April 29, 1966.

David Herlihy
Robert S. Lopez
Vsevolod Slessarev

BIBLIOGRAPHY OF ROBERT L. REYNOLDS

compiled by JANE ACOMB LEAKE

EDITIONS OF DOCUMENTS

Hall, Margaret W.; Krueger, Hilmar C.; and Reynolds, Robert L. *Guglielmo Cassinese (1190-1192)*, in *Notai Liguri del Secolo XII*. 2 vols.; Turin, 1938.

Eierman, Joyce E.; Krueger, Hilmar C.; and Reynolds, Robert L. *Bonvillano (1198)*, in *Notai Liguri del Secolo XII*. Genoa, 1939.

Hall-Cole, Margaret W.; Krueger, Hilmar C.; Reinert, Ruth G.; and Reynolds, Robert L. *Giovanni di Guiberto (1200-1211)*, in *Notai Liguri del Secolo XII*. 2 vols.; Genoa, 1939–40.

Krueger, Hilmar C.; and Reynolds, Robert L. *Lanfranco (1202-1226)*, in *Notai Liguri del Secolo XII e del XIII*. 3 vols.; Genoa, 1951–53.

BOOKS

Europe Emerges: Transition toward an Industrial World-Wide Society, 600–1750. Madison, Wisconsin, 1961.

Clagett, Marshall; Post, Gaines; and Reynolds, Robert L., eds. *Twelfth-Century Europe and the Foundations of Modern Society*. Madison, Wisconsin, 1961.

ARTICLES

"The Market for Northern Textiles in Genoa, 1179–1200," *Revue Belge de Philologie et d'Histoire*, VIII (1929), 831–51.

"Merchants of Arras and the Overland Trade with Genoa, Twelfth Century," *Revue Belge de Philologie et d'Histoire*, IX (1930), 495–533.

"Genoese Trade in the Late Twelfth Century, Particularly in Cloth from the Fairs of Champagne," *Journal of Economic and Business History*, III (1931), 362–81.

"Some English Settlers in Genoa in the Late Twelfth Century," *Economic History Review*, IV (1933), 317–23.

"Genoese Sources for the Twelfth Century History of Liège, with Special Attention to John of Liège," in *Etudes d'Histoire Dédiées à la Mémoire de Henri Pirenne* (Brussels, 1937), pp. 291–98.

"Two Documents Concerning Elementary Education in Thirteenth-Century Genoa," *Speculum*, XII (1937), 255–56.

"Gli studi americani sulla storia genovese," *Giornale Storico e Letterario della Liguria*, XIV (1938), 1–25.

"A Business Affair in Genoa in the Year 1200; Banking, Bookkeeping, a

Broker (?) and a Lawsuit," in *Studi di Storia e Diritto in Onore di Enrico Besta,* vol. II (Milan, 1938), pp. 167–81.

"In Search of a Business Class in Thirteenth-Century Genoa," *Journal of Economic History,* Supplement V, (1945), 1–19.

Lopez, Robert S.; and Reynolds, Robert L. "Odoacer: German or Hun?" *American Historical Review,* LII (1946–47), 36–53; 836–45.

Jensen, Merrill; and Reynolds, Robert L. "European Colonial Experience: A Plea for Comparative Studies," in *Studi in Onore di Gino Luzzatto,* vol. IV (Milan, 1950), pp. 75–90.

"Bankers' Account in Double-Entry in Genoa, 1313 and 1316," *Bollettino Ligustico per la Storia e la Cultura Regionale,* III (1951), 33–37.

"Gli Archivi notarili genovesi: Lavori in corso ed in programma," *Bollettino Ligustico per la Storia e la Cultura Regionale,* III (1951), 104–07.

"Origins of Modern Business Enterprise: Medieval Italy," *Journal of Economic History,* XII (1952), 350–65.

"A Brief Survey of the Indians of the United States of America: Pre-Columbian Indians with Comments upon the Effects of European Contacts with Them," in *Studi Columbiani,* vol. I (Genoa, 1952), pp. 139–55.

"Le poème anglo-saxon *Widsith*: Réalité et fiction," *Le Moyen Age,* LIX (1953), 299–324.

"Town Origins," in *Great Problems in European Civilization,* ed. by Kenneth M. Setton and Henry D. Winkler. (Englewood Cliffs, N. J., 1954), pp. 173–205.

"An Echo of *Beowulf* in Athelstan's Charters of 931–933 A.D.?" *Medium Aevum,* XXIV (1955), 101–03.

"Eadhild, duchesse de la *Francia,* et Ealhhild, patronne du *Scop* de *Widsith,*" *Le Moyen Age,* LXI (1955), 281–89.

"Note on *Beowulf's* Date and Economic-Social History," in *Studi in Onore di Armando Sapori,* vol. I (Milan, 1957), pp. 175–78.

"Reconsideration of the History of the Suevi," *Revue Belge de Philologie et d'Histoire,* XXXV (1957), 19–47.

"The Mediterranean Frontiers, 1000–1400," in *The Frontier in Perspective,* ed. by Walker D. Wyman and Clifton B. Kroeber (Madison, Wisconsin, 1957), pp. 21–34.

"Handwriting, Illustrations: Some Problems in Economic-Historical Research," in *Studi in Onore di Amintore Fanfani,* vol. III (Milan, 1962), pp. 431–39.

TO THE FRIENDS OF ROBERT L. REYNOLDS

The thirty-seven years in which I have had the fun of functioning actively as my husband's secretary have been rich and rewarding. No one working and living with him for so long could fail to appreciate and enjoy his dominant characteristics as a person, a teacher, and a scholar: Unflagging intellectual curiosity with a very wide scope of interests; fascination with the events in the world around him, both past and present; a mind constantly open to new ideas and possible new approaches to old ideas, opinions, and conclusions; a devoted teacher, able to impart to his students some of the joys and interest of the intellectual life, always ready to give of himself to those who are really trying to expand their knowledge and abilities, whether on a high or mediocre scale; impatience always with the closed mind, the overly pretentious, the person who is trying to "get by" without an effort. His pleasure in his work is best summed up by his own remark, "How many people are lucky enough to be able to spend their lives working on their hobby?"

Along with the above have been his great pride in, and love and loyalty for, his family, his friends, his country, and his university; his personal and intellectual courage throughout his life and in the past decade despite what might have been allowed to become a devastating and embittering lack of health. Through all the years his wit and kindly approach have made living and working with him a delight, and endeared him to those about him.

On my part, I am deeply grateful to the people who have made this volume in tribute to him possible.

Sarah Chickering Reynolds

MEDIEVAL "SLAVERS"

CHARLES VERLINDEN

University, Ghent Academia Belgica, Rome

According to a common belief, slavery in the Middle Ages served exclusively domestic purposes and consequently the slave trade had only slight commercial interest. Aboard the ships traversing the Mediterranean, slaves reputedly occupied a place of scant importance among the cargoes. No doubt that is partly true, but the following pages attempt to show that some ships carried cargoes of captives, which made them *negriers*, or black slavers, before the word existed, or even the color! For among the slaves transported, Negroes still held only a restricted place.

In an article entitled "Traite des esclaves et traitants italiens à Constantinople," which appeared in *Le Moyen Age* in 1963,[1] I considered certain entries concerning the slave trade in the account books of the Venetian Giacomo Badoer,[2] regarding the years 1436–1439. In certain cases, numerous groups of slaves were apparently sent from Constantinople across the entire Mediterranean as far as Spain. Thus, from an entry of 1438 involving a "compagnia fata per el viazo de Maioricha [Majorca]," we learn that Ser Zuan Mozenigo had an investment in no less than 150 slaves, representing a capital of 16,125 hyperpers; Ser Alesandro Zen invested in 19 slaves, or 2,042 hyperpers; and Badoer himself in 13 slaves, or 1397 hyperpers.[3] Needless to say, this was large-scale commerce, at least for those times. Ser Zuan Mozenigo mentioned above insured a shipment of slaves from Modon in the Morea to Sicily, and with a partner paid 200 hyperpers for it at a 9% rate. This proves that we are dealing with a substantial shipment, probably as large as thirty heads, to judge by the average of prices mentioned in Badoer's accounts.[4] A new "Viazo de Maioricha," in which a certain Ser Marco Balanzan, whom one finds elsewhere trading at Canea in Crete, participates, involved 164 slaves. Some ships carrying similar human cargoes are already true "slavers." These voyages were long, as the ships went from the northern ports of the Black Sea (from whence came nearly all the slaves mentioned in Badoer's accounts) to Constantinople, and from there to

Chios, to Crete, to Sicily, and of course to Venice and even to Majorca and to Catalonia.[5]

A considerable number of slave cargoes were loaded in the ports of the Black Sea. On August 20, 1427, the Venetian Senate discussed the matter of 400 captives, "men and women slaves," whom the galleys "which come from the region of Tana" (that is, from the Venetian colony of Tana at the mouth of the Don) were to bring to Venice.[6] That is obviously quite a group, but we know that the Venetian *mude* or convoys were made up of many ships, and it is therefore difficult to form an idea of the number of captives who constituted the cargo of each of them. None the less, it would seem that some ships were entirely loaded with slaves. Thus, on July 26, 1410, we see in the instructions the Venetian Senate gave to its representative in Constantinople that the sultan had promised to allow a deduction of 508 ducats from the tribute paid him by the Venetians of the Bosporus "for the damage of the ship, carrying female slaves, of the noble man Nicolaus Barbus."[7] A negotiation relating to a purchase in 1416 proves that in this case it was a matter of a cargo of some 100 female slaves.[8]

Let us consider another deliberation of the Venetian Senate, dated April 30, 1423.[9] Every year, we are informed, ships from Constantinople and from Tana bring a large number of slaves to Venice. Since these ships remain for long months at sea, the captains are demanding from the owners of the slaves substantial sums for their support. The Senate consequently decided that the owner shall pay four and one-half ducats for passage and the same for food for slaves traveling from Tana to Venice; from Constantinople to Venice, it will be three and one-half ducats, twice over. If some slaves die during the voyage, their passage need not be paid, but only expenses really encountered for the support of the slave until the time of his death. For such measures to be taken certainly indicates a transport in numbers. Here is another clear instance. On January 28, 1444, the Venetian government directed a protest to the Genoese doge Raffaele Adorno concerning an attack upon the ship of Francisco Venier in the port of Chios. The 95 slaves of both sexes which Venier was taking from the Crimea to Crete had been carried off.[10]

Let us turn from the Venetian trade to that of Genoa. On May 21, 1396, a ship of Nicoloso Usodimare arrived at Genoa coming from Romania, or the Byzantine Empire. She carried, besides other merchandise, "female and male slaves, 80 heads."[11] This figure does not appear in the least bit exceptional, for in 1410 an account book from the Genoese colony of Caffa in the Crimea carries the following notation:

> Also, on May 29, for the said income of Saint Anthony in 176, So. 34, Sa. 19, and they are for Chiriachus Vellatus, master of a ship going from Sinope with 84 captives, that is, 21 from Sinope, also 18 slaves from Sinope, also for 30 captives from Bursia, also for one slave from Bursia, also for 13 captives from Samos, and others mentioned in the attached list, written by the hand of Matheus de Bargalio, notary.[12]

Here is then a cargo of 84 slaves, who doubtlessly had been purchased from the Turks whether at Sinope, Bursia, or Samos. The "income of Saint Anthony" is a tax laid on ships loaded with slaves by an office of the same name. We learn more about this office in a letter of February 1, 1424, addressed by the *officium provisionis Romanie* of Genoa to the consul at Caffa. It states that the "officium capitum Sancti Antonii" levied a tax on vessels carrying slaves in the Black Sea. From that time, this office would have agents "in whatever place from whence slaves are exported, whether in Tanai or Sevastopol or elsewhere, wherever you send ships."[13] The same text informs us that these duties are charged on the Muslim traders as well. Now, these latter frequently had Alexandria as their destination. We see this principally by a decision of 1429 by which the Genoese government abolished the tax of 3 per cent which its consul had established at Alexandria "for certain slaves detained at Caffa." These slaves were doubtlessly destined to enlarge the ranks of the Mameluke troops of Egypt, who were comprised, as is known, of slaves, in the majority Caucasians and imported preeminently by the Genoese. They had been detained at Caffa. With this, the Egyptian authorities had imposed on the Genoese of Alexandria 16,000 ducats of "outrage" [*avania*]. These latter hoped to recover the loss by imposing a tax of 3 per cent on the import and export of Genoese merchandise.[14]

On February 1, 1431, instructions were given to a Genoese embassy for presentation to the Mameluke sultan. The ambassadors were to make known the unhappiness of Genoa with the abuses perpetrated by the sultan's officers, "both in the recent scandal of the slaves and in the taxing of spices and other daily harrassments." The slaves had been detained at Caffa under the pretext that there were Christians among them, but in fact the Genoese were quite content to use this means of pressure in order to obtain necessary facilities for their commerce in spices at Alexandria. The passage we have just cited already makes us suspect this. It becomes even more evident when we examine the continuation of the ambassadorial in-

structions. The ambassadors were, in effect, to demand from the
Mameluke sovereign the restitution of the 16,000 ducats required
from the Genoese merchants of Alexandria "for the scandal of the
slaves of Caffa." If he accepts this condition and some others which
have no connection with slave trading, Genoa will again allow him
the "*tractus* of slaves from Caffa," on the condition that he agrees to
pay customs and duties. The *tractus* meant the permission for the
Muslim merchants to take from Caffa Russian, Tartar, and Cauca-
sian slaves, and to bring them to Egypt on Genoese vessels.[15]

A letter from the Genoese government to the pope, dated February 13, 1434, shows clearly that this was really the way it was in
regard to transport:[16] "From the letters of Your Holiness which we
have reverently received, we have learned that it has been calum-
niously reported against us that Genoese hands have carried Christian slaves from Caffa into Egypt and other realms of the infidel."
Genoa at once denied that her ships were transporting Christian
slaves, but not at all that she was engaged in the slave trade between
the Crimea and Egypt. Caffa, in effect, had become a "pillar of the
Christian faith," but she had concluded treaties for the slave commerce with neighboring lords, usually Tartars. According to these
treaties, slaves could be transported "beyond the limits of the Black
Sea" only on a Genoese vessel having its home port at Caffa. According to a specific law concerning this traffic, they were first of all
to be counted, then the *vectigal* or tax was to be collected for them.
Only after these two operations could they be shipped. At any rate,
before the departure of the vessel, the bishop, accompanied by religious and laymen, came aboard, called in turn the slaves, and asked
them to what nation they belonged, and whether they weren't Christians or wished to embrace the Christian faith. A slave who responded
affirmatively was taken off and sold to a Christian "in order to favor
his conversion." If these treaties and this law had not existed, one
would see "from Trebizond, Tanai, the Bosporus [Vosporo, or
Kerch], Phasis [Poti in the Caucasus] and the other ports of the
Black Sea" large numbers of Christian slaves departing for Egypt.
The Genoese, the letter concluded, merit praise rather than blame.
We can see what a subtle game the Genoese were playing with the
local powers on the northern shores of the Black Sea, with the Mameluke sultan of Egypt, and even with the papacy, in order to keep their
slave ships moving between Caffa and Alexandria. On the other
hand, the traffic was important enough to serve, to some extent, as a
counterweight in the negotiations regarding Genoese commerce at
Alexandria in general.

In the statutes of the *Officium Gazarie* of Genoa of 1441, various regulations touch upon the slave trade. They have been published by J. M. Pardessus in his *Collection de lois maritimes antérieures au XVIIIe siècle,*[17] but we have amended the text on the basis of the manuscript preserved at the *Biblioteca Civica Berio* at Genoa:

That no slaves be carried on a ship. . . . We decree and order, that no master of any galley from the Byzantine Empire or from Syria, equipped with three oars per bench, of no matter what station he may be, should dare or presume in any part of the world to carry on that galley any male or female slave, for reason of bringing or transporting them from the island of Chios and beyond, under the penalty of 25 Genoese pounds for each male or female brought or carried in violation of the said regulation. And if any notary, person aboard or officer of the said galley should place aboard her, or cause to be placed aboard her, any male or female slave without the consent of the master, he shall incur the penalty of 25 Genoese pounds.

However, the said master, notwithstanding the above regulations, may take and carry for each merchant coming with him, one slave only, whom the merchant may bring for a servant.

In ships sailing with slaves through various parts of the world, no Genoese master nor anyone who is judged as a Genoese nor anyone who enjoys a stipend from the Genoese in any part of the world, of no matter what condition or station he may be, should dare or presume in any way which can be said or imagined in any part of the world to load, place or take with him in the said vessel or carry male or female slaves beyond the number given below, under the penalty of 10 Genoese pounds for each male or female slave loaded, placed or carried beyond the said number, in order to transport them or take them from the island of Tenedos in the region of the Byzantine Empire beyond, in any part of the world, and this notwithstanding any chapter, statute or ordinance established or made to the contrary. The number beyond which it is forbidden to transport is given below.

To wit, that the master of a vessel of one deck, of no matter what condition, may legally in the said vessel transport, place, load and bring male or female slaves, or both together, to the number of 30 and no more.

The master of a vessel of two decks may legally load in the said vessel and bring male and female slaves to the number of 45 and no more.

The master of a vessel of three decks may legally place in the said vessel and bring male and female slaves to the number of 60 or no more.

However, the said masters, and each of them, may legally take in their said vessels, for each merchant sailing with them without a wage, one masculine slave, who should not be counted in the said number, it being understood that they should not incur any penalty for this.

It being excepted and reserved that any master of any navigable vessel, in which there is no cargo, saving salt and ballast, which could not be considered a cargo, may legally place in his said vessel, load, transport and bring such number of the said male and female slaves which seems better to the master and pleases him, and put them or bring them in whatever part of the world may seem good to him and please him, without that the said master should incur any penalty for this.

However, the *Officium Gazarie* is obligated and required under penalty of later review, upon the arrival of any ship carrying male or female slaves, to send to the said ship and make diligent inquiry concerning the said regulations. And if it should find any master has violated the above or any of the above, it should condemn him and hold him condemned, and must do so, for the above-mentioned penalties.

Thus, the Genoese galleys could not transport gangs of slaves beyond the island of Chios, whether they came from the Byzantine Empire or from Syria. The first category evidently included ships which came from the Black Sea too, while those from Syria meant ships from Egypt as well. It was at any rate perfectly licit for these galleys to carry slaves from the north of the Black Sea to Alexandria. It was only beyond Chios and towards the central Mediterranean where they could not transport captives. Further, we should not forget that the Genoese made very little use of galleys.

For other ships, that is to say practically for the entirety of the Genoese fleet, they could transport beyond Tenedos—the difference in route should be noted—only 30 slaves if they were of one deck (*coperta*), 45 if they had two, and 60 if they had three. But any vessel sailing in ballast could carry any number of slaves anywhere at all.

Therefore, the great stream of slave trading between the Black Sea and Egypt was affected not at all by this legislation, and even the slave trade in general was in practice scarcely touched, since the checking could be done only at Genoa by the *Officium Gazarie*. The *Officium Sancti Antonii* which received from the colonies taxes on the transported slaves had no interest in limiting the number. Let us further consider whether this legislation, elastic as it was already, was respected.

We have, for example, the ship of Marino Cigalla which arrived at Chios in 1455 with 114 slaves, which he had loaded at Cembala, that is to say, Balaklava in the Crimea. The ship was not a galley, and he therefore should not have been able to pass Tenedos with more than 60 slaves, even if his vessel had three decks, unless he was sailing in ballast (*saburra*). But who then was going to check that at Chios, which according to the legislation of 1441 occupied from that time a key position on the route from the Black Sea to Egypt, at least with regard to the slave trade? It is particularly interesting to note that the ship was valued at 75,000 hyperpers, while the slaves amounted to 136,530 hyperpers, that is to say, 180 per cent of the value of the means of transport.[18]

Information relative to the conditions of transport for the slaves is not especially abundant, but the ships plying the trade must often have been floating tombs like the Atlantic slave ships in the modern epoch. We can note, for example, 24 slaves (4 children and 20 Abkhaze women) from the Caucasus, between 12 and 28 years of age, loaded on the ship of Gaspare Judex in 1455 by Ambrosio de Benedetto. He also had on the same ship some "fusti" from Sevastopol, that is, some wood, a bulky commodity. Of course, there was other merchandise aboard, and perhaps too additional slaves belonging to other merchants. In any event, the transport cost was one ducat per head as far as Chios. Food also had been purchased for these slaves, consisting of biscuits, cheese, fish, and a barrel of Malmsey wine, which was purchased only at Pera. There was also some linen for shirts and some cloth from Catalonia of poor quality for clothes. But of the 20 young women, 8 died in the course of the trip.[19] We can only conclude one thing, that is, like on the slave ships of modern times, available space was quite restricted and epidemics rampant. Deaths then amounted here to 30 per cent, counting the children, of whom no word is given to show if they survived.

Another example in 1455 reveals how little the legislation of 1441 was respected. That year, Pietro Lomellini loaded at Rhodes to the account of a Catalonian no fewer than 74 slaves, destined for Syracuse.[20] The Genoese also conducted traffic in slaves for Moslem countries other than Egypt. Thus, in 1456, a Genoese ship in the service of the *Officium Gazarie* found itself outside Syracuse with "fevers" raging aboard. The decision was made to go, not to Tunis where the ship was supposed to land, but to Genoa. The owners of the slaves it was carrying were to pay 370 Genoese pounds, at the rate of two pounds per "head," to the other merchants in compensation for the change of itinerary. There were at this time still 185 slaves on board,[21] and it is certain that considerable numbers were already dead, for otherwise they would not have taken such an extreme measure as changing the route. It should be remembered, in fact, that a loss of 30 per cent did not stop the ship we mentioned above from landing at Chios.

The carrying of slaves destined for Moslem countries by Genoese ships coming from the Levant was not then limited to the eastern

Mediterranean, nor to Mameluke Egypt. It also supplied the Moslem countries of the western Mediterranean basin. And this draws our attention to an aspect of colonial trade in the late Middle Ages which hitherto has not been sufficiently studied: the role of Christian merchant fleets (principally Venetian, Genoese, Catalonian, and Provençal) in the Mediterranean carrying trade linking Moslem countries. This is a natural phenomenon in the colonial economy. Did not the Portuguese, and later the Dutch, serve the commerce among various Asiatic countries in a similar capacity, once they recognized their needs and the possibilities they offered to their carrying trade?[22] In the matter of the slave trade the Genoese already had clearly perceived the advantages which were thus offered them.

The *Treatise of Emmanuel Piloti on the passage to the Holy Land*, which dates from 1420, gives valuable information on the slave trade and its connections with Mameluke Egypt as a great consumption market. From the "pays du roy de Tune," that is, from Tunisia, from Barbary, and from Tripolitania came "little black slaves, 1000, or 1500, or 2000 every year, about 10 years in age, and they make them all pagans,"[23] that is to say, Moslems. Thus, young black slaves were coming from regions of the Sudan which were still not or little touched by Islam. Trans-Sahara caravans brought them to the shores of the Mediterranean, notably to the Barbary coast of Africa, and especially to Tripolitania (Barca mountains). From there, Christian ships, principally Genoese and Catalan, carried them not only into Christian countries to the north of the Mediterranean, but also from Moslem land to Moslem land. The Portuguese from 1448 would try to capture this cross-Sahara commerce at Arguim in Mauritania, and divert it towards the Atlantic.[24] They did not bother about the slave trade on the Mediterranean itself, as the small size of their fleet did not allow them to participate in it.

But let us return to the *Treatise* of Piloti, and to Alexandria as a center of the slave trade. "From Sathalia and Candilore, which are part of Turkey and border with the land of Syria" came "male and female slaves."[25] The same commerce came from Pallatia, also in Asiatic Turkey.[26] From "Gallipoli, which is on the bank of the narrows of Romania," come "much merchandise and especially Christian slaves."[27] Obviously here are countless prisoners which the Turks had taken for decades in the course of their Balkan campaigns.[28] They arrived at Gallipoli on the Dardanelles by way of Adrianople.

Here, in effect, are the words of Piloti:

Thus, in the regions of Turkey, and in the court of the Grand Turk, as it is in Adrianople and Gallipoli, there are found many great pagan merchants, who do no other business but the purchase of young slaves, male and female,[29] at an age which corresponds with the wishes of the sultan, in order to conduct them to Cairo. Some of these merchants may have 100 souls, and others 200, and they bring them to Gallipoli and load them on ships of pagans, and sometimes on ships of wicked and evilly disposed Christians.[30]

These last adjectives are understandable from the pen of the author of a pilgrimage guide, but the examples which we have cited prove sufficiently that, among these "bad Christians," the Genoese were not the least numerous.

And they take them [Piloti continues] sometimes by way of Damietta, but more frequently by way of Alexandria (where Christian merchants resided!) and from there they are carried to Cairo. And when they have arrived at Cairo in the presence of the sultan, there are some old and experienced assessors, who set the price per head. And they make a large difference from one nation to another: so much so that the most prized are the Tartars, so that one Tartar may be worth 130 or 140 ducats,[31] a Circassian may be worth 110 or 120 ducats; a Greek 90 ducats; Albanians, Slavs, Serbs from 70 to 80 ducats, more or less according to the heads.[32]

This text is extremely interesting because it shows that the overland trade route coming from the Balkans crossed the maritime route coming from the Crimea at Gallipoli. Since the same ships brought not only the Tartars and Circassians from the Black Sea to Alexandria, but also the Greeks, Albanians, Slavs, and Serbs from the Balkans, therefore it was Genoese ships above all which handled the bulk of the traffic from Caffa to Egypt, as we have already learned.

In addition, Piloti is well informed on the slave trade leaving Caffa. From there the sultan "acquired every year 2000 souls, more or less according to the times."[33] Elsewhere, Piloti speaks again of Caffa and shows how well he is aware of the slave trade carried on there:

The city of Caffa is Genoese, and is very close to and surrounded by pagan lands, such as those of the Tartars, Circassians and the Russians, and other pagan nations. To these regions the sultan of Cairo sends his agents and has them purchase slaves. These have no other way of attaining the sea but through the city of Caffa. And when these or other slaves are brought to the said place, the Genoese governors of the city inquire of them whether they wish to be Christians or pagans. Those who say that they wish to be Christian are detained; those who respond

> that they wish to be pagan are allowed to depart, and remain under the disposition of the agent of the sultan. He has them loaded on ships of very false and very wicked Christians, which take them to Alexandria, or rather to Damietta and from there to Cairo.[34]

Here Piloti does not mention carriers other than the "very false and very wicked Christians." Furthermore, what he says concerning the Christian slaves matches rather well the contents of the letter from the Genoese government to the pope which we cited above,[35] as well as that giving instructions to the consul of Caffa in 1431.[36] Piloti also knows that the sultan was sending "agents and servants" to Caffa for the slave trade.[37] Are we to believe that he is making a distinction and that the former are Christians and the latter Moslems? Perhaps that would be going too far, although we know at least one Genoese agent, Gentile Imperiali, whom Bertrandon de la Broquière met in 1432.[38]

It is worth the trouble to consider briefly the Moslem sources concerning all this traffic. We can now do something in this direction, thanks to the material recently collected by S. Y. Labib, in his *Handelsgeschichte Agyptens im Spätmittelalter (1171–1517).*[39]

We see there first of all that, at the epoch with which we are concerned, the importation of Mamelukes in Egypt was already a very ancient trade. By a decree of Baibars in 1260, we learn that the importation of slaves from the Black Sea was already considered vital by the Mameluke power of Egypt. Labib also translates an important passage of the edict as it appears in the collection of Al Qalqasandi:

> The importers of Mamelukes and young female slaves sell their merchandise at higher prices than calculated; they have, exactly as those importers who come from neighboring lands and distant regions, the right to set their prices at their discretion. Our wish aims only and exclusively at increasing our troops, and the importers of Mamelukes, supported by our generosity, observe the said right. Whoever is able to do so, let him increase the number of shipments, for our perseverance pursues as its unique goal the enlargement of the Islamic army In fact Islam owes it to these armies, that its banners have been unfurled. The Mamelukes, whom we have employed for us in this fashion, have stepped from darkness into light, and the shame of their unbelief has given place to praise which is due to their present faith. And they battle for the victory of the family and the population of Islam.[40]

Thus, the sultan consented to pay "abnormal" prices for the Mamelukes, of which Islam in Egypt had so great a need for its army. We should also emphasize equally the Moslem proselytism which served in some measure as a justification for the slave trade. One might have thought that this was a Portuguese chronicler at the beginning of the African slave trade: between the Islamic and Christian worlds, the difference, from this point of view, is minimal.

At that moment, this commerce was still not in the hands of the Italians, especially the Genoese, who only after the fall of the Latin Empire of Constantinople obtained a footing in the Black Sea. This is shown by the treaty between Byzantium and Egypt concluded in 1281, which opened the route of the Bosporus to Moslem slave merchants.[41] But it may be stated that from the end of the thirteenth century the role of Italian carriers did nothing but grow, so much the more since their commercial navigation dominated from that time the entire east and center of the Mediterranean. The intensive exploitation of the notarial and commercial archives of Genoa and of Venice would certainly permit the collection of an extended documention on this commerce, which was both important for Italian navigation and vital for the very existence of the Egyptian Mamelukes. S. Labib, who utilized only unpublished Arab documentation, gives us nothing of the sort, and the few indications which he furnishes concerning the termination of this slave trade are negated by the documentation assembled in this brief article. Thus, it cannot be stated that the destruction of Caffa and Tana in 1395 "led to the decline of the slave trade in Egypt"[42] and that the negotiations of 1431 between Genoa and the sultan, with which we were occupied above, were only, too, a passing episode.[43] In reality, it was the Turks who, shortly after the conquest of Constantinople, made an end to the importation of slaves from the Black Sea in Egypt by the Italians. They wished thereby to weaken Mameluke Egypt, the conquest of which they would undertake a few decades later.

Besides, for a long time and in quite different circumstances, notice had been taken that the suppression of the slave trade was the best means of ruining the Mameluke strength in Egypt. Already in 1311, during the General Council of Vienna, a memoir had been sent by the ambassadors of the king of Cyprus to Pope Clement V concerning the means of reconquering the Holy Land and destroying the power of the sultans of Egypt.[44] This document called attention to the necessity of intercepting and seizing Christian ships which were carrying slaves into Egypt and thus were supplying the Mameluke battalions.[45] These Mamelukes, the text added, were imported into Egypt from Turkey, which is to say at that moment, from Asia Minor and the Black Sea. They constituted the principal support of the military strength of Egypt.[46] The king of Cyprus knew all the more the truth of what he said, as his own merchants actively participated in the slave trade towards Egypt, generally following raids on the islands inhabited by their coreligionists in the Aegean Sea. The papacy heard the appeal by the Lusignan sovereign, and in fact forbade Christian merchants and navigators from participating in the slave trade with Egypt in 1317, 1323, 1329, 1338, and again in 1425. The multiplicity of these interventions sufficiently shows how small was their effect. Moreover, the profits realized by the Italians aroused the emulation of the southern French and the Catalans. The result was that the slave trade to Egypt became truly an international commerce, in which all the Christian commercial navies of the Mediterranean world participated.

Among these fleets, none, however, seems to have played a part comparable to that of the Genoese, first of all because none seems to have had at its command a tonnage comparable to Genoa's.[47] Secondly, the fleet which might have been able to offer some competition, that of Venice, had, in regard to the slave trade, entirely divergent interests to defend. For Venice, the slave trade with Egypt was incidental, for she had her own agricultural colony in the eastern Mediterranean, Crete, to supply.[48] When she transported slaves elsewhere, it was above all towards Venice herself or towards the western basin of the Mediterranean.[49] However that may be, the "slavers" of the late Middle Ages were a reality in the Mediterranean, a reality without which Mameluke Egypt doubtlessly could not have survived, any more than the Spain of the Ommayad caliphs could have lasted without the *sakaliba* slaves some centuries before.

NOTES

1. Vol. LXIX, pp. 791–804.

2. *Il libro dei conti di Giacomo Badoer*, ed. U. Dorini and T. Bertelé, (Il Nuovo Ramusio, 3; Rome: Istituto Poligrafico dello Stato Italiano, 1956).

3. Verlinden, "Traite," p. 802.

4. *Ibid. passim.*

5. *Ibid.* p. 803.

6. C. Verlinden, "La colonie vénitienne de Tana, centre de la traite des esclaves au XIVe et au début du XVe siècle," *Studi in onore di Gino Luzzatto,* II (Milan, 1950), p. 185.

7. N. Jorga, *Notes et extraits pour servir à l'histoire des croisades au XVe siècle,* 1st series, I (Paris, 1899), p. 185.

8. *Ibid.* p. 245, 5 ducats per head.

9. F. Thiriet, *Regestes des déliberations du Sénat de Venise concernant la Romanie,* II (*1400–1430*), (Paris-The Hague, 1959), p. 202, no. 1879.

10. *Ibid.* III (*1431–1463*), (Paris-The Hague, 1961), p. 106, no. 2626.

11. R. Livi, *La schiavitù domestica nei tempi di mezzo e nei moderni* (Padua, 1928), p. 262, no. 53.

12. Jorga, *Notes,* p. 24. The "in 176" probably refers to a page number in another account, *so.* are sommi, and *se.* are unknown coins—Tr.

13. *Ibid.* pp. 354ff.

14. *Ibid.* pp. 493ff.

15. Silvestre de Sacy in *Notices et extraits des manuscripts de la bibliothèque du Roi,* XI, p. 74: " . . . obtentis itaque omnibus suprascriptis vel iis saltem quae in principio diximus nobis videri necessaria, et cum modificationibus quas prudentiae vestrae relinquimus, et prout superius diximus, placet nobis ut soldano ac suis tractum sclavorum ex Caffa concedatis, ipsis solventibus dritus et cabellas consuetas et ordinatas, hac tamen declaratione semper praecedente, quod scilicet si quis ejusmodi sclavorum vellet cristianus fieri, id ei liceret, dummodo ejus domino solvatur pecunia in Caffa constituta. Scribimus itaque consuli Caffae et novo consuli in mandatis dabimus ut de tractu talium sclavorum disponat ac faciat juxta commissiones vestras. Et ad uberiorem cautelam binas vobis litteras mittimus annexas, quas, cum volueritis, consuli Caffae transmittatis per aliquem ex his Sarracenis qui Caffam iturus sit." It is humorous to note that the instructions to the consuls at Caffa, meant to put the Genoese on the good side of the Holy See by limiting to some extent the slave trading of Christians, were carried to the Crimea exactly by Moslems from Cairo, no doubt some agents of the sultan charged with the bringing back of Mamelukes.

16. Jorga, *Notes,* p. 566.

17. Vol. IV (Paris, 1837), p. 436.

18. J. Heers, *Gênes au X Ve siècle* (Paris, 1960), p. 370 and n. 5.

19. *Ibid.* p. 371.

20. *Ibid.* p. 403.

21. *Ibid.* p. 404. It would be worth the effort to study the report closely (Archivio di Stato, Genoa, Not. Giudiziali, Pilosio Benedetto).

22. See, for example, the role of Portuguese merchants of Macao, as it is described in the recent volume of R. A. Boxer, *Portuguese Society in the Tropics. The Municipal Councils of Goa, Macao, Bahia and Luanda, 1510–1800* (Madison, 1965), and my review in the *Revue belge de philologie et d'histoire,* XLIV (1967), pp. 1084–86. For the Dutch, see K. Glamann, *Dutch-Asiatic Trade* (*1620–1740*) (Copenhagen, 1958) and my review in *Revue belge . . .,* XXXIX (1961), pp. 956–58.

23. Ed. H. Dopp (Publications de l'Université Lovanium; Louvain-Paris, 1958), p. 135.

24. C. Verlinden, "Les débuts de la traite portugaise en Afrique (1433–1448)," *Miscellanea mediaevalia in memoriam J. F. Niermeyer* (Amsterdam, 1967), pp. 365–377, and "Esclavage noir en France méridionale et courants de traite en Afrique," *Mélanges Renouard, Annales du Midi* (1966), pp. 325–343.

25. Piloti, p. 137.

26. *Ibid,* p. 140.

27. *Ibid.* p. 141.

28. Many of them were sold in Venetian Crete from the end of the fourteenth century. Cf. my study, "La Crète, débouché et plaque tournante de la traite des esclaves aux XIVe et XVe siècles," *Studi in onore di Amintore Fanfani,* III (Milan, 1962), pp. 593–669.

29. The example of what is seen in Crete and elsewhere proves that not even in Egypt was it a matter solely of children.

30. Piloti, p. 52.

31. The price of an adult.

32. Piloti, p. 52.

33. *Ibid.* p. 54. Therefore, the same annual number (2000) as that of the black slaves coming from the ports of Barbary. And this regards only the purchases of the monarch!

34. *Ibid.* p. 143.

35. See above, n. 16.

36. See above, n. 15.

37. Piloti, p. 52.

38. C. Schefer, *Le voyage d'Outremer de Bertrandon de la Broquière* (Paris, 1892), p. 68, n. 1.

39. Beiheft 46 of Vierteljahrschrift für Sozial-und Wirtschaftsge-schichte (Wiesbaden, 1965).

40. Labib, pp. 85 ff.

41. M. Canard, "Un traité entre Byzance et l'Egypte au XIIIe siècle et les relations diplomatiques de Michel VIII Paléologue avec les sultans mamlouks Baibars et Qala'un," *Mélanges Gaudery-Demombynes* (Cairo, 1937), and "Le traité de 1281 entre Michel Paléologue et le sultan Qala'un," *Byzantion,* X (1935).

42. Labib, p. 329.

43. See above, n. 15.

44. L. de Mas Latrie, *Histoire de l'île de Chypre sous le règne des princes de la maison de Lusignan,* II (Paris, 1852), pp. 118 ff.

45. ". . . debeat premitti quantitas galearum que capiant malos et falsos christianos qui dictis Sarracenis portant homines armorum scilicet Mamo-lucos, lignamina, ferrum, picem, victualia et alias merces necessarias eis." *Ibid.* p. 119.

46. "Cum terra Egypti non ginnat homines fortes in armis, si non ha-beret dictos pueros Mammolucos qui de Turquia et mari Pontico portantur eisdem, de quibus soldanus facit suas gentes armorum, cito imminueretur eorum potencia, quantum ad gentes armorum, per quos Christianos im-pugnant." *Ibid.* p. 120.

47. Cf. Heers, *Genes,* pp. 280–82.

48. C. Verlinden, "La Crète, débouché et plaque tournante de la traite des esclaves aux XIVe et XVe siècles," *Studi in onore di A. Fanfani,* III, pp. 593–699, especially pp. 605–09, and 667.

49. Cf. my study cited in n. 1 above.

THE CAMBIUM MARITIMUM CONTRACT ACCORDING TO THE GENOESE NOTARIAL RECORDS OF THE TWELFTH AND THIRTEENTH CENTURIES

RAYMOND DE ROOVER
Brooklyn College

The Genoese notarial records are one of the most important sources—perhaps the most important and certainly the most abundant source—for the study of the roots of capitalism and the origins of many business institutions. Around the turn of this century, some of these records became available and were first utilized by German legal and institutional historians, such as Levin Goldschmidt, Heinrich Sieveking, and Adolf Schaube, to whom economic history perhaps owes its existence as an independent discipline. Since the available records were fragmentary and incomplete, it was inevitable that their interpretation was sometimes incorrect and gave rise to the formulation of hypotheses which were unsubstantiated by adequate evidence and led to quite bitter controversies. Even now that nearly all the extant notarial records of the twelfth century and many of the following century are available in print, although some progress has been made, it would be rash to state that all problems have been solved.

The late Professor Eugene H. Byrne, realizing the historical value of the Genoese records, had entire notarial cartularies photographed and formed a collection of photostats at the University of Wisconsin. Not to be outdone, the Italians then created the collection *Doucumenti e studi per la storia del commercio e del diritto commerciale italiano* under the editorship of Federico Patetta and Mario Chiaudano. Several volumes were published, beginning with the contracts of the earliest and most famous of the Genoese notaries, the cartulary of Giovanni Scriba. When this undertaking ran into trouble because the expected financial support was not forthcoming, Professor Robert L. Reynolds took the laudable initiative of making arrangements for continuing publication in collaboration with the R. Deputazione di Storia Patria per la Liguria. As a result, the acts of several more notaries were published. In the meantime, a Belgian scholar, Madame Renee Doehaerd, began doing research in the Genoese archives and eventually published a selection of notarial contracts of the thirteenth century under the auspices of the Academia Belgica in Rome.

The present study is based mainly on this printed material. I have also made use of the records of Amalric, a notary active in Marseilles around 1248. No attempt has been made to consult any unpublished sources, since there are so many good examples of *cambium maritimum* in the published volumes. The purpose of this study is twofold. The first intent is to show how the *cambium maritimum,* or the *cambium nauticum,* contract differed from the sea loan, on the one hand, and from the ordinary *cambium,* on the other hand. The second purpose is to illustrate how the lender's profit, since it was not stated openly, was cleverly concealed in the exchange rate or rates, so that the usurious character of the contract was not apparent at the first glance. In the course of this demonstration an attempt will be made to clarify the dispute of long standing between Levin Goldschmidt and Adolf Schaube about the origins, the legal nature, and the economic character of the exchange contract, because misunderstanding on this point can only lead to hopeless confusion. In truth, this dispute is part of a broader controversy which was not started by those two German scholars but dates back to the time of the Genoese notaries, when some rigorous theologians argued that the *cambium* was essentially a loan, while others, more kindly disposed toward business, held the view that it was a *permutatio* or a conversion of currencies.

Many Italians use the phrase *cambio marittimo* rather loosely by extending its meaning to cover any kind of sea loan including the bottomry loan. This is not what I mean here. This study deals exclusively with the *cambium maritimum* in a narrow and well defined sense. Like the sea loan, or *foenus nauticum,* such a contract always contained a conditional clause which made the repayment of a loan contingent upon the safe arrival of a ship or of a cargo at the port of destination. In addition to the credit risk, the lender therefore assumed the sea risk, that is, the risk of losing any claim to repayment of the loan if the goods or the ship pledged as security failed to reach port safely because of an act of God, the fortunes of the sea, or the assaults of men-of-war, such as enemies, corsairs, or pirates. This is what was understood by the formula *ad risicum et fortunam Dei, maris et gentium.*[1]

The *cambium maritimum* contract differed, however, from the *foenus nauticum* or sea loan in one important respect: instead of being repayable in the same currency upon safe return or arrival of a certain ship or a certain cargo, the *cambium maritimum* always involved an exchange transaction and was repayable not in the same, but in a different, currency, usually that circulating at the place of destination. On the other hand, the *cambium maritimum* differed from an ordinary *cambium* because implementation of the contract was conditional and depended upon the fulfillment of an uncertain event: the safe arrival of a ship or of its cargo.

The *cambium maritimum* was thus a hybrid form of contract that combined some of the features of the *cambium* and others of the sea loan or *foenus nauticum*. Such a contract may be defined as a covenant between a lender and a borrower by which the latter promised to repay the former in a foreign port and in a foreign currency on condition that a certain ship or the major part of its cargo made port.[2] If not, the borrower was freed from any further obligation. Usually the contract did not stipulate how much the lender would earn by lending his money and assuming a rather heavy risk. As we shall see, his profit was determined by undervaluing the foreign currency in which the loan was repayable.

Before going more deeply into the matter of the *cambium maritimum* proper, let us have a look at the two contracts whose characteristics were merged in it, and first at the *foenus nauticum* or sea loan. This is a very old contract whose origins date back to Greek and Roman times.[3] It is even likely that the Phoenicians knew this contract. It was still very popular in the twelfth century and up to 1234 when it was branded as usurious in the famous decretal *Naviganti*, promulgated in that year or earlier by Gregory IX.[4] Many examples of sea loans are found among the acts of John the Scribe or Giovanni Scriba, the earliest of the Genoese notaries whose cartulary has come down to us. A typical contract is the one dated August 6, 1156, by which a merchant named Tado acknowledged receipt of six pounds, Genoese currency, and promised to repay eight pounds one month after the ship on which he was sailing to Alexandria had safely returned to Genoa or after his own safe return, should he decide to come back on another ship.[5] This loan was apparently secured by the goods which Tado carried to Alexandria and those which he intended to purchase there and bring back to Genoa. In this period most merchants were still peregrinators who accompanied their own goods on sea or on land. According to the above figures, the lender earned two pounds or $33\frac{1}{3}$ per cent for interest and risk-taking on a round trip from Genoa to Alexandria that, it is true, might have lasted several months.[6] Nevertheless, this figure may seem high, and it is.

However, one should not forget that the twelfth century was a period of rapid economic expansion, that capital was scarce, and that the perils of the sea were still very real. On shorter trips from Genoa to Provence or to Sicily, the rate was lower but still as high as 25 per cent.[7]

As the reader will notice, the profit made by the lender is stated quite openly. Prior to 1234, it could still be argued that the sea loan was not usurious, because the lender ran the risk of losing his capital through disaster at sea; but the canon *Naviganti* altered the situation by refusing to recognize *periculum sortis* as a valid title to interest. The promulgation of this decretal had therefore an adverse effect on the popularity of the sea loan.[8] In so far as I am able to judge from the Genoese records, its use declined in favor of the *cambium maritimum* to which the ban did not extend.[9] It should, however, be emphasized that the *cambium maritimum* contract did not owe its existence to the tightening of the usury prohibition, since numerous examples are found in the cartulary of John the Scribe, long before the appearance of the *Extravagantes,* the collection of canons issued by Gregory IX (1234).[10] The early medieval sea loan usually applied to a round trip, for example the successful completion of a voyage to Alexandria and back to Genoa (*navi sana eunte Alexandriam et inde redeunte*).[11] The *cambium maritimum* contract, on the other hand, usually applied only to an outbound or an inbound voyage, seldom to a round trip. Moreover, the use of this contract presupposed a more sophisticated organization of foreign trade, since the lender needed to have a representative abroad to transact his business, unless he travelled on the same ship as the borrower.

Ordinary *cambium* contracts occur less frequently in the Genoese notarial records than sea loans and then only with reference to the fairs of Champagne or inland towns, such as Milan or Pavia, exceptionally in connection with Pisa. Levin Goldschmidt, around 1900 the most prominent German specialist on the history of commercial law, saw in the *cambium* contract only a transfer instrument to effect international settlements.[12] His thesis was promptly challenged by Adolf Schaube, who pointed out that such a contract could also be used to cover up a loan and to grant credit.[13] Since Adolf Schaube was only a simple *Gymnasiallehrer* (high school teacher) in Brieg (Silesia), his boldness created quite a scandal in Wilhelminian Germany where hierarchy was so strictly observed not only in the army but in all fields. How did such an unimportant pedagogue dare question the opinions of Professor L. Goldschmidt of the University of Berlin, author of the celebrated *Universalgeschichte des Handelsrechts* and editor of the *Zeitschrift für das gesamte Handelsrecht*, called Goldschmidt's *Zeitschrift*, even sometimes in reference notes?[14] This was inadmissible. Nonetheless, Schaube was right and Goldschmidt wrong. Of the two, Schaube was the better historian whose strong point was that he read documents with meticulous care and did not allow himself to be influenced by preconceived legal theories.

Despite evidence to the contrary, Goldschmidt was firmly convinced that the usury doctrine of the Church did not affect business practices and was simply disregarded.[15] He refused to admit that, since usurious contracts were invalid at law, the merchants were compelled to resort to subterfuges in order to conceal, more or less successfully, the true character of their credit operations—if possible, in a manner approved by the theologians. The *cambium* contract offered the merchants such a possibility and they did not fail to seize this golden opportunity.

Here is the text of a typical exchange contract taken from the cartulary of the Genoese notary Giovanni di Guiberto (1200–1211):

> Petrus Pixis of Pavia acknowledges that he has received in loan [*mutuo*] from Bergonzo Ruba, also of Pavia, 9 pounds, Genoese currency, and promises to pay him and Johannes, his partner, or one of them, or the certain attorney of either one of them [*vel certo misso alterius eorum*], 14 pounds 5 sol., Pavese currency, in Pavia at the coming feast of All Saints. And if he [Petrus] does not carry this out, he promises to indemnify them for all expenses, damages and interest which they might incur after the said term in connection with the collection of the said debt, and they are to be given credence on their word without oath. And in security he obligates all his property, present and future. Witnesses: Benzo Guastoni and Jacob of Como, both of Pavia. Done in Genoa under the Bakers' Gallery on September 25, 1203.[16]

As is clear from the text of this contract, a debtor confessed that he had received nine pounds in Genoese currency on September 25, 1203, and promised to repay the equivalent, 14 pounds 5 sol., in Pavese currency on the coming first of November. This contract consequently involved a conversion of Genoese currency into Pavese currency as well as a loan, since money borrowed on September 25 in Genoa was repayable about five weeks later in Pavia. According to the figures given, the exchange rate was 19 denarii, Pavese currency, for one sou or shilling Genoese. No interest was explicitly stipulated, but it was presumably hidden by estimating the Pavese currency below its real value, say 19 den. per sou instead of 18 den. or

18½ den. per sou, although this is merely a guess, since the contract does not give this information.

The above contract is one among many similar ones and may safely be regarded as typical.[17] If so, a *cambium* may be defined as a contract involving an advance of funds in one place and its repayment in another place at a *later* date and in a different currency. By definition, such a contract involved both an exchange transaction and a credit transaction which were so closely interlocked that they could not be separated.

In this connection, L. Goldschmidt made several mistakes. First of all, he called such a contract an *Eigenwechsel,* which is the German term for promissory note.[18] It is true that the contract took the form of a promise to pay, since the bill of exchange in draft form was not yet in use.[19] Nevertheless, Goldschmidt used terminology that is not only wrong but positively misleading. The Latin expression found in contemporary documents is *instrumentum ex causa cambii,* which may be rendered in English as an exchange contract in notarial form.[20] Instead of being an informal note, the above contract is a deed written in the verbose style of the medieval notaries.

Second, the primary purpose of a *cambium* contract, Goldschmidt contended, was to transfer funds from one place to another place.[21] This might, or might not, be so: all depended on the intentions of the contracting parties in each particular case, and notarial contracts usually do not reveal intentions. In any case, the exchange contract might serve the purpose either of transferring funds or of granting credit. It was even possible to cancel a first exchange transaction by re-exchange in the opposite direction, as it is possible today to convert dollars into English pounds and then to reconvert those pounds into dollars. Such exchange and re-exchange transactions could easily lead to abuse and be transformed into a device for concealing a loan, pure and simple, as in the case of dry exchange and fictitious exchange.[22]

Last, Goldschmidt advanced the opinion that in the *cambium maritimum* the lender received a premium for assuming the sea risk, but that in the ordinary *cambium* it was the *Wechselgeber,* that is, the borrower or the seller of a draft, who collected a commission supposedly as a reward for shipping specie or making it available in a distant place.[23] Goldschmidt was right about the *cambium maritimum,* although he failed to explain exactly how the lender earned his premium or compensation for risk. With regard to the ordinary *cambium,* Goldschmidt's theory applied only to the special case of

bankers who sold letters of credit to travelers going abroad. The same
is still true today: the American Express Company charges a commission when issuing travelers' checks payable by its agencies in
other countries. In the normal course of business, however, it was not
the *Wechselgeber* (the debtor) but the *Wechselnehmer,* the creditor
or the buyer of a foreign draft, who gained at the expense of the
seller.[24] In reality there was no difference between the ordinary *cambium* and the *cambium maritimum* in this respect: in both cases, the
lender's profit was adroitly concealed in the exchange rate by placing
a higher value on the local than on the foreign currency or, as the
medieval theologians put it, by estimating present money more than
absent money.[25] The only difference is that, in the case of *cambium
maritimum,* the margin of profit was even greater because an insurance premium was added to interest.

Goldschmidt's theory was promptly challenged by Schaube, who
used ingenious ways to prove that the remitter, or *Wechselnehmer,*
far from paying a commission to the *Wechselgeber,* earned interest
by accommodating some one who needed local currency but who had,
or expected to have, funds available abroad.[26] The remitter, in one
of the cases cited by Schaube, happened to be the Venetian *bailo* of
Trebizond who, in 1320, had a surplus of funds to remit to his government. According to the records, he concluded for this purpose an
exchange contract with merchants and disbursed 1958 pounds 4 sol.
3 den. *ad grossos* for a promise to pay 2164 pounds 14 sol. thus
making a profit of nearly 9 per cent for the Venetian government.
Circumstantial evidence shows definitely that the *bailo's* primary
purpose was to remit to Venice without running the risk and the expense of shipping specie (*salvos in terra sine periculo*), whereas the
other party viewed the transaction in a different light, as a means
of financing a business venture with borrowed funds.[27] This confirms
what has been said before about the dual character and the dual purpose of exchange transactions.

Recently published documents fully corroborate the correctness
of Schaube's viewpoint. One of the most convincing proofs is afforded by a contract dated October 31, 1252, according to which
Roffredo Bramanzoni, the representative in Genoa of the powerful
Sienese banking house of the Bonsignori, acknowledged in his own
name and that of his partners that he had received 1416 pounds 13 sol.
4 den., Genoese currency, from Gherardo Oltramare and promised
to repay the equivalent, 1000 pounds of Provins, at the forthcoming
fair of Troyes *ad rectum pagamentum,* on December 3, 1252. How-

point of interest is the way in which this profit was determined by manipulating the exchange rates and setting arbitrary values on the Byzantine perper. At par this coin was worth about 7 sol. 6 den., Genoese currency, or about 2.7 perpers to a Genoese pound. Yet the contract under discussion rated the perper *below* its value (5 sol.) when it was lent out and *above* its value when it was repayable (10 sol.).

A more normal and less puzzling contract, also found in the cartulary of Giovanni Scriba, is a *cambium maritimum* dated July 19, 1157.[36] According to its provisions, Amico de Mirta and his spouse, Alda, acknowledged having received 100 pounds Genoese and promised to pay 3 perpers per pound, or 300 perpers in all, in Constantinople before Carnival, upon condition that Ruffino's ship and the major part of the specie it carried (*vel maiori parte pecunie que in ea portat*) arrived safely at destination. However, if this payment did not take place, the debtors were expected to repay the creditor, a certain Guglielmo de Candida, at the rate of 9 sol. 6 den. Genoese per perper one month after the safe return of the ship on which Amico de Mirta and the said Guglielmo chose to come back to Genoa. Apparently both debtor and creditor intended to make a trip to Constantinople and to travel on the same ship.[37] Using the data given in the contract, I figure that it called for the repayment in Genoa of 142 pounds 10 sol., Genoese currency, which corresponds exactly to a profit of 42.5 per cent. This is less exorbitant than the preceding contract but still well above normal.

Most likely, this anomaly is due to the fact that trade and political relations between Genoa and the Byzantine Empire were still uncertain. Amico de Mirta, other sources reveal, was actually sent as an ambassador to Constantinople to negotiate a settlement.[38] His mission was a failure, because the Republic of Genoa had concluded a treaty of non-intervention with the King of Sicily in January 1157, and the disappointed Greek Emperor was not going to make concessions without obtaining in return some tangible aid against his enemy.

At this time trade relations between Genoa and Sicily or between Genoa and Syria were much more active than with Constantinople where the Pisans still occupied a well entrenched position and hampered Genoese efforts to gain a firmer foothold. The cartularies of the Genoese notaries contain quite a number of contracts (partnerships, commendas, and sea loans) concluded for the trade with Sicily where the Genoese sold mainly "French" cloth and made returns in wheat. The *cambium maritimum* contract was also used as a method to finance this trade. Here is a literal translation of such a contract enacted by the Genoese notary Lanfranco:

> I, Henglesius, draper, acknowledge that I have received as a loan [*mutuo*] from you, Gisulfo, 55 pounds, Genoese currency. Renouncing all exceptions, I promise that either I or my representative will pay in Sicily to you or your certain attorney 25 ounces of gold of old tari according to the weight of Messina, free from duties and any expenses or charges, upon safe arrival of the ship on which you are sailing or most of the cargo of the said ship. For this purpose, I pledge to you the security that you acknowledge to have in your possession, namely a bale containing five capes of Montreuil and one piece of blue Stamford cloth. This pledge is entrusted to you to be carried to the said country [of Sicily] and to be sold there in the presence of witnesses in discharge of the said debt, and if there is a deficiency after deducting the proceeds of the goods pledged as security, I promise to pay you 65 sol., Genoese currency, for each unpaid ounce, one month after your return to Genoa upon safe arrival of the ship on which you and the witnesses decide to return or upon safe arrival of the major part of this vessel's cargo. If I fail to do this, I bind myself and all my property, with penalty of twice the amount due, etc. And you promise me to invest in merchandise any surplus [above the amount of the loan], to bring it back to Genoa at my risk, and to hand it over to me. Enacted in Genoa on September 21, 1210.[39]

The surprising feature of this contract is that the debtor stayed at home in Genoa and that the creditor accompanied the goods that were pledged to him as security. Moreover, they were not only entrusted to his care but he was in charge of selling them at the best price obtainable. Therefore he was entitled to a commission as a selling agent, in addition to interest for paying in advance, and to a premium for assuming the sea risk. This contract is consequently more than a loan; besides involving a *cambium* it embodies some traits of a partnership agreement.

As in preceding *cambium* contracts, the lender's profit was determined by manipulating the exchange rate of the foreign currency. In this period, the Sicilian ounce of 30 tari was worth about 50 sol. or 2½ pounds, Genoese currency, but the contract valued it at 44 sol. when borrowed and at 65 sol. when repayable. There was consequently a margin of 21 sol. which corresponds to nearly 48 per cent of the principal. This is far above the normal rate of 25 per cent charged on ordinary sea loans according to many examples in the Genoese notarial records.[40] Since the contracting parties certainly would not ship goods to Sicily if they did not intend to sell them there, the provision about repaying the loan or rather part of it in Genoa was introduced only as a penalty clause that was not expected to enter into play unless something went seriously wrong.

The cartulary of the notary Lanfranco contains a similar contract, dated September 18, 1210, involving a *cambium maritimum* of only 8 pounds 8 sol. Genoese currency, or four Sicilian ounces, secured by twenty pieces of fustian.[41] This corresponds to a rate of 42 sol. per ounce repayable at the rate of 60 sol. in Genoa, if the sale of the fustians failed to cover the loan, which was not expected to happen. The difference of 18 sol. between the two rates represents 43 per cent, not much less than the preceding contract.

The terms of a third contract were much more favorable to the borrower than those of the other two by giving him the benefit of a high exchange rate in converting the Genoese pounds into Sicilian ounces. In this case, the loan amounted to 75 pounds, Genoese currency, equivalent in Sicily to 30 ounces.[42] Simple arithmetic will show that this equation is based on a rate of 50 sol. per ounce. Settlement of any unpaid balance was to take place in Genoa at the rate of 60 sol., a difference of only 20 percent against 40 percent in the other two cases. The debtor received the same favorable treatment in still another contract enacted by the notary Cassinese in 1192. It relates to a loan of 800 pounds which called for the payment of 410 ounces in Sicily, that is, at the rate of 39 sol. an ounce.[43] An unpaid portion was repayable in Genoa at the rate of 50 sol. per ounce, which would be a difference of only 28 per cent. This document is unfortunately unreliable because the reading of the figure "50" is uncertain. Why there existed these discrepancies is hard to explain without knowing the circumstances attending each case or the conditions prevailing in the money market at a given time.

The notarial records by their very nature give little information about the state of the money market, although such an organization was emerging in important trading centers, such as Genoa, Marseilles, and Siena, and at the fairs of Champagne. Certainly different rates were quoted according to whether the foreign currency was payable *salvos in terra* or subject to sea risk. It is, however, difficult to secure positive evidence. Nevertheless, I was able to find some information among the records of the notary Amalric of Marseilles. On April 14, 1248, some one borrowed 100 sol., or 5 pounds mixed money current in Marseilles, and promised to repay 4 pounds Genoese currency, in Genoa eight days after the safe arrival of the borrower's ship named "Bonaventure."[44] According to these data, the exchange rate was 15 den. currency of Marseilles, for 12 den. or one sou Genoese currency. Four days later, on April 18, the same notary drew up another contract, also *ex causa permutacionis seu cambii,* involving a straight *cambium* of 130 pounds Marseilles currency, equal to 100 pounds Genoese currency, repayable in Genoa *salvos in terra,* that is, unconditionally without risk, on May 1.[45] On this latter transaction the rate was consequently 15¾ den. of Marseilles for 12 den. or one Genoese sou. If one assumes that during the four days from April 14 to April 18, there was no major change in the conditions of the money market—which is most likely—there was a difference of three-fifths of a denier between the rate *salvos in terra* and the rate on a *cambium maritimum* including the sea risk. This corresponds exactly to a premium of 4 per cent to cover the perils of the sea. This would be excessive today for the short voyage from Marseilles to Genoa, but was quite normal in the thirteenth century when navigation was still surrounded by many dangers.

In their excellent collection of commercial documents, Robert S. Lopez and Irving W. Raymond publish a Genoese exchange contract which they label somewhat facetiously "Dry" Sea Exchange.[46] I hate to disagree with the authors, whose work I greatly esteem, although they must have known that their label is somewhat contradictory and that the sea far from being dry is a watery expanse. The contract, it is true, mentions Benedetto Zaccaria, a Genoese admiral in the service of the Byzantine Empire, who is one of the contracting parties. Nevertheless, it does not mention the sea risk and is strictly dry, since it refers to exchange from Genoa to Constantinople and rechange from Constantinople to Genoa. It has, however, the interesting feature that it does not reveal how much the borrower actually received and states only that he borrowed an unspecified sum in Genoese currency (*tot denarios Januinos*). Without this vital information, it is impossible to figure out how onerous this loan was. The appearance of this formula indicates, however, the growing impact of the Church's usury doctrine.

The actual influence of the Church's attitude in the matter of usury has been another bone of contention among economic historians. Some, who question Max Weber's thesis, go even so far as to deny that it had any effect at all. The Genoese records seem to indicate, however, that the teachings of the Church in economic matters did not remain without some repercussion on business practices. The thirteenth century was a great century of intellectual ferment and the codification of the canon law brought forth attempts to enforce its regulations and to apply its provisions to the matter of contracts. It is within this framework, *de contractibus,* that economic questions were considered. It is not surprising that the new contracts that were gaining ground in the bustling sea ports and in particular in Genoa came under the scrutiny of the canonists and of the theologians. The canon *In civitate tua* condemning credit sales at increased prices is an excerpt from a letter addressed by the Pope to the Archbishop of Genoa (1213) and the famous *Naviganti* is directly aimed at the sea loan and at similar deals concluded in the trade with the fairs of Champagne.[47]

The effect of the usury doctrine is perceptible in a subtle change in the terminology used in the Genoese records. In Giovanni Scriba's cartulary and in the earlier notaries, the word *mutuum* is commonly found in connection with straight loans as well as with other contracts.[48] This was a dangerous word to use, because it had the same effect on canonists and theologians as the waving of a red banner in front of a bull. A *mutuum* was always usurious, if it ceased to be gratuitous *(gratis et amore).* It is amazing that the canon *Naviganti* was not stretched to outlaw the *cambium* contract as well. The canonists, for example Geoffrey of Trani (d. 1245), Henry of Susa, Cardinal Hostiensis (d. 1271), and Monaldus Justinopolitanus (d. 1288), were already moving in this direction by defining the *cambium* as a disguised loan, especially if the lender intended to make a profit by buying for cash a foreign currency payable at the fairs or in another place at a future date.[49]

To counter this undesirable development, the Genoese notaries began gradually to drop the objectionable word *mutuum* and to adopt more innocuous formulas such as *nomine cambii* or *nomine venditionis.*[50] The Marseilles notary Almaric favored the formula *ex causa permutacionis seu cambii.* Often the amount borrowed is not specified and the contract states only that the borrower received an undetermined amount of Genoese pennies *(tot januinos).*[51] Even if full information was given, the contract was drafted in such a way that one often needs paper and pencil in order to figure out how the lender's profit was determined. This was presumably done to befuddle the theologians.

It was Alexander Lombard, or Alexander of Alexandria, O.F.M. (d. 1314), who saved the situation by arguing in his *Treatise on Usury* that the Church condemned usurers but protected exchangers and that, moreover, a *cambium* was not a *mutuum* but a *permutatio pecunie* which was not usurious, if there was the least doubt about the

future course of the exchange rate.[52] By making this qualification, he opened the door to a flood of evasions. Since his doctrine
was accepted from then onward by all the leading theologians, it
had the important consequence that banking activities could henceforth be carried on under the cloak of exchange. Alexander Lombard
was certainly well informed about Genoese business practices and
his treatise was most probably composed in connection with a *quodli-
betic* debate held in Genoa in 1306 or 1307, in which the whole
matter of licit and illicit contracts came up for discussion.[53] It was
the start of a heated controversy which, originating in the type of
contracts drafted by the Genoese notaries of the period of the Crusades, was to last until well into the eighteenth century. One may even
say that it is still going on today and stirring up conflicts among
historians interested in the development of banking, the origins of
credit instruments, and scholastic economic doctrines, not to mention
the supporters and the opponents of the Max Weber thesis.

NOTES

1. Enrico Besta, *Le obbligazioni nella storia del diritto italiano* (Padua,
1937), p. 234.
2. *Ibid.*, p. 235. Besta is one of the few legal historians who distinguishes
clearly between a *foenus nauticum* and a *cambium maritimum*.
3. Ugo Enrico Paoli, "Prestito a cambio marittimo," *Nuovo Digesto
Italiano* (Turin, 1939); George M. Calhoun, "Risk in Sea Loans in Ancient
Athens," *Journal of Economic and Business History*, II (1930), 561–84. Note
the title of Paoli's article, which deals with sea loans, not with *cambium
maritimum* as defined above.
4. *Corpus juris canonici, Decretales:* canon *Naviganti*, Extravagantes
Gregory IX, V, 19, 19.
5. *Il cartolare di Giovanni Scriba*, eds. Mario Chiaudano and Mattia
Moresco (Turin, 1935), I, 56, No. 104.
6. An additional clause of the contract stipulated that, should Tado
decide to stay in Egypt longer than usual, the loan became due nevertheless
in the summer of 1157, if most of the Genoese fleet returned safely from
Alexandria.
7. *Ibid.*, p, 116, No. 218; p. 130, Nos. 239, 240; p. 319, No. 588, and
passim. To Tunis the standard rate was 33⅓ per cent, the same as to Alexandria.
8. This is the opinion of Riniero Zeno, *Storia del diritto marittimo
nel Mediterraneo* (Catania, 1915), pp. 160–161. It is not shared by Calvin
B. Hoover, "The Sea Loan in Genoa in the Twelfth Century," *The
Quarterly Journal of Economics*, XL (1926), 495–529.
9. Florence Edler de Roover, "Early Examples of Marine Insurance,"
Journal of Economic History, V (1945), 175–76.

10. The influence of *Naviganti* on the development of the *cambium maritimum* contract is rather overstressed by Adolf Schaube, "Der Versicherungsgedanke in den Verträgen des Seeverkehrs vor der Entstehung des Versicherungswesens," *Zeitschrift für Social- und Wirtschaftsgeschichte*, II (1894), 176–77. However, Schaube is not entirely wrong. He is certainly right in criticizing L. Goldschmidt for seeing in the *cambium maritimum* a *Remittierungsgeschäft*, or a transfer-of-funds device. See L. Goldschmidt, *Universalgeschichte des Handelsrechts*, I (Stuttgart, 1891), 354. Only one volume published.

11. *Cartolare di Giovanni Scriba*, p. 56, No. 104.

12. In German: "Es ist ein Rimessengeschäft." (*Universalgeschichte*, pp. 403-408). Even if the granting of credit may be involved, the primary purpose of *cambium* was to transfer funds (*Geldzuweisung*). For a discussion of Goldschmidt's views, see André-E. Sayous, "L'histoire universelle de Lévin Goldschmidt et les méthodes commerciales des pays chrétiens de la Méditerranée aux XIIe et XIIIe siècles," *Annales de Droit commercial français, étranger et international*, XL (1931), 199–217 and 309–22. On p. 205 the author makes the following statement: "Le renom de l'auteur (Goldschmidt) en impose aux étudiants et aux Américains au point d'aider à la propagation d'erreurs." This is a dart aimed at the "Wisconsin School."

13. Especially in his article, "Studien zur Geschichte und Natur des ältesten Cambiums," *Jahrbücher für Nationalökonomie und Statistik*, LXV (1895), 153–91 and 511–34.

14. To the great annoyance of American students who do not find Goldschmidt's *Zeitschrift*, Hildebrand's *Jahrbücher*, or Schmoller's *Jahrbuch* in any library catalogue.

15. *Universalgeschichte*, pp. 140–141, esp. n. 168. Goldschmidt criticized Wilhelm Endemann sharply for stressing the persistent influence of the usury doctrine in general and, especially, in connection with the early development of marine insurance. For a rebuff of Goldschmidt on this point, see Richard Ehrenberg, *Das Zeitalter der Fugger* (Jena, 1922), I, 32n.

16. *Giovanni di Guiberto (1200–1211)*, eds. M. W. Hall-Cole *et al.* (Turin, 1939), I, 409, No. 882.

17. Other examples in Goldschmidt, *Universalgeschichte*, pp. 420–427. These examples are not all taken from the Genoese records.

18. *Ibid.*, pp. 418–419. More precisely Goldschmidt used the term "domizilirter Eigenwechsel."

19. For the transition from the *instrumentum ex cause cambii* to the bill of exchange, an important document is a contract dated February 26, 1253, and published by Roberto S. Lopez, *La prima crisi della Banca di Genova, 1250–1259* (Milan, 1956), p. 153, No. 98. This is a notarial contract already drafted in the form of a letter missive addressed by the drawer to the drawee.

20. On this whole question consult also Raymond de Roover, *L'évolution de la lettre de change, XIVe-XVIIIe siècles* (Paris, 1953), ch. 1, esp. pp. 29–31.

21. *Universalgeschichte*, p. 403. Cf. Schaube, "Studien," p. 156, and R. de Roover, *L'évolution*, pp. 12–13.

22. On this whole question of the bill of exchange there has been a long and tortuous controversy, extending over the past seventy-five years and involving W. Endemann, L. Goldschmidt, Adolf Schaube, Carl Freundt, André-E. Sayous, A. P. Usher, and others. Although some points are now well established and generally accepted, differences of opinion persist and the quarrel is still smoldering. For bibliography, consult R. de Roover, *L'évolution*, pp. 161–170. An up-to-date Spanish edition of this book is in preparation.

23. *Universalgeschichte*, p. 415.

24. The use of these terms by Goldschmidt has created endless confusion, since foreigners have even given them the reverse of their real meaning. I am therefore giving here the equivalents in several languages in the vain hope of avoiding further misunderstanding:

Wechselnehmer = Valutageber = remitter = buyer of a draft = *bailleur de fonds = datore = remittente.*

Wechselgeber = Valutanehmer = drawer = seller of a draft = borrower = *tireur = prenditore* (old meaning) = *traente.*

In the Middle Ages, *prenditore* always referred to the drawer, not to the beneficiary, of a bill of exchange.

25. John T. Noonan Jr., *The Scholastic Analysis of Usury* (Cambridge, Mass., 1957), pp. 317–327.

26. Adolf Schaube, "Studien," *op. cit.*, pp. 153–191, 511–534.

27. *Ibid.*, pp. 154–155.

28. The text of this contract is published by Renée Doehaerd, *Les relations commerciales entre Gênes, la Belgique et l'Outremont* (Rome, 1941), II, 418–419, No. 775. Cf. *ibid.*, pp. 419–420, No. 776 for another contract of the same kind between the same parties. The contract is discussed in R. de Roover, *L'évolution*, pp. 32–33.

29. The computations are as follows:

	Pounds	Sol.	Den.	Genoese
Amount repayable in Genoa 1000 pounds of Provins or 20,000 sous at 19 den. per sou.	1583	6	8	
Deduct: amount borrowed 1000 pounds or 20,000 sous at 17 den. per sou.	1416	13	4	
Profit: 2 den. per sou or 40,000 den.	166	13	4	

30. Doehaerd, *Relations*, II, 63, No. 131. Cf. *ibid.*, p. 57, No. 119.

31. Six times 3 den. is 18 den. a year; 18 den. interest on 13 den. capital corresponds to 135 percent a year and more, because interest was compounded and added to principal at each renewal.

32. The amount of the loan, 6 pounds Genoese, is modest, which suggests that Beltranus Bertaldus made personal loans to small people who had no security to offer but whom he could exploit. Bertaldus always called himself banker and had a partner, Wilhelmus Scarampus of Asti, who was

engaged in trade rather than in banking. See Robert L. Reynolds, "Genoese Trade in the Late Twelfth Century, Particularly in Cloth from the Fairs of Champagne," *Journal of Economic and Business History*, III (1931), 378.

33. *Cartolare di Giovanni Scriba*, I, 45, No. 84. The borrowers were Amigono de Curia and two brothers, Raimondo and Ribaldo. Cf. Goldschmidt, *Universalgeschichte*, p. 420.

34. The normal rate on sea loans for Constantinople was 33⅓ per cent *(de tribus quattuor)*. See *Cartolare di Giovanni Scriba*, I, 233 and 249, Nos. 438 and 468.

35. Adolf Schaube, *Storia del commercio dei popoli latini nel Mediterraneo* (Turin, 1915), p. 280, No. 177; Wilhelm Heyd, *Histoire du commerce du Levant au moyen âge* (Leipzig, 1923), I, 202–204.

36. *Cartolare di Giovanni Scriba*, I, 117, No. 219. This contract is discussed by R. de Roover, "The organization of Trade," *Cambridge Economic History of Europe*, eds. M. M. Postan *et al.*, III (Cambridge, 1963), 55–56.

37. " . . . sana veniente illa navi quam ego Amicus tecum Wuilielme, eligero Constantinopolim ad mensem post quam venero. . . . "

38. Heyd, *Commerce du Levant*, I, 204; Schaube, *Storia*, p. 281, No. 177.

39. *Lanfranco (1202–1226)*, eds. H. C. Krueger and R. L. Reynolds (Genoa, 1951), I, 336–337, No. 752; Doehaerd, *Les relations commerciales*, II, 126, No. 260.

40. *Cartolare di Giovanni Scriba*, I, 130, Nos. 239 and 240; 157, No. 295; 159, No. 298; 229, No. 430; 240, No. 451, *et passim*.

41. *Lanfranco*, I, 331, No. 739.

42. Doehaerd, *Relations*, II, 176, No. 348.

43. *Notai liguri del secolo XII: Guglielmo Cassinese* (1190–1192), eds. Margaret W. Hall *et al.* (Turin, 1938), II, 235–236, No. 1701.

44. *Documents inédits sur le commerce de Marseille au moyen âge*, ed. Louis Blancard (Marseilles, 1885), II, 67, No. 497.

45. *Ibid.*, II, 94, No. 553.

46. *Medieval Trade in the Mediterranean World* (New York, 1955), 172–173, No. 81.

47. *Corpus juris canonici, Decretales:* canons *In Civitate tua* and *Naviganti*, Extra. of Gregory IX, V, 19, 6 and 19.

48. *Giovanni Scriba*, I, 17, No. 32; II, 54, No. 917; *Giovanni di Guiberto*, I, 79, No. 136; 110, No. 206; 252, No. 544; 262–263, No. 558; 270, No. 572, *et passim*. The formula *mutuo nomine cambii*, sometimes used by Giovanni di Guiberto, made matters worse: p. 215, No. 454; 251, No. 542; Doehaerd, *Relations*, Nos. 260, 303, 348 *et passim*.

49. R. de Roover, *L'évolution*, pp. 186, 187; Noonan, *Scholastic Analysis of Usury*, p. 181.

50. Examples of *nomine cambii*: Doehaerd, *Relations*, Nos. 570, 577, 587, 588, 620 *et passim*. *Nomine vendicionis*: *ibid.*, Nos. 603, 616, 824 *et passim*.

51. Examples: *ibid.*, Nos. 118, 297, 347, 577, 721. According to Alessandro Lattes, the presence of the formula *tot januinos* or its equivalent always indicated that the contract was a concealed loan, presumably

usurious (A. Lattes, "Di una singolare formula genovese nei contratti di mutuo," *Rivista del diritto commerciale,* XXII (1924), 542–50.)

52. Alonzo M. Hamelin, *Un traité de morale économique au XIVe siècle: Le tractatus de Usuris de Maître Alexandre d'Alexandrie* (Louvain, 1962), pp. 179–180, 181, 182, 185; Raymond de Roover, "Les doctrines économiques des scolastiques: à propos du traité sur l'usure d'Alexandre Lombard," *Revue d'histoire ecclésiastique,* LIX (1964), 858–60.

53. Alexander Lombard probably visited Genoa when, in 1306 or 1307, he went from Rome to Paris to succeed John Duns Scotus as professor at the university (Hamelin, *Un traité,* pp. 60–63).

STARS AND SPICES: THE EARLIEST ITALIAN MANUAL OF COMMERCIAL PRACTICE

ROBERT S. LOPEZ

Yale University

"When you see a merchant to whom the pen is a burden," says Benedetto Cotrugli in his description of an ideal business man who would almost match Baldassar Castiglione's ideal courtier, "you may say that he is not a merchant."[1] As a matter of fact, the heaps of medieval commercial records that have survived, in spite of so many factors conspiring to their destruction, lend support to the suggestion that merchants, not clergymen, were the greatest consumers of ink and paper in the later Middle Ages; to say nothing of the fact that such a large proportion of Italian literature was produced by and for merchants.

Half way between the extremes of the *Decameron* and the bill of exchange, we come across a sizable group of reference works which economic historians still designate by a title invented for them by an eighteenth-century scholar: *Pratica della Mercatura*, that is, manuals of commercial practice.[2] Often (but not always) designed for the private use of employees of a specific commercial company, these manuals do not usually aim at artistic distinction any more than would a modern primer of business administration. Even the drabbest among them, however, contain some lively economic, sociological, and geographic comments beside their tightly packed factual information. Francesco di Balduccio Pegolotti was not a professional writer, but the youthful power and charm of fourteenth-century Florentine language and imagery embellishes many pages of his *Libro di divisamenti di paesi*; much later, Daniel Defoe could not help remaining an artist when he wrote *The Complete English Tradesman*. The learning and sophistication of Arab Syria transpire, however clumsily, through Abu al-Fadl al-Dimishqi's *Beauties of Commerce* (written some time between the ninth and the twelfth century); the erudition and refinement of the early Renaissance make their way through the involved sentences of the already mentioned

Della mercatura et del mercante perfetto by Cotrugli of Dubrovnik (Ragusa), in the fifteenth century. Countries and wares are graphically described in the Chinese *Chronicle of Various Foreign Lands* by Chau Ju-kua (early twelfth century), and, of course, more so in the book of Marco Polo, which may be mentioned here if we accept Professor Borlandi's brilliant contention that its core was a "pratica della mercatura."

This brief enumeration indicates that the genre was not strictly limited to the Italian Middle Ages, and that it could go well beyond sheer handbooks. In its narrower sense, however, the term "pratica della mercatura" covers only a very homogeneous group of manuals, nearly all of them compiled in Italy (more often than not, in Florence or by a Tuscan writer) between the late thirteenth and the late fifteenth century. Apart from a few digressions, they devote their entire space to practical data about weights and measures, moneys and exchange, commodities and techniques, markets and fairs, customs, transportation, and other details a merchant should keep ready at hand. It has often been claimed that each manual was intended to be a secret possession of the commercial company for which it had been compiled; but this contention is tenable only in the sense that no company would be unselfish enough to lend its tools to a business competitor. Most of the material could not possibly remain a secret, because it came from official tariffs or statutes, well known books of elementary arithmetic, and the daily experience of every assayer or merchant; moreover, some employees moved from one company to another, and others liked to publicize their knowledge, through manuscript copies and, as soon as it was invented, through the printing press. Indeed, a modern reader is struck by the fact that every manual reproduces almost verbatim entire pages of earlier manuals, without any apparent effort at bringing the information up to date. No doubt weights, measures, and many other data hardly ever changed, and a competent reader could easily tell the difference between live and obsolete information; but reproducing the latter was a waste of time and paper. One wonders, for instance, why the man who copied in 1472 an earlier copy of Pegolotti's manual, originally compiled between 1310 and 1340, took the trouble of including even the material on Acre "when it was in the hands of the Christians," that is, before 1291.

Nevertheless, all changes in methods and institutions sooner or later found their way in the numerous compilations preserved in various Italian archives and libraries. Unfortunately, only five of them are now available in modern, scholarly editions: the often mentioned manual of Pegolotti, which is the earliest and most important "pratica" in print; an anonymous *Tarifa zoè noticia dy pexi e mexure*, written in Venice a few years later (after 1345); an anonymous and untitled manual from the Datini archives in Prato, completed in 1385 or 1386; a manual written in Genoa, 1396, by the Florentine merchant Saminiato di Guciozzo de' Ricci and completed between 1416 and 1418 by an agent of the Medici company; and, last in time, *El libro di mercatantie et usanze de' paesi*, compiled in Dubrovnik (Ragusa), 1458, by the Florentine Giorgio di Lorenzo Chiarini on the basis of earlier manuals.[3] To these five texts we may hope that Professor Armando Sapori will soon add a critical edition of a *Libro d'avisi di fatti di mercatantia* (fourteenth century), which he has transcribed from a manuscript of the Cattedra Dantesca at the National Library of Florence; had he been less burdened with administrative work, he told me, he would have liked to publish at least an excerpt as a tribute to the memory of our common friend, Robert Reynolds.

In turn, I hope to publish in the near future a transcription of the earliest extant Italian "pratica": the *Memoria de tucte le mercantie*, compiled by a Pisan merchant or, possibly, a notary in 1279 according to the "Pisan style"—that is, in 1278. To Robert Reynolds, who in 1939 restored my liberty and strengthened my faith in the brotherhood of men by offering me a scholarship and helping me find, through Menottian consulates, a way to America, I humbly dedicate this preliminary account of a document which would have engrossed his attention, had I been ready to show it to him but a few months ago.

In Summer 1966, when I first saw in the Biblioteca Comunale of Siena the seventeenth-century manuscript which has preserved the thirteenth-century text of the *Memoria*, I was surprised that no one had yet been tempted to publish it in full. Its existence had been disclosed almost a hundred years ago to the privileged few who received a rare, privately printed pamphlet by F. Piccolomini; in 1912, Professor Monaci spread the information by reprinting in his source book of the early Italian language the meager and, altogether, ill-chosen excerpts of Piccolomini; in 1936, Allan Evans printed a few more lines and suggested some relation between the *Memoria* and the later manual of Pegolotti, of which he was giving an excellent critical edition.[4] There are, of course, some knotty problems concerning the interpretation of one or another detail; a few obviously wrong transcriptions of the seventeenth-century copyist cannot easily be amended; on the whole, however, the text is perfectly clear.

The mere fact that the *Memoria* is the oldest surviving example of an Italian "pratica della mercatura," and the only one from Pisa, would suffice to invite our attention; in addition, it includes data which cannot be found elsewhere and, above all, its organization is unique. As a matter of fact, the original from which the *Memoria* was copied did not contain only a "pratica della mercatura," but also a number of "formulae of civil suits, legal instructions . . . and other formulae for [notarial] instruments," a do-it-yourself handbook of practical astrology, and a skeleton chronicle of Pisa down to 1278. It was, hence, a well rounded repertory of all things a merchant ought to know, with the possible exception of practical arithmetic, which we may suppose the compiler of the booklet knew well enough to need no reminder. Who he actually was, we do not know; he may have exercised the notarial profession, which was not incompatible with commercial activities, but more probably he was only a well-read merchant.

The formulae are the only part of the original which the seventeenth-century copyist omitted to transcribe. The chronicle, which unlike the "pratica" and the astrological notes was printed in full by Professor Monaci, consists of very brief entries recording the dates of construction of the most important buildings (such as, "The foundation of the port of Pisa was laid in 1163"), of memorable battles and conquests (such as, "The Pisans took Sardinia from Mujahid, the Arab king, in 1016"), of the death of great personages (such as, "Messer Giovanni, judge of Gallura, died in Fucecchio, 1276, while taking part in the rebellion of the Guelphs and the Lucchese"), and a few other events shedding luster on Pisa. It may be worth noting that one of the entries refers to the capture of the famous manuscript of Justinian's Digest in Amalfi, 1140. Apart from indicating that the author was a good patriot and had an eye to the architectural embellishment of his town, the chronicle has little interest for the historian of commerce.

The "pratica" proper is much shorter than that of Pegolotti and is more loosely organized; evidently it represents an early stage of the genre, when the material was thrown together without a strict order. It does, however, try to group the information according to the following sub-headings:

1) "This is a memorandum of all commodities as they are loaded on ships in Alexandria, and of the weights according to their interrelation from one place to another";

2) "This is the memorandum of commodities as they are bought in Alexandria and of the weights used in buying them";

3) (untitled): A list of commodities and weights in other ports ranging from Acre to Ceuta, Marseille, and Southern Italy;

4) (untitled): A short list of coins;

5) "This is a memorandum of the fairs in France";

6) (untitled): A list of standard sizes for French and English cloth;

7) (untitled): Another short list of Western and Eastern coins;

8) "These are the [commodities on] sale and the weights in Laiazzo, Armenia";

9) "This is a memorandum of [duties on] sales of goods and commodities taken to Alexandria," followed almost immediately by "A memorandum of [expenses] involved in the commodities you buy there";

10) (untitled): Weights of grain, wine, and silk in Sicily and the Levant.

A large number of unrelated entries, which may have been later insertions in the margin of pages (the neat order of the copy gives no inkling of the probable irregularities of the original manuscript), add confusion to a plan which was rambling at the outset. It would be impossible for us to compress in a few lines an adequate analysis of the contents. We can only point out that the main directions of Pisan trade at the time are reflected in the comparative abundance of details on Egypt, Syria and Cilician Armenia, North Africa, and the "Regno" (that is, the kingdom of Sicily, then embracing both the island and the southern third of the Italian peninsula). Significantly, the "Regno" vies with Alexandria for the first place in the number of entries. Its chief exports are heavy and inexpensive foodstuffs, whereas Alexandria, Acre (which comes third in the number of entries) and, in general, the Levant are noted especially for spices and other light and valuable goods. On the other hand, Constantinople is mentioned less frequently than one might have expected— obviously the Pisans had lost much ground to the Genoese and the Venetians—and French cloth, later the most precious counterpart of imports from the Levant, does not seem to play as large a role as it does in later manuals.[5]

There are a few interesting details on costs and duties, but most of the entries aim at providing some guidance through the bewildering maze of discordant weights, measures, and coins. Why do a hundred *salme* of wine from Scalea, in Calabria, correspond in Tunis to 95 *mezzaruole*, whereas a hundred *salme* of unspecified Calabrian wine correspond only to 82 *mezzaruole*? Why does a *centenario* (hundredweight) of hazel-nuts from Naples correspond to between 150 and 155 *cantari* in Tunis but to 145 *cantari* in nearby Bougie, whereas a *centenario* of walnuts from Naples corresponds to 140 *cantari* both in Tunis and in Bougie? We do not know, but a merchant had better be informed. Perhaps the difference depended on tares: "brazil-wood [is bought in Alexandria] by the *cantare fulfuli* (the pepper cantar), and you have to give six *cantari* in the place of five, and this is for allowance made for the wood." Perhaps the difference depended on local port uses: "When freighting, 225 *cubelle* of Salerno are reckoned at one *centenario* of Naples, but [actually] they are more than that." When a merchant had the good surprise of coming across familiar measures, he noted it with the greatest pleasure: "In Morea (Peloponnesus) people weigh by the Lucchese pound, which is one fifth of an ounce larger than the Pisan one." It does not matter that the Moreans had made no conscious effort at borrowing their pound from far away, land-locked Lucca; the weight was the same, and a Pisan merchant, neighbor and hence enemy of the Lucchese, when traveling abroad acknowledged his kinship.

All in all, the material in the Pisan "pratica" bears a great resemblance to the richer material in Pegolotti, whose manual was compiled in nearby Florence some fifty years later. A large proportion of the entries reappear in Pegolotti, usually with the same numerical equivalences, but with a different wording and order, which leads us to doubt that there may have been direct borrowing. But this does not in the least diminish our interest in reading an earlier version of the same information. Moreover, there is a sufficient number of entries—especially on Acre, Laiazzo, and some southern Italian ports—which cannot be found elsewhere, so that the *Memoria*, even in its "pratica" core, will not read like a duplication of other published manuals.

Still, the most striking feature of the *Memoria* is its astrological appendix, which is almost one-half as long as the "pratica" proper. Such a close connection of spices and stars does not occur in any other manual, and it certainly gives food for thought. After a strictly businesslike directory of weights, commodities, and tariffs, which *mutatis mutandis* would fit the most rational commercial handbook of our time, we are suddenly thrown deep into the Middle Ages. No doubt it was known that astrology played a great part in the decisions of princes, clergymen, philosophers, and physicians; but it did not readily occur to our mind that it might influence so strongly an ordinary merchant. We know that he tried to foretell the prospects for the harvest; the *Memoria* drives us to wonder whether his purchases of grain on the stalk were arranged according to the following forecasts:

"If the calends of January fall on a Sunday . . . grain will be neither cheap nor expensive. If they fall on a Monday . . . there will be plenty of grain. If they fall on a Tuesday . . . grain will be dear"; and so forth and so on.

Again, merchants were aware of seasonal fluctuations in prices; the fifteenth-century manuals of Chiarini and Uzzano, in particular, include a most detailed account of the places and dates where and when "money is dear." Sailors, in addition, had to keep in mind the prevailing winds and storms at different times of the year. How did all this agree with astrological lore? Were its previsions a mere "rationalization" of observed facts, or did the science of the stars disagree with the experience of travelers? "When the moon is in Gemini, it is good to get out of a port if the voyage had already begun . . . but if it has not, you should not sail, for it is a token of wind." "Libra: it is good to begin all travel by ship or on land, to buy and to sell, for this is a token of air." "Virgo: do travel by sea and land, buy, sell, begin anything, for this is a token of land." Nor is this the only meaning of the constellation, for under Virgo "you must not marry a maiden; if she is not a maiden, go ahead."

How typical was this advice? How closely was it followed? We cannot tell: the correspondence between employees of great companies of merchant bankers (such as the Sienese Tolomei, the Pistoiese Partini, the Pratese Datini, and the Florentine Medici) hardly ever includes horoscopes among the innumerable pieces of advice on what to buy or not to buy. Sailors, however, even today gaze at the stars more often than bankers. Be that as it may, it is a comforting sign that according to the *Memoria*, eight constellations out of twelve are especially favorable to shipping, and only one, Scorpio, is unfavorable to all kinds of work. After all, the medieval merchant was entitled to a month of vacation.[6]

NOTES

1. B. Cotrugli, *Della mercatura et del mercante perfetto* (Venice, 1573), p. 36; transl. in R. S. Lopez and I. W. Raymond, *Medieval Trade in the Mediterranean World* (New York, 1955), p. 375 ff.; see also p. 409 and 413–18.

2. The best short introduction to this kind of works is F. Borlandi's preface to his edition of *El libro di mercatantie et usanze de'paesi* (Turin, 1936), with bibliography; see also A. Sapori, *Le marchand italien au moyen âge* (Paris, 1952), p. lxvi f.; A. Fanfani, *Storia delle dottrine economiche dall'antichità al XIX secolo* (Messina-Milan, 1955), p. 78; Lopez and Raymond, p. 342 f.; F. Borlandi, "Alle origini del libro di Marco Polo", *Studi in onore di A. Fanfani* (Milan, 1962), I, 107 ff., etc.

3. F. di B. Pegolotti, *La pratica della mercatura*, edited by Allan Evans (Cambridge, Mass., 1936); *Tarifa . . .* , edited by the Istituto Superiore di Scienze Economiche e Commerciali di Venezia (Venice, 1925); *La "pratica di mercatura" datiniana*, edited by Cesare Ciano (Milan, 1964); *Il manuale di mercatura di Saminiato de' Ricci*, edited by Antonia Borlandi (Genoa, 1963); *El libro di mercatantie . . .* , edited by Franco Borlandi, cit. Each of these is supplied with useful introductions and critical appendixes. Two shorter fragments were published by Colangelo, "I pesi, le monete e le misure nel commercio veneto-pugliese alla fine del XIII e principio del XIV secolo," *Rassegna Pugliese* (1901, fasc. 8–9), and Piattoli, *L'origine dei fondaci datiniani in Pisa ed in Genova* (Prato, 1930). On the other hand, we cannot regard as a critical edition, though it is a useful one, that of Giovanni di Bernardo da Uzzano, *Libro di gabelle*, in G. F. Pagnini, *Della decima e di altre gravezze imposte dal comune di Firenze* (Lisbon-Lucca, 1765–66), IV; much less so, the early prints cited by Borlandi, preface cit., xvii, n. 3.

4. E. Monaci, *Crestomazia italiana dei primi secoli* (Città di Castello, 1912), p. 356 ff. (p. 405 ff. of the second edition, 1955); cf. Evans, preface to Pegolotti, p. XXXV ff.; later writers also refer to Monaci but add nothing to what he says.

5. In general, for the background of Pisan history, see D. Herlihy, *Pisa in the Early Renaissance* (New Haven, Conn., 1958) and E. Cristiani, *Nobiltà e popolo nel comune di Pisa* (Naples, 1962). On the position of Pisa in international trade see also G. Rossi Sabatini, *L'espansione di Pisa nel Mediterraneo fino alla Meloria* (Florence, 1935) and R. S. Lopez, *The Birth of Europe,* book III, ch. 1.

6. In the long interval between the delivery of this paper to the press and its publication another manual has appeared in an excellent critical edition: *Zibaldone da Canal*, with comments by A. Stussi, F. C. Lane, T. E. Marston, and O. Ore (Venice, 1967). This manual, compiled in Venice after 1320, also contains astrological material. I cannot take it up here, but I shall do so in a forthcoming paper to appear in *Revue Historique.*

ITALIAN MERCHANTS AND THE PERFORMANCE OF PAPAL BANKING FUNCTIONS IN THE EARLY THIRTEENTH CENTURY

GLENN OLSEN

Seattle University

In his *Papal Revenues in the Middle Ages,* William E. Lunt stated that the official use of Italian firms of bankers by the papacy is first observed in 1232.[1] He noted that already in the twelfth century the papacy was using outside agents, especially the Templars, to perform many of the duties which were later accomplished by the Italian papal bankers, but hesitated to call these agents cameral merchants or bankers, since it was only in the period after 1232 that the names *campsor domini papae* and *campsores* or *mercatores papae* or *camerae* appeared in the papal documents.[2] He noted one exception to his statement in the existence at the papal court of a *cambiator* at the end of the twelfth century, but did not wish to designate this person a papal banker unless he could be associated with those who were performing such tasks as the transport of *census* to the *camera* at this period.[3] This identification could not be made, and therefore the date 1232 remained as the earliest date at which an Italian merchant was officially titled *campsor domini papae.*

Since Lunt wrote, more has been learned of the earlier history of the Italian merchant-bankers, and it now seems certain that there existed special relationships between Italian, especially Roman, merchants and the papacy from before the time of Gregory VII.[4] This is of course not surprising. However, what these relationships were has not yet been analyzed in terms of the appearance of the official position *campsor domini papae.* The purpose of the present paper is to describe the functions of the agents which were being used in the later twelfth and earlier thirteenth centuries—before 1232—in order to determine the extent to which these agents already were acting as bankers for the papacy.

The functions which papal merchant-bankers performed after 1232 are many. These may, following Lunt, simply be listed as a standard against which the functions of the Templars, the Hospitallers, and the Italian merchants and societies of merchants which were used by Honorius III (1216–27) and earlier popes may be compared in the attempt to ascertain the degree to which these men and organizations were papal exchangers or merchants in function, if not in name. Papal merchants (1) transferred collectors' (of *census,* tenths, etc.) funds to the *camera*; (2) were used for the deposit of funds (pending transference to the *camera*); (3) were used for the exchange of money; (4) extended credit to ecclesiastics needing funds for their business at the Roman Curia; (5) frequently lent money to the *camera.*[5] These seem to have been the main tasks of papal merchants in the period of the mid-thirteenth century and following. Of course some of these functions are more important than others, and some gained in importance in the later Middle Ages.[6]

The use of the Templars and Hospitallers by the papacy must be considered first. The Templars were particularly well suited for the transference of money and the effecting of payments at a distance. As Léopold Delisle has pointed out, they were established in all the countries of Europe and in the Latin East, were well armed and acquainted with both land and sea routes, and were capable both of transporting physically large sums of money and, by means of correspondence, of effecting payments at a distance without any actual transportation of money.[7] Lunt has noted that in the latter half of the twelfth century the Templars were being used for the transference and exchange of funds and the contracting of loans, and that their Temples were being used as places of deposit; the latter function was retained throughout the thirteenth century.[8] A survey of the documents concerning the Templars from the pontificates of Innocent III (1198–1216) and Honorius III shows that the Knightly Orders retained their functions as the transferors of large sums of money, as well as their duties as operators of places of deposit, through Honorius' reign. These, however, were activities that could give only a modest place in papal banking activities to the Military Orders, for the Orders were not important in such vital functions as the giving of loans at the Curia, undoubtedly because they did not have a house of the Temple, or headquarters, in Rome.[9] From the beginning prelates visiting Rome turned to the local merchants for loans. There is no indication in the papal documents that the Templars at this period were lending money to the papacy, although their dealings with secular rulers, as well as abbots and bishops, involved a good deal of lending. Therefore, although the Knightly Orders retained their role as transferors of papal funds and as operators of places of deposit, we must turn to a consideration of the Italian merchants to see the development of the position *campsor domini papae.*

The Italian merchants were not used for deposit; this function remained in the hands of the Knightly Orders, monasteries, and churches. The real importance of the Italian merchants was in the field of credit operations. Before this importance can be understood, and the activities of the merchants in papal finance portrayed, some idea must be given of the credit and exchange techniques used by the Italian, and especially the Roman, merchants. Although the evidence from papal documents is vague on this point, we may assume that the Italian merchants were involved in the transference of funds by the *instrumentum ex causa cambii,* when any of their duties for the papacy involved the transmission of funds.[10] As will be seen immediately below, this was the normal instrument of transfer in their private dealings, and so we are to assume that it was also used in papal finance. Documents not connected with papal finance tend to substantiate this. In 1202 a prelate traveling to Rome exchanged his money for such an instrument at the Champagne Fairs.[11] Again, in 1225 Roman merchants were dealing with Henry III through exchange contracts.[12]

But much more specific evidence may be gained by referring to a handful of documents preserved in the Genoese archives. These are not concerned with papal finance, but they do give a clear picture of the organization and techniques of the Roman merchants at the end of the twelfth century. It seems reasonable to assume that if the financial techniques evident in these documents had been attained by 1191, the year from which they date, those Romans who were directly associated with the papacy were capable of using the same techniques in papal affairs. Since we are above all interested in Roman, as opposed to Italian, merchants, because the Romans are known to have been associated with the earlier twelfth-century popes as well as officially with the papacy after 1232, these documents provide a valuable source for the inference of Roman techniques throughout this period. They are valuable, too, simply because they show that the Roman merchants were established as merchant-bankers in the trade with the Champagne Fairs almost a generation before Schaube and earlier scholars had noted them.[13] When we have described these materials from 1191, we will turn to those Romans dealing directly with the papacy.

The merchants are met with in the Genoese documents in the

following manner. In November of 1191 Henry VI, Holy Roman Emperor, arrived in Genoa with his court. Henry himself was involved in transactions of November 12 and 17 preserved in the archives.[14] From November 11–16 seven documents survive involving Roman merchants, only one of whom was mentioned either immediately before or after these dates. This perhaps suggests that most of these Romans were travelling with the Imperial court, though in these documents they are involved in their own business.[15] The size of the loans involved shows that these men were already very important, for the transactions are for large sums of money. Although none of these Romans are found in the papal documents of Innocent III or Honorius III, two of them were probably related to men later involved in papal finance. The first of these, Petrus Ianni Zencij, only appears as a witness in one of the documents, and thus it is not certain that he was travelling with the royal court.[16] But he is undoubtedly of the well-known Cencii family of Rome, two of whose members appear in the documents of Honorius' reign given below. The other man is Nicola Iohannis Nicole, who may be related to Gerhardus Johannis de Nicolao, who frequently appears in the time of Honorius.

The simplest way to present the type of financial operations these Romans were involved in is to summarize and then comment on these brief documents in the order in which they appear in the archives. The first transaction took place on November 11.[17] Nicola Petri Ugozonis lent to Walzerus, elect of Cambrai, "tantum." Although this "tantum" may simply refer to the 450 marks of silver which Walzerus was now indebted for, often this expression was used to conceal the taking of interest.[18] In this case its use would signify that though Walzerus was indebted for 450 marks, he had received less than that amount, the difference representing the taking of interest. In any case Walzerus now owed 450 marks to Nicola Petri Ugozonis and his partners. The partners, to any of whom the loan was payable, were Manfredus Groja and Laurentius Romani Anastasij, who would each receive a hundred marks, Nicola Petri Uguzonis himself and Nicola Iohannis Nicole who together would receive 200 marks, and Oliverius Garzulino, who was to receive 50 marks. Thus a partnership or temporary syndicate of five Romans had been formed to make a loan to Walzerus. The usual precautions regarding payment were taken, and, in addition to Walzerus, his chaplain, subdeacon, and Tefo, *juratus*, also similarly swore to pay, obliging their goods in pledge under double penalty and renouncing *iuri solidi* and *iuri omni.*[19] In addition these men swore that they would make Egidius de Montibus, Nicolaus de Poncello, Balduinus, *juratus*, and Lambertum de Montibus to swear similarly that the loan would be paid back. The normal list of witnesses appears and the document closes with a sentence which allows for another possibility of taking interest. If the loan, or part of it, should not be paid on time (*ad medium januarium Laniaco*—the fair of Lagny began on January 2) it could also be paid at the fair of Bar-sur-Aube, which began on the Tuesday before mid-Lent. If this were done the rate of payment would now be 20 sterling for each mark instead of 13 sol. 4 den. per mark.

Another notarial document exists from the same day concerning the above transaction. Oliverius Garzulino, one of the members of the above partnership, named two of his partners, Nicola di Pietro Uguzone and Nicola Iohannis Nicole, as his agents (*suos missos*), who were themselves, or in turn through their agents, to collect the 50 marks due him from Walzerus, elect of Cambrai.[20] This document thus shows further the nature of the technique used by the Romans of this period. Once having formed a partnership, one member could commission another as his agent to collect for him the amount he had contributed to the loan given by the partnership. In turn this agent might also have agents.

Two days later by a similar document Manfredus Groja and Laurentius Romani Anastasij, the two other members of the partnership, also named Nicola di Pietro Uguzone as their procurator to collect the 100 mark amount which each of them was to receive. Thus one man had been designated as procurator for each of the other four in the partnership.[21]

On the next day two Romans, both of whom were involved in the loan to Walzerus of Cambrai, made a loan to the archdeacon Savarixius of Constantia and of Narentona, who from the context of the document seems to have been in the employ of the Curia.[22] This small loan of 30 marks of silver was given by Laurentius Romani Anastasii and Oliverius Garzulino, and was to be paid fifteen days after Christmas in Rome. The document closes with the taking of an oath to fulfill the conditions of the loan unless impeded by God or given new terms by the merchants. Brother Michel de Sancto Benedicto de Placentia and Master Rizardus swore, with a formula similar to the first Genoese document, to oblige themselves for the loan under double penalty. They renounced *iuri quo cavetur principalem debitorem primo conveniri.*[23] This document probably contains the taking of interest, since the archdeacon only admits to having received "tantum" while he explicitly owes 30 marks at 13 sol. 4 den. to the mark.[24]

Another document of the same day, November 14, shows that these Romans were not simply dealing in money transactions, but that they were merchants who engaged in money-lending.[25] In this document Iohannes de Romano BonoVicino acknowledged that he had received in pledge from Laurentius Romani Anastasij, who is noted for the third time, eighteen pieces of cloth "de Mensa" (Amiens) for transportation to Rome. It was agreed that Iohannes should receive for this cloth 65 pounds "bonorum previdixium de senatu" (Roman pounds) in a week when he would have brought it to Rome for the 60 pounds "den. ian." (Genoese pounds) which Laurentius acknowledged to have received from him. The remainder of the document reveals how the merchants were transporting their cloth and receiving payment before sale—for this document really is a variation of the above loans. Laurentius had received an advance payment (or loan) on the pledge (the eighteen pieces of cloth) which he had given for the loan. It was apparently not intended that the loan should be paid back, and thus finally the pledge of cloth would be sold by Iohannes. The pledge (that is, the cloth valued at 65 pounds in Rome) was to go to Iohannes as his payment, but if the cloth brought more than 65 Roman pounds the excess was to go to Laurentius. This shows that this was in fact a variation on the above loans and not an outright sale, for if it had been a sale it might be expected that Iohannes himself would receive any excess of 65 pounds. Therefore the loan was a means for effecting an advance payment on a shipment of cloth while providing for its transportation, its sale, the "salary" of the agent for these tasks, and its insurance. This is buttressed finally by the fact that Laurentius remained liable for any expense. On the matter of insurance, the loan was "insured" in the sense that the risk of loss was to be shared by both the owner and the transport agent. The conveyor was responsible for the loss of the cloth valued at 60 Genoese pounds, which was still the pledge owned by Laurentius, while Laurentius would lose the value of the cloth over its pledge value if it was lost. He would lose the *superfluum*. On this loan, if the cloth were lost Iohannes would lose 60 Genoese pounds and Laurentius the remainder of its value.

In a third document of this date the same Laurentius acknowledged himself a debtor of the afore-mentioned Oliverius Garzulino.[26]

Laurentius acknowledged that he owed 101 Roman pounds and five shillings due in a week when Oliverius would be in Rome, for a loan of "tantum" received from him. For this loan he gave as pledge ". . . pecias .18. de Mensa et pecias .12. de baldinellis [linen] et pecias .12. de vergatis et cannas .34. de Mustarolo [cloth from Montreuil] . . ."[27] Oliverius avowed having these and that he ought carry them to Rome ". . . ad suam fortunam in tantum quantum est suum pagamentum et superfluum ad fortunam Laurentii et ad expensas Laurentii." When he arrived at Rome, Oliverius promised that he would give the aforesaid pledge to Paul, the brother of Laurentius ". . . si ipse dederit sibi bonum redditorem et pagatorem de predictis libris persolvendis ad terminum." If Paul should not pay at the fixed date, Oliverius ". . . sua auctoritate et sine magistratus decreto, licentia Laurentii, vendat pignus predictum et quicquid voluerit faciat proprio iure, sine omni eius omniumque pro eo contradictione."

Thus this loan is of the same type as the last, but is more explicit. Laurentius received a sum of money from Oliverius. For this money he gave a pledge of cloth to Oliverius, who was to take this cloth to Rome. At Rome he would give the cloth to Laurentius' brother, Paul, who would pay him 101 pounds and five shillings. If he failed to do this, the cloth became Oliverius'. Any amount over 101 pounds and five shillings was to go to Laurentius, which shows that he still owned the cloth. Thus Oliverius was really a conveyor of goods who was to receive more in Rome than he lent in Genoa for the pledge of cloth. Laurentius' brother, Paul, was in fact his agent in Rome. It is possible that the preceding document also assumed an agent in Rome, but this was not explicitly mentioned.

The last document is from November 16, and concerns only a small loan.[28] Wido Segnoretus acknowledged that he would give Nigrinus Aprioculo or his agent ". . . lib. .13. bonorum previdixium . . . et expensas et dampnum et mutuum . . ." in fifteen days when Nigrinus would be in Rome. The document closes with the following statement, which permits a classification of this loan: "Et sua bona pignori obligat, salvo eunte ligno in quo ibit Wido vel maiori parte rerum ligni."[29] This phrase indicates that this was a sea loan. The phrase ". . . salvo eunte ligno . . . vel maiori parte rerum ligni" is a standard phrase indicating that the borrower, Wido, was insured against disaster. If the greater part of the goods in which he had invested the loan should fail to reach Rome, Nigrinus would lose the small amount he had invested in the cargo.[30]

From these documents it can be seen that by the late twelfth century the Roman merchants were already well-travelled and established in the commercial world. They were familiar with the Champagne fairs, may have been associated with the Holy Roman Emperor, and had enough capital to engage in money-lending as well as merchant activities. They probably had some familiarity with the formulas taken from the Roman law and used by the notaries, had developed means for taking or concealing interest, were using partnerships, and used agents both to collect and to pay debts, as well as to sell cloth. They were giving large loans and dealing in cloth in quantity. Finally they were familiar with the "cambium" or exchange loan and with the sea loan, and therefore were able to obtain at least elementary forms of insurance. It seems reasonable to assume that although the documents of twenty-five years later from papal sources are not nearly as specific as these from the Genoese archives, the developments noted in the Genoese cartularies still persisted. Above all the relationship between commerce and banking may be assumed to have persisted. The future "papal merchants" were first and foremost merchants who had obtained enough surplus capital to engage in money-lending.

Now that the techniques which the Roman merchants used before 1200 in non-papal merchant-banker activities have been shown, we may turn to the relation of the Italian merchants to the papacy. Feodor Schneider, who has dealt with the earlier papal financial organization, believes that by 1220 the triumph of the Italian merchants over the Knightly Orders in managing the papal financial affairs was assured. This triumph he attributes to the relatively cumbersome organization of the Orders, whose essential purpose was military and not financial, as compared to the business management of the merchants.[31] It would seem that the predominance of the Italians has an even simpler explanation. Although the Knightly Orders were important in deposit and transference of funds because of their early financial involvement in the Crusades, they had obtained no similar early control over loans given in connection with business at the Papal Court. The men who were related to the Curia for the purpose of money-lending were all merchants.

Though Italians had lent money to and at the Curia long before 1175, we may take this as a beginning date for our examination of their relations with the Curia.[32] For it is from about this time that the organization of the merchants among themselves, and the succession of Roman families who are later officially involved in papal finance, becomes discernable and continuous. Of primary concern here is the evidence of loans to the Curia itself, or loans at the Curia to prelates dealing in Rome on financial matters with the pope and *camera*. An especially interesting association of merchants lending to the pope is met with in 1175–76.[33] The members, besides Malabranca, O. Benedicti de Bona, and A. de Balduino, include a Bovo de Petri, who, as Schneider suggests, may be a relative of the Bobo Iohannis Bobonis and Bobo Oddonis Bobonis who appear in the early thirteenth-century documents.[34]

At least one name catches the eye in another group of Roman merchants of this period. The group varied in size and evidently combined as a varying number of partners for each transaction. At the head of these merchants was Alcheruzzus Romani de Rustico.[35] With him two merchants, one of them Petrus Cencii Petri de Nicolao, are commonly associated as partners. Again, one of these, Romanus Iohannis de Anastasio, was probably related to the Laurentius Romani Anastasio already met in the Genoese documents. These men are not called *mercatores* as later, but *cives Romani*[36] To give one example of their activity, a letter of Alexander III (1159–81) of August 10, 1179, mentions that the Lateran chapter and its prior John had paid a loan of 294 pounds incurred by the pope with three of these men, "Romanis civibus, iudicibus et advocatis."[37]

Several other examples of loans to the pope by Romans and other Italian merchants remain from this period.[38] But rather than multiply examples we may turn to the other division of moneylending and note that the Romans were also making use of their position at Rome to lend money to visiting prelates. It is certainly reasonable to assume that this dual function of lending to both pope and prelate was, at this period as earlier in the century, giving the Romans a privileged position at the papal court and was preparing for the time when they would become the official papal exchangers. Prelates came to Rome for many reasons, and often the length of their stay or the nature of their business forced them to borrow funds.[39] Thus in 1178 the Prior of the Augustinian monastery at Canterbury, having already borrowed from the merchants of Flanders, borrowed a large sum from the Romans.[40] Or again, in Celestine III's reign (1191–98) the bishop of Utrecht is seen to have contracted a debt of 1250 marks of silver with Roman and Sienese bankers.[41]

Turning to the pontificates of Innocent III and Honorius III it may be noted that these curial prelate-loans were a part of the development, already noted in the Genoese documents, in which by the late twelfth century the Roman merchants had established themselves at the Champagne fairs. For as it was natural to contract these prelate-loans with Roman money-lenders, so did it become customary to pay back these debts at the Champagne fairs.[42] As Adolf Schaube has pointed out, prominent among the loans to prelates are those to the German ecclesiastics, these loans again being tied to the development of trade relations by the Italian merchants.[43] In 1209 the Archbishop of Mainz, through his plenipotentiary at the Curia, obtained a loan from a Bolognese and a Roman merchant, Gerhardus Johannis de Nicolao, who is met again during Honorius' reign.[44] The loan was to be repaid with 150 marks of silver of Cologne at the next fair of Bar.[45]

There are several similar documents, connected with a schism which had developed in Cologne, concerning Romans dealing with the archbishopric of Cologne in the 1210's and 1220's.[46] It is not necessary to mention all these loans, but these merchants, who are met with in the Registers of Honorius, are mentioned: Matthaeus Guidonis Marronis, Angelus Johannis Judaei, Jacobus Scarsus, Petrus Sarracennus, Petrus de Paulo, his son Angelus, Johannes Pantaleonis, Petrus de Centio de Lavina, Johannes Cencii, Johannes Romani Deuteguardae, Petrus de Johanne Romani, and Johannes Bobonis.[47] At least seven loans were arranged, several of which were added to older unpaid loans. It is not definitely known that every one of these loans was made in Rome, but at least one letter of Honorius from 1217, which quit the church of Cologne of a loan of 160 marks, which had been borrowed from Johannes Bobonis, implies that this loan had been arranged at Rome and shows a close relationship between this merchant and the *camera*. The *camerarius* had arranged for the indigent Theoderic, Archbishop of Cologne, to receive a loan from Johannes Bobonis. Later the loan had been paid back through a papal subdeacon in the name of the church of Cologne. Significantly, a Bobo Johannis Bobonis is designated "exchanger of the lord pope" in 1238, twenty years after this transaction, as will be seen below. Again we see the continuing role of the Boboni family in papal finance. A later source from 1238 referring back to the debts incurred by Theoderic also states that another of these loans was contracted in Rome at the Curia with Roman exchangers.[48]

From the *Rotuli Litterarum Clausarum* of 1213 it is found that it was not only prelates who were borrowing from the merchants while at the Curia.[49] In a letter King John of England had ordered his treasurer and *camerarius* to pay to Romanus Nicolae, who was possibly related to the Nicola Iohannis Nicole of the Genoese documents, the debt which his last legation to the Curia had contracted with him and his partners for 235 marks.

A last example from the period of Innocent III may be drawn from another non-papal source, this time the *Gesta abbatum monasterii Sancti Albani* concerning the year 1215. This delightful passage has been translated by Lunt, and definitely mentions that in 1215 there were usurers at the Papal Court from which a needy prelate could obtain a loan.[50] Though this agrees with our other sources, we can not be sure of the reliability of the account, for it comes through the hands of Thomas Walsingham, writing under Richard II, or rather probably editing an account by Matthew Paris, who himself may have been using an earlier account.[51]

The pontificate of Honorius may now be considered. The first two letters in Honorius' Register concerning the Italian merchants date from December 1217.[52] Both of these letters are addressed to the Abbot of St. Loup in Troyes. In the first Honorius ordered him to compel the Bishop of Le Puy to repay a loan to Sienese merchants if the said Bishop had not already done so.[53] In the second the merchants ". . . Gregorius Alexii, Petrus de Centio, Petrus de Bove et Matheus Iohannis Darie cives Romani, necnon Rantius Spinellus, Hugolinus Urlandi Castellanus tabernarii, et Boncompagnus, Reruverus et Bulgarinus Senenses pro se sociisque . . ." had given a loan to R., master of the schools, and B., clerk, procurators of the Bishop of Vivarais.[54] Again, Honorius commanded the Abbot of St. Loup to enforce the payment of this loan. It is not known whether these loans were given at the Curia itself or at the fairs of Champagne. What is important to note is the protection which the pope was giving to these merchants, one of whom seems to have been of the Boboni family.[55]

From 1218 there is another indication of the English borrowing from the Italian merchants while at the Curia. Henry III sent Petrus Sarracenus, a Roman who has already been seen engaged in lending to prelates and who about this time appeared in the service of the English king, together with the Bishop of Chichester and two nuncios to the Curia.[56] Henry secured for them a general letter of credit which enabled them to borrow up to 6000 marks of sterling.[57] Although it is not known that this loan was transacted at Rome, it is very likely that it was, since its purpose was ". . . ad agenda nostra promovenda in curia Romana."[58]

There are again several transactions recorded in letters from

1219, two of which are of interest.[59] As Robert Davidsohn has pointed out, the presence at Rome of Florentine merchants can first be detected in 1219.[60] In this year a partnership of Florentine and Roman merchants was involved at the Curia in a dispute over a loan given to Bishop Walter of Chartres.[61] The loan, originally contracted at the Curia, was, however, principally with Romans. Besides certain unnamed Roman and Florentine merchants who were their partners, those Romans mentioned in the papal letter are Angelus Iohannis Iudei, Iacobus Scarso, Giraldus Iohannis Nycolai, Gualterus Manerio, Angelus Cathelino, and Romano Malialardi.[62] The loan was probably contracted in 1218 since in this letter of January 16, 1219, the pope declared the appointment of a procurator for the Bishop in his legal process with his creditors at the Curia. The other loan noted in this year is similar to several already described, and was obtained from a Roman, Iohannes Alexii, who has also been noted in previous loans.[63] From the letter of Honorius of August 8 it is seen that Iohannes was trying to recover from an abbot money which he had lent at the Apostolic See to his predecessor.

A letter of Honorius from 1220 mentions that the pope ordered Pandulph, his *camerarius* and legate in England, to give 150 of the 250 marks of silver which the king had deposited with him to the Roman Jacobus Siccaficoro.[64] One can only speculate whether this transaction had to do with a royal debt, the twentieth, or the *census,* and whether the Roman citizen was acting as an agent of the pope —for instance, as a transferor of funds to the *camera*—or in his own business supported by the interest of the pope.

In 1224 Stephanus de Lucy and Godefredus de Crawecombe, at the Curia on business for Henry III, borrowed from the Florentine Johannes Galfredi and the Roman Johannis Nicolai a loan which was paid back with 500 marks sterling.[65] In the next year, possibly in connection with the business of 1224, the king sent a citizen of London, presumably to one of the fairs of Champagne, with 3300 marks of sterling to be paid to the Roman merchants for a loan which had been obtained for transacting royal affairs at the Roman Curia.[66] Two weeks earlier, on June 1, Henry had directed that an order (or letter or bill of some type) for 1100 marks of sterling conveyed to him by Roman merchants be paid; this transaction also involved Henry's dealings at the Curia.[67]

Although several loans are known from the years 1226–27, it is not certain that any of these were contracted in business at the

Curia.[68] An undated transaction is mentioned in the year 1237 in a letter of Gregory IX (1227–41). All that is known from this letter is that under Honorius the university of the scholars of Paris had sent four procurators to the Apostolic See, and that a loan contracted there with Johannes de Gualfredo, Roman and Florentine citizen, had not been repaid.[69]

Before stating the conclusion two more documents from the time of Gregory IX may be introduced. For the year 1229 Matthew Paris has written that the papal collector in England, Stephen:[70]

> . . .had with him certain most wicked usurers, who called themselves merchants, cloaking usury under the name of the business of banking, who offered money to those who were poor and vexed with exactions; and the said Stephen urging, many were forced under the severest penalty to accept a loan, who afterward fell into their snares, incurring irreparable damages.

Therefore merchants, almost certainly Romans, could be found not only making loans at the Curia in Italy, but also following the principal collectors while engaged in lending.

The second passage of interest is from the *Liber censuum*. A papal receipt issued to cameral merchants in 1233 calls Angelirius Solaficu the former exchanger *(campsor)* of the pope.[71] This merchant and his Sienese colleagues had been receiving and dispensing money for the Roman Court. Thus in 1233 the title, not the function, of *campsor* was what was new.

In drawing the threads of the various developments presented above together, one fact, previously mentioned, must be emphasized. The man designated in 1238 as a *campsor domini papae* was the same Bobo Johannis Bobonis whose family name was noticed in the documents of Alexander III and who was probably related to the Petrus de Bove and related to or identified with the Iohannis Bobonis who appeared in the documents of the earlier part of Honorius' reign.[72] Therefore it may be stated that although official recognition of the relationship between certain merchants and the Curia, and the development of the title "exchanger of the lord pope" to designate this position, occurred in the 1230's, both the functions and possibly one of the men so designated appear in a steadily developing relationship between merchants and Curia from the twelfth century to the beginning of Gregory IX's pontificate. In this development the Knightly Orders retained their importance as operators of places of deposit and as transferors of funds, but by the end of Innocent III's reign the Italian merchants were well intrenched in the financial functions which were to become most important in the following years—specifically those of lending at the Roman Curia. Especially prominent was the Boboni family, which was apparently continuously involved in papal finance from at least 1175 to the 1230's. This family, related to both a pope and to several cardinals during this period, was active in extending loans at Rome, apparently with the active cooperation of the papacy, and produced one of the first men entitled *campsor domini papae* in the 1230's.

To summarize the functions of the Italian merchants during Honorius' pontificate in terms of the criteria proposed at the beginning of this study: (1) They were transferring collectors' funds to the *camera*. (2) They were not noticeably used for deposit. (3) By the very nature of their transactions they were involved in the exchange of money. The probabilities based on the advanced development of the Roman merchants by 1191 make it safe to assume that the papacy was using the merchants to transfer funds well before 1233. This transference would have used the methods of merchant commodity exchange and loans described in the Genoese documents. (4) They had gained a monopoly of the loans to prelates made at the Curia. (5) They were not, as apparently was no one else either, lending funds to the *camera* itself. These functions were not being performed solely by any one group or syndicate of merchants, and this is also true of the pontificate of Gregory IX. Rather, certain merchants and groups of merchants, predominantly Romans, appear to have been favored by the pope. These merchants, appearing repeatedly in the documents, evidently combined and recombined as various loans were desired by prelates at the court, or as the papacy had funds to be transferred to Rome from other countries. Certain men appear together more than once, but by and large each loan or assignment seems to have been negotiated by a partnership or syndicate set up for that purpose. Whether some of these men were physically situated at the Curia, as the *Gesta abbatum monasterii Sancti Albani* from 1215 says, or whether such officials as the *camerarius* ordinarily directed their business to them, as has been seen in the letter of 1217 in which the loan was given " . . . by the noble man Johannis Bobonis, Roman citizen, through the hand of our beloved son S[tephan], cardinal priest of the Basilica of the Twelve Apostles and *camerarius* of the Roman Church. . .," can not definitely be established.[73] But it is certain that by the end of the twelfth century they were the customary source for raising loans needed in expediting business at the Roman Curia.

NOTES

1. The following study was suggested by the late Prof. Robert L. Reynolds, who introduced me to the Genoese documents used in it, and with his consistent graciousness and skill directed me in their interpretation. See William E. Lunt, *Papal Revenues in the Middle Ages* (2 vols., New York, 1934) I, 51. Lunt's discussion of papal bankers is based on E. Jordan, *De mercatoribus camerae apostolicae saeculo XIII* (Rennes, 1909) which uses a few of the materials discussed in the following pages, but is very incomplete.

2. Lunt, *Papal Revenues,* I, 51–2. "Banker" is not an exact translation of the Latin *campsor* or *mercator.* I will use instead the Shakesperean word "exchanger," or the general terms "merchant" or "merchant-banker." This will stress the point that the Italians under discussion are essentially merchants who also perform some financial tasks for the papacy. See Raymond de Roover, "New Interpretations of the History of Banking," in *Journal of World History,* II (1954), 38–39.

3. Lunt, *Papal Revenues,* I, 51–52. Paul Fabre, *Le Liber censuum de l'église romaine* (2 vols., Paris, 1905) I, 306.

4. See especially for bibliography Robert S. Lopez, "A propos d'une virgule: le facteur économique dans la politique africaine des papes," in *Revue historique,* CXCIX (1947), 178–188. This article shows that Roman merchants were associated informally with the papacy already in the time of Gregory VII. Also helpful are Demetrius B. Zema, "The Houses of Tuscany and of Pierleone in the Crisis of Rome in the Eleventh Century" in *Traditio,* II (1944), 155–75; Feodor Schneider, "Zur Älteren Päpstlichen Finanzgeschichte," in *Quellen und Forschungen aus Italienischen Archiven und Bibliotheken* (Rome, 1906) IX, 1–9; and Volkert Pfaff, "Die Einnahmen der römischen Kurie am Ende des 12. Jahrhunderts," in *Vierteljahrschrift für Sozial-und Wirtschaftsgeschichte,* 40 (1958), 97–118.

5. Lunt, *Papal Revenues,* I, 47, 51–3, 55, 56.

6. *Ibid.,* 46–55.

7. Léopold Delisle, *Mémoire sur les opérations financières des templiers* (Paris, 1889), p. 20. On all topics touching the Templars see also the more recent and complete Jules Piquet, *Les Templiers: étude de leurs opérations financières* (Paris, 1939).

8. Lunt, *Papal Revenues,* I, 51. For a more thorough treatment of the twelfth century see Glenn Olsen, The Performance of Papal Banking Functions under Honorius III (Unpublished thesis; University of Wisconsin Library, Madison, 1962), chapter three.

9. The following is a list of references to the use of the Templars and Hospitallers by popes Innocent III and Honorius III: Delisle, *Mémoire,,* pp. 21–22; Piquet, *Les Templiers,* pp. 19–22; J. P. Migne, ed., *Patrologiae Cursus Completus, Series Latina* (221 vols., Paris, 1844–90) CCXVI, 37–38; Horoy, *Honorii III Opera Omina* (6 vols. in *Medii Aevi Bibliotheca Patristica seu Ejusdem Temporis Patrologia, Series Prima,* Paris, 1879) III, 198, 300, 460–1; Peter Pressutti, *Regesta Honorii Papae III* (2 vols., Rome, 1888) has summarized all the letters of Honorius known to him, whether they are found in the Vatican registers or not. Any letter of Honorius referred to in this study may be found in Pressutti, but he is only referred to in

the footnotes when his summary of a letter is the only source obtainable; Carolus Rodenburg, ed., *Epistolae Saeculi XIII e Regestis Pontificum Romanorum* (3 vols., Berlin, 1883–94, in *Monumenta Germaniae Historica*) I, 88–91; Martin Bouquet, ed., *Recueil des historiens des Gaules et de la France,* new edition published under the direction of L. Delisle (24 vols., Paris, 1869–1904) XIX, 705.

10. On the instruments used for exchange contracts see Raymond de Roover, *L'évolution de la lettre de change, XIV -XVIII siècles* (Paris, 1953), pp. 12 ff; and "The Organization of Trade," in *Cambridge Economic History* (Cambridge, 1963) II, 49–56, 66–71.

11. Adolf Schaube, *Handelsgeschichte der Romanischen Völker des Mittlemeergebiets bis zum Ende der Kreuzzüge* (Munich and Berlin, 1906), p. 348 on a bishop from Wales who obtained an exchange contract for 20 gold marks at the Fair of Troyes from Bolognese merchants. On the Fairs of Champagne see the unpublished dissertation of Richard David Face at the University of Wisconsin, The Caravan Merchants and the Fairs of Champagne: A Study in the Techniques of Medieval Commerce, (1957) which was summarized in an article "Techniques of Business in the Trade Between the Fairs of Champagne and the South of Europe in the Twelfth and Thirteenth Centuries," *Economic History Review,* Second Series, X (1957–58), 427–38. For other examples see also the following articles by Schaube on the exchange contract: "Studien zur Geschichte und Natur des altesten Cambium" in *Zeitschrift für Nationalökonomie und Statistik,* LXV (1895), 153–191, 511–534; "Einige Beobachtungen zur Entstehungsgeschichte der Tratte," in *Zeitschrift der Savigny-Stiftung für Rechtsgeschichte, Germanistische Abteilung,* XIV (1893), 111–51; "Das angeblich älteste Campsorengeschäft" in *Zeitschrift für das gesamte Handelsrecht,* XLI (1893), 353–60; "Die Anfänge der Tratte," *ibid.,* XLIII (1895), 1–51.

12. Schaube, *Handelsgeschichte,* p. 404. This is described below.

13. *Ibid.,* 364.

14. See under these dates in Margaret W. Hall, Hilmar C. Krueger, and Robert L. Reynolds, eds., *Notai Liguri Del Sec. XII, Guglielmo Cassinese (1190–1192)* (2 vols., Turin, 1938, in *Documenti e Studi per la Storia del Commercio e del Diritto Commerciale Italiano 12* and *13),* II, 1323, 1337.

15. *Ibid.,* II, 1318, 1319, 1325, 1327, 1328, 1329, 1333. Manfredus Goja or Groja is frequently mentioned throughout the documents of Cassinese, both before and after November 1191, and his sons may have had a house in Genoa. He, at least, was not travelling with the Emperor.

16. *Ibid.,* II, 1327.

17. *Ibid.,* II, 1318. The Walzerus mentioned in this loan never became bishop. An account of the disputed election in which he was involved is found in *Gisleberti Chronicon Hanoniense,* ed. Wilhelm Arndt, in *MGH, Scriptores,* vol. XXI, 573–77. Brief discussions of this election are found in Wilhelm Reinecke, *Geschichte der Stadt Cambrai bis zur Erteilung der Lex Godefridi (1227)* (Marburg, 1896), pp. 254–55 and H. Lancelin, *Histoire du Diocese de Cambrai* (Valenciennes, 1946), p. 122.

18. On this and the problem of whether the *cambium,* or exchange, contract was usurious or not see the following works of Raymond de Roover, *L'évolution,* pp. 12, 15–16, 19–20, 28–41; *The Rise and Decline of the*

Medici Bank, 1397-1494 (Cambridge, Mass., 1963), pp. 10-11. 108 ff.; "Les doctrines économiques des scolastiques: à propos du traité sur l'usure d'Alexandre Lombard," *Revue d'Histoire ecclésiastique*, LIX (1964), 854-66. Also John Noonan Jr., *The Scholastic Analysis of Usury* (Cambridge, Mass., 1957), pp. 17-20, 31-44, 105-8, 112-16, 128-38, 175-80; and Alonzo-M. Hamelin, O.F.M., *Un traité de morale économique au XIVᵉ siècle, le Tractatus De Usuris de Maître Alexandre d'Alexandrie* (Louvain, 1962), pp. 5-6, 67-114. From the point of view of the usury prohibition, the validity of the *cambium* contract was still in question during our period. The first writer to deal with this issue specifically was Geoffrey of Trani (d.1245). From his time the usual position of the theologians was that, while interest in all loans was disapproved of, the *cambium* was admitted as a legitimate contract because it was not a *mutuum*.

19. On *iuri solidi* and *omni iuri* see Peter Riesenberg, Roman law; renunciations and the rise of capitalism (M.A. thesis, University of Wisconsin, 1949), pp. 15-16, 70-71. A somewhat altered version of this thesis was published as "Roman Law, Renunciations and Business in the Twelfth and Thirteenth Centuries," *Essays in Medieval Life and Thought, Presented in Honor of Austin Patterson Evans*, eds. John Mundy, Richard Emery, and Benjamin Nelson (New York, 1955), pp. 207-225. This version does not include the discussions of the renunciations important for the present paper, but may be referred to for criticism of the general theories of the older writers on renunciations. Of these earlier writers, see especially Renée Doehaerd, *Relations commerciales entre Gênes, la Belgique et L'Oultremonts* (3 vols., Brussels, 1941) I, 52-60. This last book is of considerable value for understanding all aspects of the organization of trade during this period. The renunciation *iuri solidi* means that the men who have obliged themselves for the payment of the loan may only be held to pay their part if all are solvent, but if a partner cannot pay—obviously in this case Walzerus the other partner or partners may be held for the whole amount. The renunciation *omni iuri* is a helping phrase which does not mean all rights are renounced, but that any right connected with the *iuri solidi* is also renounced.

20. Hall, Krueger, and Reynolds, *Guglielmo Cassinese*, II, 1319.

21. *Ibid.*, II, 1325.

22. *Ibid.*, II, 1327. Perhaps Constantia is Coutances, and Narentona is a mistake for the Barentona near Coutances. Savary is a Norman name, but the name Savarisus occurs in Venetian documents and the Michel associated with Savarixius is probably from Piacenza. This could suggest an Italian origin or the possibility of "Constance," but I have found no conclusive identification, and Savarixius and Michel may simply be accidentally associated in the common employ of the Curia.

23. Riesenberg, *Roman law*, pp. 14-15. This is another form of renunciation. If by chance the principal debtor can not be located by the creditor, any of those who have obliged themselves may be forced to satisfy the creditor.

24. On this see Robert S. Lopez and Irving W. Raymond, *Medieval Trade in the Mediterranean World* (New York, 1955), pp. 162-7. The introductions to the various documents in this book are very useful for

understanding the types of loans, means of taking interest, and forms of merchant association used by the Italians.

25. Hall, Krueger, and Reynolds, *Guglielmo Cassinese*, II, 1328.

26. *Ibid.*, II, 1329.

27. The 18 pieces of cloth of Amiens may be the same as those mentioned in the previous document (no. 1328). However, this document (no. 1329) also mentions other pieces and kinds of cloth. On the meaning of *baldinellae* see Doehaerd, *Relations commerciales*, III, 1294, who states that they are linen (*toiles*).

28. Hall, Krueger, and Reynolds, *Guglielmo Cassinese*, II, 1333.

29. On the significance of the phrase see Lopez and Raymond, *Medieval Trade*, 168. See also the older discussion of the sea-loan in Calvin B. Hoover, Capital and Contract in Genoa in the Twelfth Century (Ph. D. dissertation, University of Wisconsin, 1925), 26–41. In this same work see also the section on loans involving pledges, 41 ff.

30. Hoover, *Capital and Contract*, p. 27, on the insurance features of the sea-loan. Hoover, p. 38, notes that what is essential to the definition of the sea-loan is the fact that its repayment is contingent on safe arrival.

31. Schneider, *Quellen und Forschungen*, IX, 3.

32. For earlier examples see note four above and *ibid.*, pp. 4–8 and Robert Davidsohn, *Geschichte von Florenz* (4 vols., Berlin, 1896) I, 798.

33. Schneider, *Quellen und Forschungen*, IX, 8–9. This was probably a form of partnership. The details of the loan are not clear. Schneider conjectures that an original loan of 600 pounds was made, divided in four parts between the partners. Since the debt was actually for 630 pounds, 30 pounds was taken as interest or for renewing the debt. As in earlier debts, Roman church-incomes were pledged.

34. *Ibid.*, p. 8. If this identification of Bovo de Petri can be made—and I have no further evidence that it can—this would mean that from this time the Boboni family was closely connected with papal finance, and was continually associated with the papacy until the 1230's, when Bobo Johannis Bobonis is designated as *campsor domini papae*. The Boboni were connected with the Orsini family, of whom Celestine III (1191–98) was a member, and themselves produced several cardinals in the late twelfth and early thirteenth centuries. See Ferdinand Gregorovius, *History of the City of Rome*, trans. from the 4th German edition by Annie Hamilton (London, 1896) V, part 2, 626.

35. Schneider, *Quellen und Forschungen*, IX, 9.

36. *Ibid*.

37. J. von Pflugk-Harttung, *Acta pontificum Romanorum inedita: Urkunden der Päpste vom Jahre 748 bis zum Jahre 1198* (3 vols., Stuttgart, 1881–86), III, 273, no. 289. See Schneider, *Quellen und Forschungen*, IX, 9–11 for further loans contracted with the Romans—several of which seem to have borne about a 10 per cent interest rate.

38. Schneider, *Quellen und Forschungen*, IX, 9–12 has listed these instances.

39. *Ibid.*, pp. 12–13. Lunt, *Papal Revenues*, I, 55.

40. Schneider, *Quellen und Forschungen*, IX, 13. Schneider says this is the first prelate-loan known to him.

41. Migne, *Patrologiae*, CCXV, 242–43. Davidsohn, *Florenz*, I, 798. It is not certain that this debt was contracted in Rome.

42. Despite comments by Honorius during the earlier period of his pontificate that the *camera* was without funds, no evidence has been found that either Innocent or Honorius was in debt to the Italian merchants. Since it has already been noted that the Curia was not in debt to the Knightly Orders at this period, there is no evidence that this function of a papal banker may be assigned to anyone during these pontificates. This may be because the documents no longer exist, but it should not be forgotten that, despite the fact that huge sums might be sent to the Holy Land, thus leaving the *camera* empty, equally large sums were being raised to replenish the papal resources. A. Gottlob, "Päpstliche Darlehensschulden des 13. Jahrhunderts," *Historisches Jahrbuch* XX (1899); 713–15, in his list of documents indicating papal loan indebtedness, lists only one document prior to the pontificate of Gregory IX, and this is of no importance.

43. Schaube, *Handelsgeschichte*, pp. 364, 421, 422.

44. *Ibid.*, pp. 348, 364.

45. I have been unable to consult a full text of the original document, but see *ibid.* and Aloys Schulte, *Geschichte des mittelalterlichen Handels und Verkehrs zwischen Westdeutschland und Italien mit Ausschluss von Venedig* (2 vols., Leipzig, 1900), I, 244.

46. Schaube, *Handelsgeschichte*, pp. 364, 422–3 on the men involved in this schism.

47. *Ibid.*, p. 364. Judaei, Pantaleoni, Cencii, Bobonis, and Scarsus are Romans, as are also probably Centio de Lavina and Romani; see also below n. 62. Petrus Sarracennus also seems to have been a Roman (see below note 56), but Saracini is a Sienese name; Elisabeth von Roon-Bassermann, *Sienesische Handelsgesellschaften des XIII. Jahrhunderts* (Mannheim, 1912), p. 28. Deuteguardae is also Sienese; *ibid.*, p. 50. Von Roon-Bassermann, p. 2 ff. considers some of the same loans as here and below involving Roman and Sienese merchants. I have been unable to see some of the collections in which these documents appear, but several may be found in Schulte, *Geschichte des mittelalterlichen Handels und Verkehrs*, I, 235–7; II, no. 422, and in Rodenberg, *Epistolae*, I, 621–2, and Schaube, *Handelsgeschichte*, p. 423 n. 7.

48. Schulte, *Geschichte des mittelalterlichen Handels und Verkehrs*, I, 236–37. For the final settlement of the loans resulting from this schism, a process which took over twenty years, see: Schaube, *Handelsgeschichte*, pp. 349, 364–65, 422–24, 427; Pressutti, *Regesta*, I, 1297, 1351, II, 6185. Additional credit was extended in the process of settling these loans, and the well-known Roman family of Manetti became involved (Pressutti, II, 6185). On them see M.D. O'Sullivan, *Italian Merchant Bankers in Ireland in the Thirteenth Century* (Dublin, 1962), pp. 35, 37, who mentions the Roman firm of Manetti as one of the earliest operating in England and Ireland in papal fiscal business.

49. Thomas Hardy, ed., *Rotuli Litterarum Clausarum In Turri Londinensi* (2 vols., London, 1833. Record Commision.) I, 146. Schaube, *Handelsgeschichte*, p. 403. I believe Schaube's figure of 325 marks for this loan should be 235 marks. John had several loans from various Roman and

Sienese bankers, and one of these of July 25, 1213, for 235 marks is printed on the same page of the *Rotuli*, probably accounting for the confusion with the letter of four days earlier concerning the 235 marks.

50. Lunt, *Papal Revenues*, II, 236, no. 356. The moralizing Matthew Paris might easily regard exchangers as usurers.

51. See the introduction to the *Gesta abbatum monasterii Sancti Albani a Thoma Walsingham, regnante Ricardo secundo, ejusdem ecclesiae praecentore, computata*, ed. Henry Riley (3 vols., London, 1867–69. Rolls Series.) I, ix–xvii.

52. Pressutti, *Regesta*, I, 935, 939. Gino Arias, *Studi e Documenti di Storia del Diritto* (Florence, 1902), pp. 78–80 has made a list of letters dealing with the relationships between the Italian bankers and the Curia and ecclesiastics under Honorius, but the list is not complete.

53. Pressutti, *Regesta*, I, 935. Schaube, *Handelsgeschichte*, p. 353.

54. Pressutti, *Regesta*, I, 939. Schaube, *Handelsgeschichte*, pp. 353, 365. Von Roon-Bassermann, *Sienesische Handelsgesellschaften*, p. 26 corrects the text to read that the following Sienese were involved in this loan: Ranuchio Spinelli, Hugolino Orlandi, Castellanus Tabernarii, Boncompagnus, Recoverus and Bulgarinus. She knows of no other references to a Hugolino Orlandi or a Castellanus Tabernarii. If Pressutti's reading were retained, the use of *tabernarii* would indicate that some of the merchants were usurers.

55. Having given this example of loans which cannot be ascertained to deal with arrangements made at the Curia or for curial business, but which show how Honorius was protecting these merchants, I shall give further loans of this type in the notes only.

56. Schaube, *Handelsgeschichte*, pp. 403–04. Pressutti, *Regesta*, I, 1876 is a confirmation by Honorius of a hereditary rent of forty pounds given to this Roman by the chancellor, Richard, Bishop of Durham, for his service.

57. *Patent Rolls of the Reign of Henry III Preserved in the Public Record Office* (2 vols., London, 1901–03. Rolls Series), I, 181. Schaube, *Handelsgeschichte*, p. 404.

58. *Patent Rolls*, I, 181.

59. I have not discussed Pressutti, *Regesta*, I, 2133, 2158, which are not directly related to the theme I am developing. See Schaube, *Handelsgeschichte*, pp. 353, 365 and the letters in their complete form in Horoy, *Honorii III Opera*, III, 256, 269. Schaube is certainly correct in stressing the fact that these two letters show how the zeal of the pope for the crusade often aided the merchants in expanding their operations.

60. Davidsohn, *Florenz*, I, 798.

61. Pressutti, *Regesta*, I, 1902. See Schaube, *Handelsgeschichte*, 359, 365 and Davidsohn, *Florenz*, I, 798 n. 4.

62. Pressutti, *Regesta*, I, 1802.

63. *Ibid.*, 2173. Schaube, *Handelsgeschichte*, p. 365.

64. Pressutti, *Regesta*, I, 3293.

65. Schaube, *Handelsgeschichte*, pp. 407–8, Hardy, *Rotuli Litterarum Clausarum*, I, 627, 652.

66. *Patent Rolls*, I, 535. Schaube, *Handelsgeschichte*, p. 404 has dated this letter June 15, 1224, but the *Patent Rolls* date it to June 15, 1225.

67. Hardy, *Rotuli Litterarum Clausarum*, II, 42. Schaube, *Handels-geschichte*, p. 404. One other document exists from 1225, but seems to have nothing to do with the Romans as papal bankers; see Horoy, *Honorii III Opera*, IV, 879 and Schaube, *Handelsgeschichte*, p. 427. Like other instances already discussed, the pope shows in this letter a special concern to protect the interests of the Roman merchants—to the extent that Honorius ordered the Archbishop of Mainz to collect all the incomes of the church of Worms to help pay off a debt of 1620 marks contracted by that church. For the origin of this debt see Horoy, II, 880 n. 1. The three loans from 1226 mentioned in Pressutti also seem to have no direct connection with loans received while negotiating business at the Curia; *Regesta*, II, 5979, 5980, 6006 and Schaube, pp. 346, 348, 349, 351, 353, 365. If some of these loans may be identified with those mentioned in Lucien Auvray, *Les Registres de Gré-goire IX* (3 vols., Paris, 1896), II, 2490–97, they may well have been negotiated in connection with business at the Curia. In any case, these letters from 1235 show that there were still several debts contracted with Roman merchants during Honorius' time which had not been paid. Evidently several of these had been contracted at the Curia.

68. Pressutti, *Regesta*, II, 6184 and Schaube, *Handelsgeschichte*, p. 428.

69. Henri Denifle, ed., *Chartularium Universitatis Parisiensis* (Paris, 1889), I, 330 no. 116. Arias, *Studi e Documenti*, p. 78.

70. Lunt, *Papal Revenues*, I, 301–2. Stephen, the papal collector, is almost certainly to be identified as Master Stephen of Anagni, described by O'Sullivan, *Merchant Bankers*, p. 36 ff. The merchants associated with Stephen were probably Romans, because the Roman firm of Manetti, already mentioned above (n. 48), was already working with the papacy in England.

71. Lunt, *Papal Revenues*, I, 314. On Angelerius Solaficu as the head of a Sienese syndicate of merchants see von Roon-Basserman, *Sienesische Handelsgesellschaften*, pp. 38, 48 ff. Unfortunately very little is known of Solaficu. His relations to the Bonsignori of Siena, and that he was active in England and France on behalf of the papacy, are known, but the precise nature of these activities is not known. One can only suggest that he was probably called a *campsor papae* because he was involved in the collection of papal revenues, as the Bonsignori were to be, rather than because he was closely associated with the Curia in Rome for the purpose of extending credit: see O'Sullivan, *Merchant Bankers*, p. 27 ff.

72. Schulte, *Geschichte des mittelalterlichen Handels und Verkerhrs*, I, 239, II, no. 426. This document is not a papal letter, but a complaint by a merchant of Siena, preserved in Cologne. This merchant in describing a loan given at the Curia called Bobo Johannis Bobonis the *campsor* of the pope. This Boboni is probably to be identified with the *Bobo fil. Johis Bobonis* whom Gregorovius lists as one of the Roman senators in the 1240's, *Rome*, V, part 1, 258 n. Of course the Boboni had also been senators in the twelfth century: *ibid.*, IV, part 2, 620 n.

73. See above note 48. The Stephan mentioned is Stephan of Ceccano, who was promoted in 1212 to the title of the Basilica of the Twelve Apostles as a cardinal priest, and who died in 1227.

THE DRAPERS OF LUCCA AND THE MARKETING OF CLOTH IN THE MID-THIRTEENTH CENTURY

THOMAS W. BLOMQUIST
Northern Illinois University

Despite the importance of the development of the woolen industry to the economy of the High Middle Ages, the processes by which cloth was marketed locally to the consumer remain largely obscure. We are, to be sure, relatively well informed about the merchandising of cloth in distant markets—the penetration of northern cloth in Mediterranean markets, for example[1]—yet the distributive channels through which woolens travelled after leaving the hands of importer or local manufacturer are still unknown.[2] That such a lacuna should exist is due primarily to the fact that traffic in cloth at the consumer level was based upon over-the-counter cash sales and has subsequently left few traces in contemporary records.

The State Archives of Lucca, however, preserve an extensive run of notarial acts of the year 1246 which help to fill this gap.[3] The evidence is fragmentary, for we are dealing with the partial production of one notary, Filippus Notti, spanning only a seven month period; yet these contracts serve to reveal one further step in the process of placing cloth in the hands of the consumer and also underscore the economic interdependence between a growing urban center, Lucca, and her neighboring countryside in the thirteenth century.

The notarial contracts deal with a part of the business carried on by a group of cloth merchants, referred to as *pannarii* in the Lucchese sources,[4] a segment of whose trade derived from credit sales developed among a group of buyers hailing from the countryside. Most of the latter in their turn dealt directly in the retail distribution of cloth in the Lucchese *contado*.[5] The cartulary of the notary Filippus Notti contains among its seventy-five folio pages 117 contracts for the purchase-sale of woolen cloths reflecting the credit business of fifteen partnerships of Lucchese drapers in the period from January 3 to July 30, 1246.[6] In the main these sales were small, averaging on a total volume of 1,108 *bracchiae* Lucchese a bit less than 10 *brac.* in quantity and 1 pound 14 sol. 5 den. in value for each transaction.[7] The smallest sale involved 4½ *brac.* of peach colored *(persi)* Florentine cloth while the largest in terms of quantity consisted of 12 pieces of both dyed and undyed cloth *(barracani albi et tinti)* and 6 *brac.* Florentine woolens sold to two inhabitants of the rural commune of Montecalvoli.[8] The majority of the recorded sales were, however, nearer in quantity to the above averages. All transactions were based upon short term credit; payment due usually within a month and seldom exceeding two months.

The 141 individuals appearing as buyers in the contracts were all residents of the *Lucchesia,* the Lucchese *contado.* They came from all corners of the surrounding countryside to the shops, *apothece,* maintained by the various drapers and their partners in Lucca.[9] From the Valdarno and Valdinievole to the southwest, the upper Valley of the Serchio, Garfagnana and the Valle della Lima to the northeast, and from the lower Serchio and Camiore to the northwest, as well as from the western *contado* bordering upon Pisan territory, men of the country sought woolen cloth in the city.[10] They usually made their purchases jointly, in temporary partnerships of two or three individuals from the same rural locale, and a draper's shop on most working days must have had a decided rustic flavor as buyers and witnesses crowded about the draper negotiating sales and settling old debts.

In general it would seem that the contracts reflect a wholesale rather than a retail trade; that is, it would appear that most of the cloth purchased in the city was intended ultimately for resale in the country. Although there are a number of obvious exceptions, such as the sales of tailored articles of clothing which were clearly destined for consumption by the buyer,[11] the credit nature of the transactions and the rural clientele involved lead to the conclusion that the majority of buyers appearing in the contracts were in fact rural peddlers. A credit transaction, of course, presumes the intent to repay, and in the case of these rural customers this meant a second journey from the country to Lucca. Had the draper's credit customers been buying solely to satisfy their own needs they undoubtedly would not have obligated themselves to undertake such a journey. Rather, they would have paid cash for their purchases, thus avoiding the inconvenience of an arduous trip. Nor, on the other hand, would a draper, were he selling retail, have been likely to advance short term credit, with all the risks involved, to individuals dwelling in some cases miles away from Lucca.

Furthermore, although none of the individuals appearing as buyers of woolen cloth was mentioned in more than one of the surviving contracts, it is nevertheless evident from the language of the documents that these men were regular visitors to the urban cloth shops. Thus, on April 5, when one Belluomo from Villorbano promised to pay the draper Ranuccio Ughieri 14 sol. 6 den. on or before the end of May as the price of 5¼ *brac.* of cloth, he also stipulated that he would also pay those monies owed from earlier transactions with Ranuccio (". . . alios denarios quos se in alia parte dare debere confitetur").[12] The record of this earlier business, preserved no doubt in another cartulary, has been lost to us, yet reference to such business conclusively establishes that our rural buyers were not infrequent visitors to Lucca and the urban drapers.

In all probability such rural merchants shopped about, buying small lots of woolens from a number of drapers with whom they maintained regular credit accounts. They also may have visited the shops of other merchants and artisans in the city, acquiring their pack of merchandise in much the same way that *mercanti ambulanti* today replenish their stock at the weekly market held in Lucca. For their part, urban drapers regularly extended credit to these merchants of the country who marketed their cloth in the rural communes, parishes, *castelli, rocche,* and farms of the *contado* before returning to the city to settle their accounts and to acquire new merchandise.

The shop of the Lucchese draper was the focal point of distribution for cloth of both foreign and local origin. Among the foreign stuffs, Florence provided the most popular of those cloths distributed in the *contado.* Florentine woolens of various qualities figured in 28 contracts reflecting the sale of 146.2 *brac.* traded at an average price of 6 sol. 5 den. per *brac.*[13] Cloth of Verona also weighed heavily in the rural Lucchese market. Veronese woolens, the most popular type was known as *santellore,* were on the average somewhat cheaper than those of Florence; 121.5 *brac.* were sold through 26 transactions and brought a median per *brac.* price of 4 sol. 8 den.[14] Nearer to Lucca, cloth of Bolognese manufacture, figuring in only one sale, traded at a price of 2 sol. 8 den. per *brac.*[15]

The documents unfortunately throw no light upon the means by which Lucchese drapers acquired their supplies of foreign cloth. To judge from the almost continuous mention of individual drapers in the contracts, it would seem that they were a sedentary lot. One contract tells us that the partners Bonagiunta Bonansegne and Rainerio Bonacase kept a mule for use in their business.[16] However, the beast was probably employed in conveying the partners about the immediate *contado* rather than in long distance commerce. On the other hand, the existence of facilities for foreigners doing business in Lucca suggests that at least a part of the drapers' foreign goods were purchased locally from visiting merchants.[17] It is also probable that a portion of their stock was secured directly in the city of manufacture but more likely that Lucchese merchants imported Lombard cloth wholesale from Genoa, a major distribution point of Lombard production.[18] French woolens, which had only a minor significance in the rural Lucchese market, were in all likelihood purchased in Lucca from Lucchese importers operating in Genoa or at the fairs of Champagne.[19]

The rural market was most favorable to the cheaper cloths of local manufacture. Northern stuffs, for example, selling at a price half again that of Florentine woolens figure in only six of our contracts.[20] On the other hand, the woolen most frequently purchased by rural buyers was an inexpensive cloth known as *baracanus*.[21] In all, the sources show the sale of 356 *brac.* of both finished and unfinished baracans traded at the modest price of 1 sol. 4 den. for each *brac.*[22] Although the place of origin of these goods was not specified, it may be assumed from this very ommission that they were the products of local looms and the Lucchese finishing industry.

Of the organization of the Lucchese woolen industry in 1246 little is known. There is sufficient but scattered evidence to postulate the working of wool in Lucca at least from the beginning of the thirteenth century.[23] However, the relatively late date at which the weavers of Lucca formed a guild (the earliest certain reference to a guild of weavers is dated 1320) implies that the weaving industry was correspondingly slow in locating in the city.[24] Of the various crafts associated with the processes of converting raw wool into finished cloth, only the dyers had a formal guild organization in the thirteenth century.[25] In 1246 most of the local production apparently derived from looms situated in rural households.

The relationship of the drapers to the manufacture of woolen cloth remains unclear. Although some drapers, as Bonagiunta and Rainerio,[26] may well have travelled about the *contado* in order to organize the production of cloth, it would seem that woolens were brought to the city from the country by a group of middlemen cloth salesmen. These merchants, performing much the same economic function as the *lanarii, pannarii,* and *merciadrii* of contemporary Pisa, found a regular outlet for their cloth in the urban shops of the drapers.[27]

Involved in four of the six contracts reflecting wholesale purchases of woolen cloth by drapers was one Bonaccorso Adiuti who lived in Parlascio, a rural area in the Valdarno noted for the early production of woolen cloth.[28] Also furnishing cloth wholesale were a resident of the suburb, *Caput burgi,* and a Florentine merchant.[29] The cloth in each instance was dyed, a fact which in part explains why these entrepreneurial middlemen did not directly exploit the rural market for woolens. It was necessary to bring the cloth to the urban dyers for finishing, and once in the city the cloth salesmen found the urban drapers affording them a regular outlet for their goods. They no doubt preferred this steady market to the uncertainties of merchandising their cloth retail in the *contado.* Similarly, the drapers would seem to have preferred to acquire their cloth of local manufacture from middlemen rather than deal directly with the numerous household weavers of the country. However, there may well have been another factor. Each of these transactions was based upon credit, and thus the drapers were able to balance their own credit sales against those sums owed their suppliers.

The above sketch, based as it is upon fragmentary evidence, can present only a partial picture of the local distribution of cloth in Lucca. Yet the documents reveal the specialization characteristic of this commerce—drapers, middlemen suppliers, wholesale importers, weavers, dyers, and rural merchants all operating in a particular area of the local cloth trade. Our material also suggests something of the complexity of local business and the sophistication of the techniques employed in its conduct. The extensive use of credit, for example, implies an advanced method of keeping books. A business run on credit of necessity involves planning, that is to say a business rationale existed even at this modest level of medieval enterprise. In addition, the importance of the developing Italian woolen industries clearly emerges from a study of the contracts, showing Florence, Verona, and Bologna the seats of a cloth industry organized for export to distant markets. Finally, the documents reveal a clear picture of the city as the focal point of distribution to a significant consumer market in the surrounding country. If the *contado* was a source of foodstuffs and raw materials, it was also a market for the expanding industrial and financial resources of the city.

NOTES

1. For the distribution of northern cloth in the Mediterranean, see especially R. L. Reynolds, "The Market for Northern Textiles in Genoa, 1179–1200," *Revue Belge de Philologie et d'Histoire*, VIII (1929), pp. 831–851; "Merchants of Arras and the Overland Trade with Genoa in the Twelfth Century," *idem*, IX (1930), pp. 495–533; "Genoese Trade in the Late Twelfth Century, Particularly in Cloth from the Fairs of Champagne," *Journal of Economic and Business History*, III (1931), pp. 362–381; H. Laurent, *Un grand commerce d'exportation au moyen-âge: la draperie des Pays-Bas en France et dans les pays méditerranéens, XIIe-XVe siècle* (Paris, 1935); R. Doehaerd, *Les relations commerciales entre Gênes, la Belgique et l'Outremont d'après les archives notariales aux XIIIe et XIVe siècles* (3 vols., Brussels-Rome, 1941); and A. Schaube, *Storia del commercio dei popoli latini del mediterraneo sino alla fine delle Crociate*, tr. P. Bonfante (Turin, 1915).

2. A. Sapori, *Le marchand italien au moyen-âge* (Paris, 1952), pp. 24–26 contains a brief bibliography of the major works dealing with the woolen industry. More recently, see the discussion of the wool industry in thirteenth-century Pisa in D. Herlihy, *Pisa in the Early Renaissance: A Study of Urban Growth* (New Haven, 1958), pp. 150–159 and Maureen Fennell Mazzaoui, "The Organization of the Fine Wool Industry at Bologna in the Thirteenth Century," unpublished Ph.D. dissertation, Bryn Mawr College, 1966.

3. On the notarial archives of Lucca, see R. S. Lopez, "The Unexplored Wealth of the Notarial Archives of Pisa and Lucca," *Mélanges d'histoire du moyen-âge dédiés à la memoire de Louis Halphen* (Paris, 1951), pp. 417–443, and E. Lazzareschi, "L'Archivio dei Notari della Repubblica lucchese," *Gli Archivi Italiani*, II (1915), pp. 175–210.

4. F. Edler, *Glossary of Medieval Terms of Business: Italian Series, 1200–1600* (Cambridge, Mass., 1934), p. 202 defines the *pannaro* as a retail merchant of imported cloth. This definition based upon the fourteenth-century statute of the court of Lucchese merchants is somewhat misleading for the earlier period. Although it is undoubtedly true that the greater part of the business of a Lucchese *pannarius* of the thirteenth century was retail, he nevertheless generated a considerable trade among the peddlers trafficking in the country.

5. The term *contado* is herein used as a geographical rather than a juridical expression to include all territories beyond the city *(civitas)* and immediate environs *(burgus)* considered by the Lucchese to be in their sphere of influence. For the territorial organization of the Lucchese state, see G. Tommasi, *Sommario della storia di Lucca*, in *Archivio Storico Italiano*, X (1847), pp. 140–142, and S. Bongi, ed., *Inventario del Archivio di Stato in Lucca*, (Lucca, 1876), II, pp. 342 ff.

6. Archivio di Stato in Lucca; Archivio dei Notari, Filippo Notti (1246), reg. 1, no. 1. The Lucchese drapers, and the location of their shops when known, were: (1) Bencipse quondam Rainolfi and Riccardus Raimundini *(in domo que fuit quondam Archiepiscopi de Benevento)*; (2) Matheus Orlanduccii; (3) Jacobinus Villiani Civithi *(in domo filiorum Arrigi Frangelaste)*; (4) Rainerius Benencase and Bonaiuncte Bonasegne *(in domo fili-*

orum Aimerigi Mosche); (5) Marchianus quondam Bonaccursi, Ubaldus quondam Bonaiuncte Ferandi, Cecius quondam Rodolfi and Albichus Rodolfi *(in domo que fuit quondam Archiepiscopi de Benevento)*; (6) Jacobus filius Bartholomei, Gottefredus quondam Arrigi Baldinocti and . . . . . . ite quondam Vecchii; (7) Bandius Ferolfi and Nicolaus quondam Uberti; (8) Ranuccius quondam Guidi Ugherii; (9) Ubertus Columbani, Marronghinus quondam Rainaldi and Bugianese quondam Uberti *(in domo que fuit Archiepiscopi de Benevento)*; (10) Deodatus quondam Guillielmi Rambecci *et gemini*; (11) Jacobus Lunardi; (12) Caccialumbardus quondam Guidi Caccialumbardi and Johannes quondam Bonaventure *(in domo filiorum et heredum quondam Mori Mordecastelli)*; (13) Bandinus quondam *Aldibrandini Aimelline*; (14) Bonaverus quondam Meliorati; (15) Jacobus Notti.

7. *Bracchia* was a linear cloth measure equivalent to an arm's length, but varying slightly from one Italian city to another; see F. Edler, *Glossary*, p. 15. In Lucca four *bracchie* made one *canna*.

8. Fil. Notti, fols. 6, 24v.

9. The drapers would seem to have rented rather than owned their shops within the city. The only contract for the rental of an *apotheca* is Fil. Notti, f. 20v. Ranuccius quondam Guidi rented a shop *"in angolo turris"* belonging to Aldibrandinus quondam Mariani, his brothers Orlanduccius and Rubeus Rubei, and his sons, for the comparatively high annual rent of 8 pounds. The drapers would also seem to have located in the same general area, as for example the three shops "in domo que fuit Archiepiscopi de Benevento."

10. The below listed localities appear in the contracts. In parentheses are the number of contracts in which each is mentioned. I have retained the original case and spelling of the documents. Batone (2), Bonanno Montis S. Julie (1), Bozano (1), Camaiore—loco Tramestari, plebano de loco Peralle (5), Cantignano (1), Capella S. Giorgii (1), Capella S. Laurentii ad Vacchole (1), Capella S. Martini in Colle (1), Capella S. Michaelis de Villorbano (5), Capite burgi (2), Carraia (1), Cassano (1), Castagnone (1), Castro Vetrii, Castro novo plebani Conputi (3), Ceraliano Rocche Govertelli (1), Cercilliano (1), Conputo de Loco Colli (1), Controne (3), Decimo de Loco Roncato (4), Ecclesia S. Blasii de Aldepascio (1), Ecclesia S. Marie de Pellagio Vallis Lime (1), Francca (1), Hospitale S. Alluccii (1), Lamari (1), Lopellia (1), Limano Vallis Lomo (1), Massa Pisana (1), Matraia (1), Montecalvoli (4), Monte Chiatri (1) Montefalcone (6) Moriana de Loco Factorii (1), Mocanno (1), Nave (1), Pescalia (1), Porcari (1), Porta S. Donati (1), Porta S. Petri (1), Pedona (1), Prato S. Columbani (1), Putholo (3), S. Casciano de Vico Rube (1), S. Gennuario (1), S. Johanne de Scheto (1), S. Giorgio (1), S. Martino in Fredano (1), S. Maria ad Colle (1), S. Maria de Paganico (1), S. Michele de Scheto (2) S. Petro Salaii (1), S. Prospero de Marlia (1), Seano (5), Scelinario Plebis Mostesi Gradi (2), Vallarni (1), Valle Nebule (1), Viritiano (1), Vurno (3).

11. See Fil. Notti, f. 32v for the sale of a woolen shirt to one Moricone de Carraia, intended for his son Gualfredus, for the sum of 25 sol. In this case the buyer stipulated that he had received the shirt and indeed Gualfredus was wearing it (". . . . et gonella vergata qua indorsa habebat suprascriptus Gualfredus"). For other sales of clothing out of the drapers' shops, see Fil. Notti, fols. 33v, 43, 64v.

12. Fil. Notti, f. 41.

13. For sales of Florentine cloth, see Fil. Notti, fols. 1v, 18v, 24v, 25v, 17v, 29v, 30, 30v, 31v, 32, 35, 35v, 36, 37, 45v, 46v, 47, 59, 50v, 59v, 64v, 65, 65v, 68v, 73v.

14. For cloth of Verona, see Fil. Notti, fols. 2v, 3, 5v, 6v, 23v, 32v, 35, 37, 37v, 38, 38v, 39v, 40, 40v, 41, 47v, 48, 49v, 56, 60, 62, 62v, 64v, 73v. Pegolotti mentions a cloth known as *santelarezine* called *santelaxerio* in the Venetian sources. This was a specialty of the Veronese cloth industry: see A. Evans, ed., *Pegolotti, La Pratica della Mercatura* (Cambridge, Mass., 1936), p. 429; for the specifications of the manufacture of *santelari,* see L. Simioni, ed., *Gil antichi statuti delle arti veronesi secondo la revisione scaligera del 1319,* in *Monumenti storici pubblicati dalla R. Deputazione Veneta di Storia,* 2nd ser., *Statuti.* (*Venice, 1914*), IV, pp. 7, 11, 15–18.

15. Fil. Notti, f. 18v.

16. Fil. Notti, f. 51 (April 26, 1246): Salamone quondam Sacchi de plebe S. Macharei (located three kilometers from Lucca on the lower Serchio) stipulated that he had in partnership with the two drapers for a period of five months one mule valued at 13 pounds. The drapers conferred into the partnership the sum of 34 sol. which entitled one or the other of them to use the animal two days of each month. For use of the mule beyond two days in any given month, the partners agreed to pay a per diem fee of 12 den. The terms of this arrangement imply that the partners did not envision employing the animal on extended journeys.

17. The importance of Lucca as a center of foreign commerce may be deduced from the number of brokers and money-changers operating in the city in the thirteenth and fourteenth centuries. See T. Bini, "Sui Lucchesi a Venezia; memorie dei secoli XIII e XIV," *Atti della R. Accademia lucchese di Scienze, Lettere ed Arti,* XV (1854), pp. 82, 86ff., and F. Edler, "The Silk Trade of Lucca during the Thirteenth and Fourteenth centuries," unpublished dissertation submitted to the Dept. of History, University of Chicago, Chicago, 1930, pp. 99–104 for the activities of Lucchese brokers and money-changers. I am currently collecting material relating to the money-changers of Lucca which I hope will result in a more detailed analysis of their activities.

18. R. S. Lopez, "L'attività economica di Genova nel Marzo 1253 secondo gli atti notarili del tempo," *Atti della Società Ligure di Storià Patria,* LXIV (1935), p. 195, has indicated the increasing importance of Lombard cloth in the Genoese market during the course of the thirteenth century.

19. For the close political and economic ties existing between Lucca and Genoa, see A. Schaube, *Storia del commercio dei popoli latini,* pp. 798–800, 805–806 and F. Edler, "The Silk Trade of Lucca," pp. 113–123. See also my unpublished Master's essay, "Lucchese Commercial Activities in Genoa, 1186–1226," submitted to the Dept. of History, University of Minnesota, Minneapolis, 1960. For the Lucchese at the fairs of Champagne, F. Bourquelot, *Études sur les foires de Champagne, sur la nature, l'etendue ét les règles du commerce qui s'y faisait au XIIe, XIIIe et XIVe siècles,* (Paris, 1865), I. pp. 166–175; Schaube, pp. 420–423, and Edler, pp. 93–96.

20. See Fil. Notti, fols. 45, 45v, 57v, 58v, 59, for sales of *gliscelli, verdelli,* and *crentoni* of Arras and fols. 9, 45v for *sanguinei* and *rosei* of Ypre.

21. The term *baracanus* was apparently of Arabic origin referring to a camlet of mohair. However, a Florentine tariff of the fourteenth century lists *baraccani* among the wares of the *lanaiuoli*: see A. Evans, ed., *Pegolotti, La Pratica della Mercatura*, p. 414.

22. For sales of *baracani,* see Fil. Notti, fols. 5v, 7, 23, 28, 28v, 29v, 31, 32, 33, 33v, 34, 34v, 38v, 39v, 41, 46v, 56, 69, 70v, 71v, 74.

23. T. Bini, "Sui Lucchesi a Venezia," pp. 15–24 has argued that the thirteenth-century Lucchese woolen industry was more advanced than that of Florence. Bini's thesis has been refuted by S. Bongi, "Della mercatura dei Lucchesi nei secoli XIII e XIV," *Atti della R. Accademia lucchese di Scienza, Lettere ed Arti*, XXIII (1884), pp. 445–456. However, only a cursory glance through the notarial documents in the LL series of the Cathedral Archives of Lucca is sufficient to indicate the importance of wool to the economy of Lucca in the first half of the thirteenth century. One hopes that this material will soon form the basis for a full scale study of the Lucchese industry. By 1265 woolens from Lucca were mentioned in a Venetian tariff indicating that by that date the industry was organized for export commerce as well as for local needs: see H. Laurent, *Un grand commerce d'exportation*, pp. 76–77.

24. See T. Bini, "Sui Lucchesi a Venezia," p. 62 ff. for Lucchese weavers and the formation of a weavers' gild.

25. The statute of the Lucchese dyers guild of 1225 has been edited by P. Guerra, *Statuto dell'Arte dei Tintori di Lucca del 1255,* (Lucca, 1864). A more recent edition may be found as an appendix to Edler, "The Silk Industry of Lucca." This statute was a revision of an earlier document and hence we may date the dyers guild from before 1255. For the Lucchese guilds of the Middle Ages, see E. Lazzareschi, "Fonti di archivio per lo studio delle corporazioni artigiane di Lucca," *Bollettino Storico Lucchese,* IX (1937), 65–81, 141–158.

26. See above, note 16.

27. For these early cloth salesmen in Pisa, see Herlihy, *Pisa in the Early Renaissance,* pp. 157–158.

28. Professor Herlihy, *ibid*; pp. 156–157 has stressed the importance of the Valdarno, especially Calci, as the birthplace of the Pisan woolen industry. For Bonaccursus, see Fil. Notti, fols. 24, 26v, 27. On March 19 he sold 11 *cannae, 3½ brac. celestri facti de Luce* for 14 pounds 16 sol. and 12 *cannae* of the same blue cloth for 15 pounds. Two days later Bonaccursus also vended one piece Lucchese vermilion for 10 pounds and a piece of blue cloth at a price of 17 pounds.

29. For the sale of one piece *panni bladecti facti Luce* by Armannus quondam Lamberti de Capite burgi, see Fil. Notti, f. 27, and for the sale of four pieces *panni facti Luce ad III liccias* by Meliore quondam Beliocci, florentinus, f. 40v. Noteworthy for its absence from the Lucchese sources is cloth from the Garfagnana, the *carfagnini* noted by Professor Herlihy, *Pisa in the Early Renaissance,* p. 158, note 91. If cloth was carried to Lucca from the Garfagnana it probably lost its identity in the city and became subsumed under the general *panni facti Luce.*

SYMON DE GUALTERIO: A BRIEF PORTRAIT OF A THIRTEENTH-CENTURY MAN OF AFFAIRS

RICHARD D. FACE

Wisconsin State University—Stevens Point

This brief portrait of the Genoese capitalist Symon de Gualterio grows out of a long standing interest in the activities of those merchants who controlled the overland traffic between the entrepôt of Genoa and the great fairs of Champagne in the twelfth and thirteenth centuries. From the last quarter of the twelfth century through the first quarter of the thirteenth, this commerce appears to have been almost exclusively in the hands of a composite group whom Professor Reynolds appropriately termed the "caravan merchants."[1] It was composed of Flemings from the cloth town of Arras and Italians from the town of Asti, which lay north of Genoa directly on the overland route across the Alps to Champagne. The activities of these merchants, the pattern of their comings and goings over the mountains between Genoa and Champagne in the early 1190's, are perhaps most clearly revealed in the published cartulary of the Genoese notary Guglielmo Cassinese.[2] Their business life centered itself around the fairs of Champagne; the regular, rhythmic pattern of their movement was the result of the annual cycle of the six fairs and the rigid internal schedule of each to which their activity was geared. When they appear in the Genoese notarial records, these "caravan merchants" normally engaged in just three basic kinds of business: first, they arranged loans and *cambium* contracts to be liquidated at a forthcoming fair of Champagne; second, they made numerous credit purchases of pepper, alum, and other eastern commodities from native Genoese importers; and third, they sold quantities of northern French, Flemish, and English cloth on credit to Genoese drapers. Although its successful execution required intricate maneuverings and sophisticated techniques,[3] this was in outline a simple pattern of commerce, restricted and circumscribed both geographically and in regard to the articles of trade. The early "caravan merchants" were mercantile specialists.

By the middle of the thirteenth century, however, the picture has altered dramatically. By 1250 the men of Arras and Asti have disappeared,[4] and one may no longer speak of "caravan merchants" whose business life was restricted to the overland commerce between Genoa and the fairs of Champagne. Instead they have been replaced by a conglomerate group of Italians, men of affairs, whose assets are great and whose interests are broad.[5] In striking contrast to the "caravan merchants" of the 1190's, who never engaged in nor invested in Mediterranean commerce,[6] these are men for whom the commerce with Champagne formed but one facet of their total enterprise. They are equally at home in Mediterranean trade. They import eastern goods and export northern cloth as regularly as they deal in northern commerce and finance. They have, in short, merged activities which fifty years earlier had been divided between two distinct groups of businessmen, the "caravan merchants" and their wealthier customers, the Genoese importers. Their resources and their organizations are of a size to match the broader scope of their interests.

Symon de Gualterio is a typical representative of these thirteenth-century entrepreneurs. This brief sketch, detailing but a ten-month segment of his career, is presented in the nature of a case study and with the hope that a description of this individual's activity, the diversity of his investments, the extent of his personal wealth, the breadth of his acquaintance in the world of international business, may assist in understanding the character of that complex economy and society of which he was but a small part, and may also in some small measure overcome the relative lack of individual portraits of medieval businessmen lamented by Professor R. S. Lopez and others.[7]

The nature of the sources dictated the technique employed in producing this sketch. The Genoese notarial cartularies are unique in providing the researcher with a sustained, day to day record of medieval urban life and economic activity from the third quarter of the twelfth century through the thirteenth and beyond, making it possible to trace in detail the activities of an individual over a period of months or years. Indeed, to become mesmerized by the detail is ever a trap for the researcher; to soar too freely above it is ever a temptation. Yet although the record is full, it is never complete. The daybooks of all the notaries working in metropolitan Genoa during any given month or year are not preserved, and when one reaches the mid-thirteenth century, where the number of extant cartularies increases sharply, it is not always possible to have access to the total record preserved from a given period. Consequently one must remain ever alert to the shortcomings imposed by the peculiar limitations of the sources. This writer is also deeply aware that studies involving the intensive analysis of one notary's records over a limited time span cannot purport to be more than suggestive, that statistical calculations concerning the volume of trade or investment remain incomplete and must always be presented with ample qualification. Yet it would seem altogether lamentable if out of timidity one failed to utilize to the fullest possible extent sources so rich in valuable data as are the Genoese notarial cartularies. The portrait which follows is offered, therefore, in a spirit of experiment and with an attitude of caution.

The careers of several merchants active in the mid-thirteenth century could readily lend themselves to analysis, but that of the Genoese Symon de Gualterio[8] is especially attractive because we are fortunate enough to possess, in the cartulary of Bartholomeus de Fornario, not only a detailed record of his commercial ventures between March and December, 1253, but that scribe also recorded some more intimate details in his last will and testament.

The will reveals Symon de Gualterio to have been a man of great wealth, a capitalist to his fingertips. His monetary legacies alone totaled almost 6000 pounds Genoese.[9] He had a wife and eight children, four daughters and four sons, all of whom appear to have been as yet too young to marry in 1253. His mother was still alive, though evidently aged and widowed; and he took notice in his will of two nieces and a nephew by marriage. His bequest of over 250 pounds to the Church and to charity was an act of greater generosity than some of his contemporaries in similar circumstances permitted themselves.[10] The provisions of his testament merit closer attention.

Declaring himself of sound mind and fearing God's judgment, Symon made disposition of his worldly goods. He chose to be buried at the Church of Saint Michael in Genoa. To cover the expenses of his funeral and interment and to pay for masses said for the good of his soul, he left 100 pounds to be disbursed by his wife and kinsmen. Ten pounds of this sum, however, he earmarked for the charitable works of Genoa's cathedral of San Lorenzo. Then followed several bequests to his near relatives: 100 pounds to a niece, intended for her marriage dower; an annual income of 10 pounds for his aged mother;

and a bequest of 25 pounds to a second niece, wife of his banker Andriolus Rexem.[11] To charity Symon left 125 pounds in charge of a Dominican friar, and 150 pounds to be disbursed by his wife and kinsmen. To his immediate family Symon was generous. To each of four daughters he left a handsome dowry of 500 pounds, providing that should any one of the girls die without legitimate heirs before the age of thirty, her fortune should revert to his sons. To his wife, in addition to her dower and *antefactum*, he left a cash bequest of 100 pounds plus all her clothing, ornaments, jewelry, and other finery and personal adornments, and, to insure her comfort and health, his own "fancy" bed. She was further guaranteed a comfortable place to live in his home as long as she did not remarry. Symon's principal heirs were his four sons, all minors. To them and to their future male heirs he left the bulk of his property. From his remaining fortune, however, 3000 pounds was to be deposited in the bank of Andriolus Rexem to be invested over a three-year period by the banker (who was to enjoy one quarter of the profit) in behalf of Symon's minor heirs. The arrangement might be extended beyond the initial three-year term at the discretion of the guardians appointed to care for his children. His wife and three kinsmen were given this obligation. The will was drawn up at Symon's home in Genoa on December 17, 1253, and witnessed by six distinguished Genoese.[12]

The sums of money disbursed in Symon's will are impressive and characterize him as a man of means. Yet by themselves they give no accurate measure of his assets. In his will Symon bestowed legacies totalling just under 6000 pounds, a large figure, to be sure. But over a period of less than a month our scribe records that Symon invested more than 6000 pounds in *commenda* ventures to overseas ports alone, while at the same time also risking substantial sums in the overland commerce with the fairs of Champagne. He was a big-time operator. Some measure of the broad scope and complexity of his activities may be taken if one follows their reflection from month to month and day to day in the entries of Bartholomeus de Fornario between March and December, 1253.

In March, 1253, Symon de Gualterio, in addition to appointing procurators to handle transactions in foreign parts, made investments and loans for a total of over 2811 pounds Genoese and 1319 pounds of Provins. He sold merchandise worth over 316 pounds Genoese and extended credit in *cambium* contracts for 2000 pounds of Provins. His activities in the course of this month were varied: he bought and sold wool; he purchased English cloth; he sent silk and saffron in *commenda* to "France"; he invested in trade in the western Mediterranean area; he shipped a large quantity of spices to Champagne to be sold at the May fair; and he extended and purchased *cambium* on that same fair. Through the skillful manipulation of credit, and through the use of partners and procurators, he pursued these scattered interests without abandoning the comforts of his Genoese residence.

Symon first appears on March 7 as the third party in a venture to be liquidated at the forthcoming May fair.[13] On March 11 he appointed a procurator, Ugo de Baxiano, to collect 316 pounds 16 Sol. Genoese owed him by a Piacenzan merchant for the sale of a quantity of raw wool.[14] Several days later, on March 15, Symon appointed Albertallus Mazagie his procurator to receive seventy-two bales of "washed" wool stored in the house of Lanfrancus de Pulvino in Tortona; Symon had sold the wool to Mazagie for 1005 pounds Genoese.[15]

Next Symon turned his full attention to northern commerce and the several entries which follow show him occupied with ventures involving spices, woolen cloth, and finance at the fairs of Champagne. This phase of activity began on March 17 with the purchase of thirty pieces of English woolen cloth (from Northhampton ?) from Bernardus Camorerius of Parma for 556 pounds 5 Sol. Genoese, which Symon agreed to pay in mid-July when he would have realized the profits from his transactions at the coming May fair.[16] On the same day Symon appointed two procurators, Mussus Calderarius and Wilielmus Quatuoroculis, both Piacenzan merchants of some prominence, who were to receive twelve bales of ginger from Peire Brondellus, Symon's agent at Lagny.[17] The spice had been shipped to Peire's house in Lagny by Symon's relative and business associate, Lanfranchus de Gaulterio. The procurators were to pick up the ginger at Lagny and, one may assume, sell it at the May fair in nearby Provins. The profit from such a sale would in turn be invested in northern cloth to be shipped back to Symon in Genoa, thus completing a routine cycle of commerce.

But Symon's interest in the May fair did not end here. In two exchange contracts, drawn up on March 19 and 20, he sold *cambrium* in the money of Provins for a total of 1319 pounds.[18] In a third contract, dated March 22, Symon bought *cambium* on the May fair for 1000 pounds of Provins from Johannes Ascherius, a merchant and banker very active in finance and trade between Genoa and Champagne.[19] In this instance Symon acted in the name of his associate

Nicolosus de Nigro and employed funds on deposit in the bank of Nicola Tortorini and Company, one of many banking concerns operating in Genoa at this time. Despite this flury of activity, however, Symon would not attend the May fair in person, for on March 23 he appointed Johannes Toscanus his general procurator to handle all his financial transactions "in 'France' and in the fairs of 'France' and Champagne," with authority to send merchandise to him in Genoa by land or by sea.[20] Then on March 27 Symon was again the buyer of *cambium* on the May fair, this time advancing Genoese *denarii* to the Sienese banking firm of Rofredus Bramenzoni, the Genoese representative of the great Bonsignori house of Siena. As he did earlier, Symon here represented another merchant, Wilielmus de Savignono, to whom Rofredus Bramenzoni and Company promised to pay 1000 pounds 'of Provins at *rectam solucionem* at the fair.[21]

The scope of Symon's commercial enterprises was particularly well illustrated by his purchase, on March 27, of a three-quarters interest in a ship called the *Saint Francis* for 390 pounds.[22] This was a rewarding investment which would facilitate those shipments of northern cloth that regularly absorbed a considerable portion of Symon's capital, and would also permit him to participate more directly, and with greater profit, in maritime trade throughout the Mediterranean area and beyond.

The last two days of March found Symon still concerned with trading ventures. On March 30 he sent saffron and silk worth over 770 pounds Genoese in *commenda* with Jacobinus de Gavio de Campo to "France"; possibly a visit to Champagne and the May fair at Provins was also intended. Finally, on March 31, he invested 25 pounds Genoese in *commenda* to Maiorca with the factor Bonifacius de Mari de Finario.[23]

In April the tempo of Symon de Gualterio's activities increased markedly and can be seen in part to have taken a new direction. Our scribe recorded 26 entries in which Symon figured as one of the major contracting parties. It would be tedious and of dubious value to analyze each of these entries separately, but certain significant categories and statistics emerge from the whole mass of material. One observes first that Symon, like so many of his merchant colleagues, began early in this month to invest more heavily in overseas commerce,[24] a phenomenon to be associated with the regular spring sailings of merchant fleets from Genoa for various destinations. Between April 1 and 28, for example, Symon committed slightly more than 6000 pounds to *commenda* ventures carried by various factors to distant ports.[25] Their destinations included Sicily, Sardinia, Tunis, Bugia, Acre, and the exotic African port on the Atlantic, Saphi. In the first week of April four ventures to Sicily and one to Sardinia, each carried by a different factor, claimed over 1002 pounds of Symon's capital.[26] Three ventures to Tunis were recorded in contracts drawn up on April 12, 16, and 29 for a total investment of 430 pounds.[27] These were standard *commenda* contracts wherein Symon contributed all the capital and the factors were to receive one fourth the profit.

But voyages to Bugia and Syria accounted for the greater part of Symon's capital: of 3828 pounds, he invested 2578 in three ventures to Bugia[28] and 1250 in three ventures to Syria.[29] Several of these contracts merit closer attention. The ship *Saint Francis*, of which Symon was three-quarters owner, was about to set out on a Mediterranean voyage to the port of Bugia. Aboard the ship would be Jacobus de Mari and Jacobus Frexenus, both of whom carried investments from Symon de Gualterio which, taken together, totaled more than 2500 pounds. Symon's financial arrangement with each of these men was involved. On April 19 he had received merchandise (or a loan) from de Mari valued at 1180 pounds, which sum he agreed to repay within three months after the *Saint Francis* had returned safely from her voyage to Bugia.[30] Then on the same day Symon invested his three-quarter share in that ship (here valued at 498 pounds 11 sol.) in *commenda* with de Mari, who evidently functioned in the dual capacity of creditor and partner,[31] for on April 25 he also took in *commenda* from his father, Nicolosus de Mari, the remaining one-quarter share of the ship (valued at 150 pounds).[32] It seems clear that Jacobus de Mari was to be in charge of the *Saint Francis* on her voyage to Bugia. The second factor who figures in this complicated series of agreements, Jacobus de Frexenus, besides carrying 1000 pounds from Symon in straight *commenda* agreement at one-quarter profit, also contracted to carry the 1180 pounds (in goods or money?) which Symon secured in loan from de Mari.[33] Finally, before leaving on this prolonged and possibly dangerous voyage, Frexenus took the precaution of appointing Symon his procurator for all affairs of business in Genoa.[34]

In keeping with a traditional pattern of commerce between Champagne, Genoa, and the eastern Mediterranean, many of Symon's *commenda* ventures to Syria were invested in northern cloth. Of the 1250 pounds which he committed to Syrian ventures, 1100 was invested in cloth of Chalons and Northhampton, carried to Acre by Jacobus de Galiana for one-quarter profit.[35] On April 28 Symon invested 900 pounds in a venture carried by Nicolosus de Carlo to the African Atlantic port of Saphi, recently tapped source of gold for Genoa's new coinage.[36] There remain four *commenda* ventures, contracted between April 22 and 28, in which Symon committed 514 pounds to factors who indicated no specific destination;[37] yet one may assume that most of them set sail for Mediterranean ports. These bring Symon's total investment in overseas commerce to a fraction more than 6596 pounds for the month of April, 1253. This is the heaviest investment in this area of trade which the cartulary of Bartholomeus de Fornario shows Symon to have made in that year. These entries indicate, too, that over the course of this month the volume of investment in such ventures expanded sharply. Symon, for example, committed 1002 pounds to five *commenda* ventures in the first week of April; whereas on April 28 alone he arranged six such contracts involving a total of 4150 pounds.

The pattern of Symon's activities in business and commerce continued substantially unaltered into the month of May. Although the number of contracts in which he appeared and the sums involved, as recorded in the cartulary of Fornario, diminished since April, Symon still invested more than 1054 pounds in Mediterranean trade. Over three-fifths of this was concentrated in six *commenda* contracts drawn up by the scribe on May 2.[38] As the month wore on these contracts tapered off, the last being recorded on May 20. As in April, the Mediterranean port of Bugia claimed the largest single share of Symon's capital—325 pounds distributed over three contracts recorded on May 2, 10, and 20.[39] He invested 300 pounds in two ventures to Tunis, both drawn up on May 2.[40] Sicily accounted for only one investment of almost 52 pounds also recorded on May 2, and on May 13 Symon invested 45 pounds in a venture to Maiorca.[41] There remain three *commenda* contracts, two dated May 2 and the third May 16, involving a total investment of just over 333 pounds, for which no destination was indicated.[42]

If one may accept the evidence provided by our scribe as a reliable indication of the overall volume and nature of commercial investment on the part of one merchant, a pattern begins to emerge, however dimly, from the monotonous series of nearly mute *commenda* agreements. The pattern of Symon de Gualterio's investment in overseas commerce follows a wobbly, but steadily ascending curve throughout the month of April, reaching a sharp and somewhat isolated peak on April 28 (with the expenditure of 4150 pounds in six contracts); this climax is sustained through the first days of May, after which the curve descends rapidly through the middle and latter part of that month. Evidence from one notary may be judged insufficient, but one can comment on the sharp crescendo of activity in which Symon engaged toward the end of April and the beginning of May—a flurry of activity which anticipated the annual spring sailings of merchant vessels into the Mediterranean and beyond.

Symon's interest in northern trade, particularly that with the fairs of Champagne, remained steady throughout March, April, and into the month of May. He appeared in two documents concerned with the May fair at Provins, both recorded on May 10.[43] The first was a standard *cambium* contract, but Symon was neither the buyer nor the seller. Both parties were prominent merchants in Genoa and at the fairs. Wilielmus Lercarius bought *cambium* for 902 pounds 16 sol. Provins from Johannes Ascherius and Company to be paid at *rectam solucionem* in the next May fair. However, the document goes on to state that Symon de Gualterio paid "so many" Genoese denarii to Ascherius in the name of Wilielmus Lercarius by having the sum credited to Ascherius on the books of the bank of Andriolus Rexem, *i.e.* at Symon's request a sum of Genoese denarii was transferred from his account to the account of Ascherius in the Rexem bank— wholly a paper transaction.[44] Was Symon himself serving here as a banker? Or was he merely using the facilities of a banking house in order to advance credit to a fellow merchant? Symon functioned in the very same manner once before.[45] Also his connection with the bona fide *bancherius* Andriolus Rexem is attested to in several additional entries in Fornario's cartulary.[46] Rexem was the husband of Symon's niece Jacobina, and appears to have served with some regularity as Symon's banker and trusted business associate; indeed, as we have seen, he was to be entrusted with the management and investment of the legacy of 3000 pounds which Symon left to his underage heirs.

Happily, the second document of May 10 which refers to the May fair is far less opaque concerning the business affairs of Symon de Gualterio. Its basic purpose was to authorize a procurator to represent Symon and his relative Lanfrancus de Gaulterio in the receipt and sale of merchandise in Champagne, the same purpose for which Symon had commissioned two Piacenzan merchants his procurators back on March 17;[47] indeed, the two contracts overlap. In that of May 10 Symon and Lanfrancus, who had now returned to Genoa, constitute Jacobus de Picardo, who was not present, their procurator to receive 6 bales of cloves and 2 bales of galingale from Peire Brondellus, who also appeared in the earlier contract, or from Mussus Calderarius, who was one of the procurators authorized in the earlier contract. As before, the agreement states that the merchandise be picked up at the house of Brondellus in Lagny where it had been sent by Lanfrancus de Gualterio. But this time the procurator was expressly given license to sell the merchandise at the May fair in Provins.[48]

These documents, though commonplace in their basic intention of authorizing procurators to transact business in distant places, serve at the same time to bring into sharp focus for a brief moment the complexity and efficiency of the organizations with which merchants like Symon de Gualterio surrounded themselves. There was Symon himself, the capitalist, the head of the organization, who remained in Genoa manipulating the varied facets of his far-flung enterprise; there was Lanfrancus de Gualterio, the junior partner, one may suppose, the traveling factor, who moved about continental and Mediterranean Europe purchasing marketable goods and arranging their shipment to a central point of collection and storage in Champagne; in the north there was Peire Brondellus, merchant of Lagny, the organization's resident representative in Champagne, who at minimum received shipments and provided storage facilities; and finally, one encounters a series of procurators, temporary agents, authorized by the home office to collect, sell, and buy goods, to pay debts, and to arrange credit. Yet only when one adds to this rough description some account of Symon's heavy investment in commerce all over the Mediterranean and beyond, his purchases in Genoa of wool and finished cloth, and his active role in international banking and finance—only then does the three-dimensional figure of the thirteenth-century "man of affairs" begin to emerge from out of the vast, impersonal forest of scribal notations.

During the summer months of 1253 Symon's activities appear to have slackened off appreciably. Indeed, Fornario recorded only one contract from June in which he appeared;[49] and in July he was absent altogether from Fornario's entries. In August, however, the rhythm of Symon's activity gradually picked up once again. He appeared in six contracts between August 6 and 25. In the first of this series he appointed Fulco de Castro his procurator to collect the profit and capital from five *commenda* contracts in which he had invested 730 pounds between early October, 1252, and the beginning of May,

1253.[50] On August 13 he granted quittance to Obertus Rubeus, acknowledging to have received full payment from all *commenda* and debts.[51] Similarly on August 16 he acknowledged receipt of full payment and satisfaction from Obertus de Cariis and Company of Piacenza for a series of payments which the firm's representatives had collected in Symon's name from Nicolosus Pelicia in Montpellier.[52] Here Symon had employed the facilities of a Piacenzan banking house to liquidate his distant ventures. One may conjecture that Symon less frequently did business in Montpellier than he did further north in Lagny where his own representatives were permanently stationed.

By August 18 Symon had again turned his attention to Mediterranean affairs. On that date he figured as the principal party in a contract of maritime exchange (*cambium nauticum*). Symon acknowledged receipt of *tot de tuis rebus* from Ugetus Lomellus for which he promised to pay *nomine venditionis* 3895 Syrian Gold bezants[53] to Ugetus or his agent at Acre within the month of January next upon the safe arrival there of the ship *Saint Gabriel* or the greater part of its cargo. In a supplementary clause Symon agreed that should the said bezants not be paid at Acre as stipulated, he would then pay the debt in Genoa, at the rate of ten Genoese *solidi* for every bezant, within one month after any ship of Ugetus' choosing, or the greater part of its cargo, should arrive safely back in Genoa. Jacobus de Gualterio acted as guarantor for Symon in the transaction.[54] As the "seller" of foreign exchange in this agreement, Symon was shifting the risk of sea transport from himself to Lomellinus, payment to whom was contingent upon the safe arrival of a ship and its cargo in Acre, or on return, in Genoa. The exchange was customarily made at a rate which would provide the lender or "buyer" of *cambium*, Lomellinus, with both interest and compensation for risk. Such agreements were regularly expressed in the form of a sale (*nomine venditionis*).[55]

This entry differs mildly from the majority of maritime exchange contracts in that it contained a clause permitting repayment in Genoa at a specified rate of exchange if the "seller" of *cambium* so desired. Normally, too, the settlement of such an agreement was stipulated within one, or perhaps two, months after the arrival of the specified ship at its destination. Here, however, settlement of a contract drawn up in Genoa on August 18 was not to be made in Acre until the following January—fully five months away—or later than that, should the contract be settled back in Genoa. The date on which the ship

Saint Gabriel was scheduled to depart Genoa for the eastern Mediterranean cannot be determined, and one can only conjecture whether or not Symon himself intended to sail with her—or, indeed, whether he intended himself to go to Syria at all. Our scribe recorded his last appearance in a business contract on October 11, but he must have remained in Genoa at least until December 17 when he prepared his last will and testament. However appropriate such a precaution might have been on the eve of so long and hazardous a voyage, it seems altogether unlikely that the sailing of the *Saint Gabriel* would have been delayed three months for the pleasure of Symon's company.

On August 18 Symon attempted to make himself sole owner of the ship *Saint Francis*, three-quarters of which he had purchased back in March.[56] The contract records Symon's purchase of one-quarter of the *Saint Francis* from Nicolosus de Mari for 125 pounds to be paid within two months after the coming Christmas; however, for reasons unknown, on November 2, before payment was made, the agreement was cancelled. Symon's last appearance in Fornario's cartulary in the summer of 1253 occurred on August 25 when he acknowledged receipt of 20 pounds owed him by Ruffinus de Sancto Donato and paid by the latter's agent, Nicolosus Becusrubeus.[57]

During the autumn of 1253 Symon continued to interest himself with business ventures in the Mediterranean area. He figured in eight entries between September 15 and October 11.[58] Half of these consist of *commenda* contracts in which Symon invested just over 1560 pounds Genoese in ventures to Bugia, Maiorca, Sicily, and an unspecified destination. Among these is an agreement in which Symon Grillus would carry over 311 pounds from Symon on a venture to Sicily. This entry figured in a complicated group of contracts which require further attention.[59]

Between October 8 and 11 Fornario prepared a series of contracts the central figure of which was the same Symon Grillus, who was about to undertake a trading venture to Sicily, sailing to Messana on the ship *Supeta*. On this trip he arranged to carry sums in *commenda* from Vencigentis de Gualterio, from Symon de Caritate and his brother Andrea, and from Symon de Gualterio.[60] He also served Symon as procurator,[61] in which capacity he contracted a maritime exchange (*cambium nauticum*) with Symon de Caritate on October 9. Grillus acknowledged that he received over 302 pounds Genoese from Caritate, for which he promised to pay (*nomine venditionis*) 113½ ounces of gold in Sicilian "tari"[62] to Caritate, or to his procurator (Symon de Primontorio)[63], within two months after the ship *Supeta* should arrive in Messana.[64] The Genoese money was apparently invested in northern cloth.[65] From this tangled series of pledges and agreements in familiar pattern of Symon de Gualterio's *modus operandi* in the world of Genoese business and finance emerges clearly. As he had done on August 18, Symon again, though this time indirectly, acted as the "seller" of foreign exchange, perhaps as a device to "insure" himself against the loss at sea of a shipment of northern cloth; for one can assume that the majority of such contracts of maritime exchange involved more than the permutation of monies which the document overtly expresses. Here as elsewhere Symon's extensive employment of agents, partners, and procurators is obvious. His personal involvement in business dealings and high finance stretched from the county of Champagne in the north, to the distant shores of Syria in the east, and Saphi on the African shore of the Atlantic Ocean in the west; and, at least in the majority of cases,[66] he manipulated all this without abandoning his Genoese palazzo.

In conclusion perhaps some statistical data of a general and comparative nature might be of value. According to the entries of our scribe, between March and October, 1253, Symon de Gualterio invested over 9400 pounds Genoese in overseas commerce (including ventures to Sicily, Sardinia, Tunis, Bugia, Syria, Saphi, and several unknown destinations). That is almost 18 per cent of a total investment in such commerce of nearly 53,000 pounds Genoese on the part of that group of 278 merchants who may be identified by their participation in trade with the fairs of Champagne. At the same time, however, Symon was also very active in northern commerce. He was a principal in five substantial *cambium* contracts drawn on the May fair of Provins between March and May, 1253, whose sums totaled over 4220 pounds of Provins, and one *commenda* venture to "France" in March for 770 pounds Genoese. The former figure constitutes almost 9½ per cent of the more than 46,000 pounds of Provins invested in exchange agreements by the same merchant group among 181 contracts drawn on the fairs of Champagne in Fornario's cartulary. That figure may profitably be compared with the record of the early "caravan merchant" group in the cartulary of Guglielmo Cassinese. Between January, 1191, and February, 1192, the "caravan merchants" invested only 1840 pounds Genoese and 1069 pounds of Provins in 60 loans and exchange contracts drawn on the fairs of Champagne.[67] Having tabulated in detail the records of only two notaries, one may resist the temptation to term such an increase in the volume of trade staggering, but it could not be out of order to assert that it is uniquely demonstrative of the increasing tempo of economic life which characterized the thirteenth century.

NOTES

1. See his two pioneer articles on the cloth trade: "The Market for Northern Textiles in Genoa, 1179–1200," *Revue Belge de Philologie et d'Histoire*, VIII (1929), 831–851; and "The Merchants of Arras and the Overland Trade with Genoa, Twelfth Century," *ibid.*, IX (1930), 495–533.

2. *Guglielmo Cassinese* (1190–1192), eds. M. W. Hall, H. C. Krueger, R. L. Reynolds (2 vols., in *Documenti e Studi per la Storia del Commercio e del Diritto Commerciale Italiano*, Turin, 1938). Clearly this notary catered to the northern merchants in Genoa; his records contain over 500 contracts touching upon their business and commerce.

3. I have discussed the techniques employed in this commerce in two earlier articles: "The Techniques of Business in the Trade Between the Fairs of Champagne and the South of Europe in the Twelfth and Thirteenth Centuries," *Economic History Review*, X (1958), 427–438; and "The *Vectuarii* in the Overland Commerce Between Champagne and Southern Europe," *ibid.*, XII (1959), 239–246.

4. The vicissitudes, both political and economic, which account for the changes in the personnel and composition of the merchant groups who controlled the overland commerce between Genoa and Champagne over the years make an intriguing story in themselves which I hope soon to relate in a separate study. Suffice it to say here that by the second quarter of the thirteenth century the men of Arras and Asti virtually disappeared from the trade with Champagne. The period during which the Asti men almost totally drop out of the Genoese records coincides very closely with the turbulent reign of the Emperor Frederick II, and may be explained primarily by the fact that Asti's orientation in the Papal-Imperial struggle was Ghibelline while the Genoese were deeply committed to the Guelph cause. The disappearance of the men of Arras is more difficult to account for, but it seems most likely that rather than being forced out of the trade, they voluntarily retired from it. Having made their fortunes as "caravan merchants," they evidently graduated to the more lucrative profession of financiers. This solution is suggested in part by Georges Bigwood's study of the financiers of Arras in the thirteenth and fourteenth centuries, where particular attention is given to the Crespin family, once very important members of the "caravan merchant" group. See "Les financiers d'Arras," *Revue Belge de Philologie et d'Histoire*, III (1924), 465–508.

5. Using as my criterion their appearance as principals in a contract drawn on a fair of Champagne in the fourth volume of the unpublished cartulary of the Genoese notary Bartholomeus de Fornario for the year 1253 in Genoa's Archivio di Stato (ASG), I have identified 278 individuals as belonging to that group of merchants who dominated the trade between Genoa and Champagne in the middle of the thirteenth century. The general cohensiveness of the group is further born out by an examination of Volume II of

Fornario's cartulary for 1250–1251, by examination of Volume II of the un-published cartulary of Januinus de Predono for 1253, and by checking the selected entries from the period published in Renée Doehaerd, *Les Relations commerciales entre Gênes, la Belgique et l'Outremont d'après les Archives Notariales Génoises aux XIIIe et XIVe siècles*, (Vols. II and III, Brussels-Rome, 1941). Of these 278 individuals, 146, or approximately 52½ per cent are Genoese; 50, or approximately 12½ per cent are Florentines; 21, or ap-proximately 7½ per cent are Sienese; 7, or approximately 2½ per cent are from Lucca; 6, or just over 2 per cent are from Parma; 4, or almost 1½ per cent are from Pistoia; and 3, or a shade over 1 per cent are from Cremona. In contrast there remain only 6 Asti men who comprise a fraction over 2 per cent of the total. To my knowledge there are no longer any men from Arras in the group.

6. Indeed, in the records of Cassinese there are only two individuals whom I can clearly identify as "caravan merchants" who in one instance jointly participated in Mediterranean commerce. Most of the principals in this document are merchants of Asti. On March 17, 1192, Bartholomeus Alfer agreed to carry 200 pounds Genoese from Enricus Alfer and 260 pounds from Belardus Belardungus in *commenda* to Sicily (*Cassinese*, No. 1757). Both Belardungus and Enricus Alfer appear as principals in a series of contracts drawn on the May fair of Provins for 1192 (*Cassinese*, Nos. 1358, 1408, 1614, 1690, 1697). To the best of my knowledge, however, in the entries of Cassinese this document provides a unique example of known "caravan merchants" investing in Mediterranean ventures. A more puzzling figure is Raimundus Unaldus whom for some time I incorrectly assumed to be a merchant of Asti and a member of the "caravan merchant" group. He appears both in contracts concerning Mediterranean commerce and in those dealing with the fairs of Champagne (*Cassinese*, Nos. 760, 829, 924, 1701). More recently, however, Vsevolod Slessarev has established his Provençal origin; he was a merchant and draper from St. Gilles (see his, "Die sogenannten Orientalen im mittelalterlichen Genua. Einwanderer aus Südfrankreich in der ligurischen Metropole," *Vierteljahrschrift für Sozial-und Wirtschaftsgeschichte*, LI, (1964).

7. See, for example, the concluding remarks to R. S. Lopez's masterful collective portrait of Genoese mercantile society, "Le merchand Génois. Un profil collectif," *Annales: Economies, Sociétés, Civilisations*, XIII (1958), 501–515.

8. Professor R. S. Lopez, who originally considered Symon a Genoese (see "L'attivita economica di Genova nel marzo 1253 secondo gli atti notarili del tempo," *Atti della Società Ligure di Storia Patria*, LXIV, Genoa, 1935, 188–89), more recently placed him among that group of Piacenzan businessmen and bankers resident in Genoa (see "Concerning Surnames and Places of Origin," *Medievalia et Humanistica*, VIII (1954), 11, n. 18; and see *La Prima Crisi della Banca di Genova, 1250–1259* (Milan, 1956), 44). The evidence I have seen, however, leads me still to think him a Genoese. There is no indication of Piacenzan origin in his last will and testament, where one would expect to find it. On the contrary, he is to be buried in Genoa, he leaves charitable bequests to Genoese religious institutions only and the executors of his estate and guardians of his children are Genoese.

This may be contrasted with the provisions in the last will of a known Piacenzan merchant, Obertus Abbas de Placentia, where bequests to Piacenzan religious houses outnumber those to Genoese institutions ten to six, and where all the executors are Piacenzans (see ASG, Bartholomeus de Fornario, II, f. 125v–126). The de Gualterii may well have been naturalized Genoese, but if so, their residence in Genoa would appear to extend back at least one generation earlier than Symon himself. The earliest reference I have encountered in the notarial registers to a "de Gualterio" is found on a mutilated page of the Cartulary of Obertus de Placentia (in Diversorum 102, f. 43 v) from March, 1197, where a ⸺ de Gualterio sells goods to a merchant of Troyes. "Gualterius" is a northern name; possibly 'the family was of north French or Flemish origin, domiciled in Genoa by the late twelfth century.

9. Some idea of the real value of that sum can be had when one observes that in Genoa in the same year (1253) one might rent two contiguous houses for 7 pounds per year (Fornario, IV, fol. 168–2); or one might purchase one "baptized, white slave girl" for 7 pounds (Fornario, IV, fol. 90v–3). Also one might purchase a house in the city for 100 pounds (Fornario, IV, fol. 115v–5), or a sea-going merchant vessel for between 500 and 600 pounds (Fornario, IV, fols. 17v–5, 18–2, 208v–4, 216v–3).

10. See, for example, the last will of the wealthy and distinguished Genoese, Ansaldus Cigala, a *judex*, who in 1264 bequeathed to the Church for the repose of his soul only 3 pounds, one tenth of which was contributed to advance the construction of the "mole" in Genoa's harbor (Leonino de Sexto in Giberto de Nervio, II, fol. 251–252v). The story revealed in this will is presented in my article "Lanfranco Cigala of Genoa: The Career of a Delinquent," *Medievalia et Humanistica,"* XV (1963), 77–85.

11. Andriolus regularly handled Symon's financial transactions. See below.

12. Fornario, IV, fol. 278v.

13. Fornario, IV, fol. 1–4. Wilielmus Tartaro takes 65 pounds 2 sol. in *commenda* from Guilielmus Bonizus invested in money of Provins, which he is to receive from Symon de Gualterio at the next May fair of Provins. The sum is derived from 118 Saracen bezants of Syria owed to Bonizus in payment for sugar.

14. Fornario, IV, fol. 3v–1. Symon's debtor is Raynucius Ayguininus, one of the Piacenzan group active in the trade with Champagne. Jacobus de Gualterio, Symon's relative and occasional business partner, is one of the witnesses.

15. Fornario, IV, fol. 7v–3.

16. Fornario, IV, fol. 8v–3.

17. Fornario, IV, fol. 8v–5.

18. Fornario, IV, fol. 10–2, 10v–7. In the first of these contracts Symon's creditor for the 319 pounds in Provins is Guilielmus Bonizus. An appended clause states that if Symon, or his agent, does not pay the sum at the fair, he may repay it in Genoa one month after the fair has ended at the rate of 20 Genoese *denarii* for every 12 Provins *denarii*. In the second contract Symon shares the responsibility of paying 1000 pounds in Provins with

Nicolosus de Nigro. Their creditor is Ottobonus Picamilia, whose associate Lanfrancus de Palma acts for him in the transaction.

19. Fornario, IV, fol. 13–4.

20. Fornario, IV, fol. 14–4.

21. Fornario, IV, fol. 18–1. In this instance Symon functioned much like a banker, which Professor Lopez has called him, but his relationship to Wilielminus de Savignono remains too opaque to be certain.

22. Fornario, IV, fols. 17v–5, 18–2. Later, on August 23 (*cf.* fol. 208v–4) Symon tried to purchase the remaining one quarter of the ship from Nicolosus de Mari, but for reasons unknown this sale was cancelled in November.

23. Fornario, IV, fols. 21–2, 22v–2.

24. Indeed, only five documents recorded by Fornario in April in which Symon appears do not concern themselves directly with Mediterranean commerce. On April 1 Symon witnessed a *cambium* transaction on the May fair at Provins between Petrus Garretus of Asti and the Florentine Jacobus de Donato (Fornario, IV, fol. 23v–2). In a document drawn up on April 4 Symon acknowledged the services of his banker Andriolus Rexem in discharging certain financial obligations in his behalf for which he gave quittance (Fornario, IV, fols. 29v–5, 30–1). On April 11 Symon sold *cambium* in Genoese *denarii* to Ugetus Lomellinus, a prominent Genoese merchant, and promised to pay 1000 pounds of Provins at the next May fair (Fornario, IV, fol. 14–4). In this cartulary Symon appears in no other transaction concerning the fair of Champagne in the month of April. At the very end of the month, on April 29, Symon bought sixteen pieces of *virides* of Chalons from the cloth importer Bernardus Camorerius of Parma for 203 pounds 12 sol. Genoese, which Symon agreed to pay by the end of August when he should have disposed of the cloth in the eastern Mediterranean market (Fornario, IV, fol. 67v–1). One additional document from April 1 may indirectly reflect Symon's activities. In that entry Lanfrancus de Gualterio (and Johannes de Marino) appointed procurators to receive a shipment of cloth from a *vectuarius* in Montpellier (Fornario, IV, fol. 24–1). One cannot determine whether Lanfrancus was here acting in his own behalf or as Symon's partner.

25. One must remember, of course, that this figure, although large, is based upon tabulations compiled from the entries of just one notarial cartulary; one cannot assume that Symon confined his business solely to the notary Bartholomeus de Fornario.

26. Fornario, IV, fols. 23v–4 (1 April); 23v–3 (1 April); 24v–6 (2 April); 28v–4 (4 April); 34v–1 (7 April).

27. Fornario, IV, fols, 42v–3 (12 April); 50–1 (16 April); 67–6 (29 April).

28. Fornario, IV, fols. 54–5 (19 April); 65v–5 (28 April); 65v–6 (28 April).

29. Fornario, IV, fols. 59v–4 (22 April); 63–6 (28 April); 63v–1 (28 April).

30. Fornario, IV, fol. 54–4. This contract does not appear to me to fit comfortably into any of the usual categories of maritime transactions. It is not a maritime exchange (*cambium nauticum*), since no permutation of monies is involved. It is possibly a sea loan (*foenus nauticum*), but if so the

roles of the borrower, customarily the travelling merchant, and the lender, the sedentary investor, are reversed; in this case Symon de Gualterio, the borrower, remains in Genoa, while the lender, de Mari, travels abroad. Or the document may also be an early example of the so-called "insurance loan," wherein the insured, or borrower, remained at home, and the loan was declared repayable upon the safe arrival of the borrower's goods. Customarily, in these contracts, however, the lender was always a ship owner and the borrower a shipper. For a lucid discussion in English of the development of such contracts, see Florence Edler de Roover, "Early Examples of Marine Insurance," *Journal of Economic History*, V (1945), 172–200, in which earlier studies, beginning with the pioneer work of Enrico Bensa, *Il contratto di assicurazione nel medio evo* (Genoa, 1884) are summarized.

31. Fornario, IV, fol. 54–5.

32. Fornario, IV, fol. 61–4. In addition Jacobus de Mari carried 703 pounds from his father in a straight *commenda* agreement for one-quarter profit, and also 66 pounds and 2 sol. from Armanus Pinellus and brothers (55v–4), 44 pounds from Nicolosus de Vendeto, *bancherius* (55v–1), 44 pounds and 12 sol. from Lanfrancus de Georgio and his brother Acetus (60–1), and 151 pounds and 6 sol. invested in silk from Wilielminus Lercarius and brothers (61–5), all in similar contracts drawn up between 19 and 25 April.

33. Fornario, IV, fol. 65v–5, 6 (28 April). Frexenus carried at least one additional sum of 40 pounds in *commenda* from Armanus Pinellus and brothers (fol. 57v–3) contracted on 19 April.

34. Fornario, IV, fol. 67v–4.

35. Fornario, IV, fol. 63v–1.

36. Fornario, IV, fol. 65–3. See R. S. Lopez, "Back to Gold, 1252," *Economic History Review*, IX (1956), 219–40.

37. Fornario, IV, fol. 59–5 (22 April); 61–3 (25 April); 61v–1 (25 April); 65–4 (28 April). The factors in the last two contracts are Symon's relatives Lanfrancus and Jacobus de Gualterio.

38. Fornario, IV, fol. 73v–3, 4, 6; 75–1, 4, 5. The first two of these, for 75 pounds each, are scheduled for unknown destinations. The third represents an investment of 100 pounds in gold to be carried to Tunis by a member of the noble Genoese Doria family. In the fourth contract Symon invests 100 pounds to be carried to Bugia by Aschinus de Colonato. The fifth is a *commenda* contract for 200 pounds to be carried to Tunis by Wilielminus de Asture, and the sixth a small investment of 51 pounds 14 sol. to be carried to Sicily by Jacobus Barlaria.

39. Fornario, IV, fols. 75–1 (2 May); 97v–2 (10 May); 115v–6 (20 May). The second of these entries is a contract involving 125 pounds in which the factor is another member of the Doria family; the third, for 100 pounds is carried by Johannes de Bissane, son of the Genoese notary Enricus de Bissane.

40. Fornario, IV, fol. 73v–6; 75–4 (see above, note 38).

41. Fornario, IV, fol. 75–5 (see above, note 38); 101v–5.

42. Fornario, IV, fols. 73v–3, 4 (see above note 38); 107v–1. This last contract involves an investment of 183 pounds carried by Wilielminus de Volta.

43. Fornario, IV, fols. 97v–1; 97v–5.

44. "Ego Johannes Ascherius nomine meo et sociorum meorum confiteor tibi Wilielmo Lercario me recepisse et habuisse a Symone de Gualterio solvente pro te et tuo nomine . . . tot denarios Jan. quos idem Symon mihi scribi fecit in bancho Andrioli Rexem . . . ."

45. Fornario, IV, fols. 34–4. On 22 March, just as in the contract of 10 May, Symon, in the name of his associate Nicolosus de Nigro, credited Johannes Ascherius and Company with "so much" in Genoese *denarii* on the books of the bank of Nicola Tarranini.

46. Fornario, IV, fols. 29v–5; 278v–1 (Symon's last will and testament).

47. Fornario, IV, fol. 8v–5.

48. Fornario, IV, fol. 97v–5.

49. Fornario, IV, fol. 132v–1. Here Symon gives and concedes the 40th part of the *ius introitum*, which Nicola Bambaxus bought in public auction from the commune of Genoa for 802 pounds. For the most recent discussion of Genoese customs duties and the publication of relevant documents from the fourteenth century, see John Day, *Les douanes de Gênes, 1376–1377*, (2 Vols., Paris, 1963.)

50. Fornario, IV, fol. 172–4.

51. Fornario, IV, fol. 181v–1.

52. Fornario, IV, fol. 189v–5. The debts collected were in goods and money: over 666 pounds of cloves and 73 pounds of Provins. Symon's nephew and personal banker, Andriolus Rexem, witnessed the document.

53. These coins are probably the "pseudo-bezants" struck by the rulers of the crusaders' states in imitation of various types of Islamic dinars; or they are possibly the "reformed" bezants, whose legend was in correct Arabic script and language, but whose content was purely Christian, issued at Acre and Tripolis beginning in 1251. See Philip Grierson, "A Rare Crusader bezant with the *Christus vincit* Legend," *American Numismatic Society Museum Notes*, VI (1954), 169–178.

54. Fornario, IV, fol. 199–5.

55. For discussions in English of the maritime exchange agreement as a prototype of the marine insurance contract, see W. S. Holdsworth, "The Early History of the Contract of Insurance," *Columbia Law Review*, XVII (1917), 85–113; and also F. E. DeRoover, *op. cit.*

56. Fornario, IV, fol. 208v–4.

57. Fornario, IV, fol. 210–6.

58. Fornario, IV, fols. 218–6 (15 Sept.); 220v–1 (16 Sept.); 223–1 (22 Sept); 234v–5 (9 Oct.); 236–1, 2, 3 (11 Oct.). With the exception of 222–6, in which Martinus Ususmaris acknowledges Symon's payment of 27 pounds in behalf of Obertus de Manfredo, each of these entries is concerned with Mediterranean commerce. October 11 marks Symon's last appearance in a business contract in this cartulary; his last will and testament, however, was drawn up on December 17.

59. Fornario, IV, fols, 218–6; 220v–1; 223–1; 236–1.

60. Fornario, IV, fols. 232v–2 (8 Oct.); 234v–3 (9 Oct.); 223–1 (11 Oct.).

61. Fornario, IV, fols. 236–2 (11 Oct.); 234v–5 (9 Oct.); 236–3 (11 Oct.). In the first of these Gualterio appoints Grillus his procurator; in the second he assures Caritate that he will act as guarantor for Grillus in the mari-

time exchange; and in the third Gualterio acknowledges to Grillus that the latter was acting in Gualterio's behalf when he contracted the said maritime exchange with Caritate.

62. For a discussion of this coinage see R. S. Lopez, "Il Ritorno all' Oro," and for a condensed version in English, Lopez, "Back to Gold, 1252," *Economic History Review*, IX (1956), 219–240.

63. Fornario, IV, fol. 234v–4.

64. Fornario, IV, fol. 235v–2 (10 Oct.).

65. Fornario, IV, fol. 234v–4.

66. Fornario, IV, fol. 236–3. The fact that Symon employed a procurator for the venture to Sicily, whereas none is mentioned in connection with that to Acre, lends further plausibility to the supposition that he intended to take the latter voyage in person.

67. Though less startling, some additional statistics illustrating the cloth trade may also be of interest. In the records of Cassinese between March and December, 1191, the "caravan merchants" made "loans" and sold northern cloth to Genoese drapers and others worth approximately 4400 pounds Genoese. Between March and December, 1253, Fornario recorded cloth sales by that group of merchants who dealt with the fairs of Champagne totaling approximately 7300 pounds, indicating an increase of slightly over 60 per cent. The comparative numbers of contracts in which these sums are recorded, however, further indicate the increasing volume of trade. In 1191 the total of 4400 pounds is spread over 95 contracts, whereas in 1253, 7300 pounds is compressed into only 60 contracts. Also the record of cloth sales in Fornario may be somewhat deceptive because of the wide ranging interests of the merchants by the mid-thirteenth century. Just as their operations were far less restricted geographically than were those of the "caravan merchants" in the late twelfth century, so were the commodities in which they traded far less specialized.

THE POUND-VALUE OF GENOA'S MARITIME TRADE IN 1161

VSEVOLOD SLESSAREV

University of Cincinnati

In his recent study on Genoa's customs John Day was able to assemble an impressive row of figures that allowed him to trace the fluctuation of Genoese maritime trade from 1341 to 1406[1] For the thirteenth century some scattered data has been provided by Heinrich Sieveking.[2] Further back in time the sources reflect a society and government too rudimentary to have cared for anything approaching statistics. The present essay attempts to supply some meaningful figures for the middle of the twelfth century. The process involves a comparison of losses suffered by the Genoese merchants during the 1162 attack on their colony in Constantinople with some entries in the cartulary of the Genoese notary Giovanni Scriba (1155–64). If successful, the resulting amounts will offer not only a point of departure toward figures given by Sieveking and Day but also a yardstick to measure an early stage of the commercial revolution.

A lengthy discussion of the Genoese colony in Constantinople would be out of place here. Suffice to say that Emperor Manuel's grand design to reestablish the Byzantine rule over Southern Italy and Sicily made him seek the good will of the Ligurian metropolis. Toward the end of 1155 ambassador Demetrio Macrembolite and the consuls of the city concluded a preliminary treaty which among other things gave the Genoese entering the empire a privileged status and promised to them a quarter in the capital.[3] The precise location of the future colony was not spelled out, yet the wording of the treaty suggested that it was expected to be near the Venetian and Pisan *emboloi*, both on the southern shore of the Golden Horn. Venice had a quarter here since 1082 and Pisa got its in 1111;[4] the arrival of a third competitor obviously increased the already existing rivalry. The notarial minutes of Giovanni Scriba show clearly that at least since 1156 Genoese merchants were trading at Constantinople and other imperial harbors, and some even seem to have combined commerce with mercenary service in the Byzantine navy.[5] Where the

merchants lived while in the capital is not clear, because officially
the quarter was not yet in Genoa's possession. In 1157 the Genoese
ambassador, Amico di Murta, was dispatched to Constantinople "to
exact the promised wharves and the quarter." Three years later
another ambassador retraced the route probably with the same assignment. First tangible notice of the quarter, in a later document
referred to as the quarter of the Holy Cross, comes with the disaster
of 1162.[6]

In spring of that year one thousand Pisans attacked some three
hundred Genoese "merchants" with the intention of "despoiling and
killing them." The Genoese resisted for a day, but on the morrow
the Pisans returned with a reinforcement of Venetians, Greeks, and
"other rabble of Constantinople." Overwhelmed by the assailants,
they abandoned their lodgings and merchandise, saving nothing but
their lives. The Pisans captured the Genoese *fondaco*[7] with its 30,000
bezants worth of goods and they killed a young nobleman, son of
Otone Rufo. The annalist Caffaro, to whom we owe this account,
said nothing about the way in which the Genoese were able to escape.
Presumably they withdrew to their ships or ship in the harbor and
sailed home thirsty for revenge.

The outrage to Genoa's pride and the sting of material loss resulted in a prolonged war between the two republics. It cost thousands
of lives, resulted in inestimable damage to trade, and ended only in
1175 when Emperor Frederick I finally induced the parties to negotiate.[8] In the meantime Genoa began to mend diplomatic relations
with Byzantium whose tacit connivance in the upheaval must have
been at least suspected. In 1168 the commune dispatched Amico di
Murta once more to the shores of the Bosporus. Restitution to Genoa
loomed large in negotiations which advanced but slowly on account of
shifting political alliances. A new quarter was assigned to Genoa in
1170 only to be destroyed again, this time by the Venetians. Though
grievances against the inept host were piling up, little was undertaken
on both sides for a number of years. Then by the latter part of 1174
the consuls gave elaborate instructions to ambassador Grimaldi, who
was to bolster his demands with a detailed list of losses. Among the
nine major items amounting together to 84,340 bezants, the losses of
the first Genoese quarter, assessed to 29,443 bezants, represented the
largest claim.[9] It is this portion of Grimaldi's instructions that will
occupy our attention.

The introductory paragraph to the losses of 1162 still echoes
bitterness: had not the Genoese gathered securely "in trust and under

the wings of the Empire" when they were despoiled?[10] The list itself
is little more than names and quantities of bezants under a laconic
title: *Ratio perditarum emboli de Sancta Cruce.* Its precise date of
compilation cannot be ascertained, except that it must have taken
place after 1165, for one prominent Genoese who was alive in that
year is referred to in the list as "late."[11] Considering the very young
age of the colony at the moment of its spoliation one can be reasonably sure that no trading agreements, of which the list is a reflection,
were concluded in Constantinople. This notion is further strengthened
by the fact that almost all names, even those of the less prominent
travelling agents, can be traced to the cartulary of Giovanni Scriba
(1155–1164).[12] Furthermore, neither in the list of losses nor in other
instructions that could relate to the year 1162 is there a mention of a
notary, without whose help no commercial agreements could have
been written down. We have thus in Giovanni Scriba a unique reflection of the *societates, commenda*-contracts, sea-loans, etc. that
had been drawn up in Genoa on the eve of merchants' departure to
Constantinople, i.e. prior to the middle of September 1161.[13]

The ultimate source of the list, that has been published twice in
modern times,[14] are two twelfth century manuscripts,[15] one known
as "small" or B version, the other as "large" or A version. Both could
have been written by the same scribe. Version A is considerably
neater and less cursive than B, it obviously represents an enlarge-
ment and partial revision of the latter.[16] The total sum of 29,443
bezants lost by the Genoese in goods and currency appear only in the
A version. Neither A nor B is free of over-sights, yet taken together
they are superior to the modern editions.[17] The manuscripts are
also helpful in revealing the rationale of the arrangement which certainly cannot be gained from the most recently printed text.

In the manuscripts each separate claim is preceded by a paragraph sign (not consistently in A) and by a capitalized *Pro.* An individual claim may contain the name of just one person, e.g., *Pro
Oberto malocello perperos cxii.* Frequently a claim included the name
of the damaged party and of the travelling agent, e.g., *Pro Stabili
perperos cclxxv quos Donundius de balneo ibidem amisit.* In some
cases one or several sub-claims, each introduced by *Item,* follow the
initial request.[18] The total number of claims following each introductory *Pro* amounts to 104 in B and 108 in A.

The value of the list for the history of Genoa's trade has been
noticed before, so too has the fact that many names mentioned in it
constituted the "flower of Genoese nobility."[19] What escaped the

older scholarship was the possibility of tracing some commercial agreements found in the cartulary of Giovanni Scriba to the list of losses. In the year 1161 Scriba recorded one joint investment to Romania, i.e. Byzantine Empire, and three to Constantinople. The one to Romania stands apart from the rest. A middle-sized *societas* of slightly more than 47 pounds was drawn up on June 18, well in advance of the late summer when most of the contracts to the eastern Mediterranean were put into writing.[20] Since the partners do not appear in the *Ratio*, they were not in Constantinople during the sack. Of no particular value in itself, the document indicates a distinction made by Genoese merchants between the empire at large and its capital.[21]

In Scriba's busiest season, on August 29, a priest by the name of Guglielmo di Langasco, Bertoloto di Campo, and Otone Barba di Latta must have approached him to validate their *societas*.[22] Each of the men contributed 80 pounds; Otone was to take the total sum (in merchandise, we presume) and in addition 10 pounds of his own to Constantinople, Alexandria, or wherever else he wished. The increment from his own money he could keep, also half of the profit from the partnership, while the other half was to go to the priest and Bertoloto. Thirteen years later Scriba's minute shrank to a single claim in the *Ratio*: "For Bertoloto di Campo 97 bezants which were lost by Otone Barba di Latta and 27 bezants also of his [i.e. Bertoloto] lost by Bernardo Catenacio."[23] The smaller sum represents undoubtedly Bertoloto's investment with another travelling agent that must have been recorded by one of Scriba's colleagues. Strangely enough, the list does not contain compensations of Otone or the priest. Even Bertoloto's restitution was calculated at 1 pound to 1.21 bezants, an impossibly low rate of exchange, as will be seen later.[24] Was the Genoese government asking for its citizens less than their due? Death of partners could be conjectured, yet if so, why did the commune fail to think of the heirs? It is more likely that the bulk of the investment, except perhaps a half or a third of Bertoloto's goods, was transhipped from Constantinople to Alexandria, as the wording of the document vaguely suggests. In such a case a number of rearrangements, such as appointing a new agent, would have been in order. For the present study it is significant to notice that the compilation of the list was not a mechanical prorating of sums of old contracts into Byzantine money.

Closer to the departure of the fleets, on September 8, Stabile and Donadeo, brother of banker Ingone, registered a *societas* of 170 pounds; the former's share was two-thirds, the latter's one-third.[25] This amount and 24 pounds invested in linen by Otone of Milan were to be taken by Donadeo to Constantinople. Otone could keep the profit from his investment, whereas the profit of the partnership was to be divided into equal shares. This time nobody was omitted from the roster of losses. Scattered among a hundred odd claims we find: "For Stabile 275 bezants lost by Donadeo *de balneo*," "For Otone of Milan 100 bezants which the banker Donadeo lost in Constantinople," "For Donadeo *de balneo* 171 bezants which his nephew Pascale lost there."[26]

A striking feature of these claims is an uneven exchange rate between the Genoese pound and the bezant. The two-thirds to one-third division of 170 pounds results roughly in 113 against 57. The ratios of two sets of figures would reimburse Stabile at 1:2.43, Donadeo at 1:3.00, and Otone at 1:4.16. A somewhat similar latitude of variation emerges from three claims of the same list. They are unique in so far as losses are given simultaneously in pounds and bezants.[27] The ratios ascend here from 1:2.46 over 1:2.48 to 1:3.00. Our difficulty lies in not knowing enough about the fluctuation of exchange rates in 1161. From one quotation it seems as if the interest-free exchange was somewhere close to 1:2.625.[28] Should this equation approach true conversion, then some Genoese were promised less than what they had lost. On the other hand Otone's rate of 1:4.16 was extremely generous. The lesson of these figures is to be wary of any mathematical operations that would entail conversions from one currency to another.

On September 9th four gentlemen pooled their resources to launch one of the biggest ventures of the year. Guglielmo Burone and Idone Mallone contributed to a *societas* 300 pounds, Guglielmotto Ciriol 200 pounds, and Ugone Elie, the travelling agent, 80 pounds.[29] Of the first three men's capital a double of 80, i.e. 160 pounds, was to form the *societas* proper, the rest or 340 pounds were treated like a *commenda-* contract from which Ugone could draw a quarter of the profit. Ugone had the option of taking the total sum "wherever he may wish." We would have never known where the investment went, if not for its mention in the *Ratio*. All the claims appear together under a *Pro*-entry without any regard to the complex arrangement: "For Guglielmo Burone, Idone Mallone, and Guglielmo (*sic*) Ciriol 1,500 bezants that were lost in their goods by Ugone Elie, this above 240 bezants of Ugone's own lost by him in the enterprise."[30] In this third and last document the rate of exchange is a uniform 1:3.00. It is important to notice that no provision was made to compensate Ugone for the loss of his labor spent on the *commenda* portion of the contract, a significant fact for the evaluation of the rest of the *Ratio*. Finally, the concealment of destination proves to be something else than letting the travelling party make the decision. Surely, the three prime investors, two of them members of illustrious Genoese families, knew well where their goods were to go. If they kept the direction of the journey secret, it was out of concern for their business venture.

The evidence from the three confrontations can be easily summarized. In some cases claims appear lower than the figures known from the minutes of Giovanni Scriba. The rate of exchange is not uniform and one may suspect that the total of losses expressed in bezants is slightly higher than the total investment in Genoese pounds taken to Constantinople. To a certain degree this raising of the rate is neutralized by the fact that the official total of 29,443 bezants when rechecked should be amended to 29,807 bezants.[31] Instead of trying to adjust all errors and distortions it would be wise to accept the figures of the *Ratio* for what they are, a rather reliable source with a margin of error no bigger than perhaps 5 per cent—not enough to cause serious alarm.

Before proceeding to the main objective of the essay, one remark is in order. Fascination with notarial minutes should not obscure the possibility that investments were taken abroad without being recorded by notaries. A reminder to this effect comes from the first entry of the *Ratio*: "Remember to ask for our chancellor 300 bezants which his son Ugone lost in Constantionple etc."[32] From Scriba we learn that on July 19, 1161, Ugone, son of chancellor Oberto, gave at the behest of his father who was personnally present *antefactum* (bridegroom's gift to his bride-to-be) to Richelda, daughter of Giovanni Golia.[33] The amount was 100 pounds and it came from Oberto's estate; Nicola Roza received it for her. Though there is nothing to indicate that Ugone took the *antefactum* to Constantinople, the circumstantial evidence favors it strongly. Since Ugone was a minor and still under his father's *potestas*, it can be maintained that no formal agreement was drawn up. With this in mind one could say that the figures of the *Ratio* are more representative of the total investment to the capital of Byzantium than all the notarial minutes of that year, even if they had been preserved.

The next step is obvious. Knowing the number of contracts to Constantinople validated by Giovanni Scriba, the total sum in

Ц4909

Genoese pounds invested by his clients, and the expected compensation in bezants, one could establish at least approximately the share of Scriba's activity in relation to the share of all other notaries put together. For the latter the only available guide is the *Ratio*. There are three ways to approach the problem. Scriba's own cartulary supplies the names of nine other notaries who lived in the city.[34] This information is of no great help, because nothing can be said about their activity, nor is the number in itself conclusive.

Had the *Ratio* been composed in a more systematic fashion, one could have reconstructed with its aid the number of all commercial agreements drawn up for Constantinople. Although this cannot be done, there is a circuitous road that leads very much to the same result. In an overwhelming majority of cases commercial contracts involve only one travelling party while the investing party may consist of several individuals. The three *societates* analyzed above are a sufficient proof, for taken together they show seven investors entrusting their capital to three travelling agents. It would be permissible thus to equate the number of travelling agents with the number of contracts. The *Ratio* records a total of seventy-four travelling agents, three of which appear in Scriba's cartulary; the resulting ration is consequently 71:3 or roughly 24:1.[35] This would indicate that Scriba's colleagues authenticated collectively twenty-four times as many contracts as he. The figure is equally of little use, for even an approximate number of contracts, unless one can compare thousands of them, does not constitute a true measure of the volume of trade.

The last and perhaps the best approach would be to compare the claims arising from Scriba's three minutes with the total figure of losses. Expressed in numbers the juxtaposition is between 2,383 bezants and 29,443 bezants.[36] Identical monetary units permit simple division resulting in 12.35, a figure midway between nine and twenty-four. Since Scriba catered predominantly to noble families of substantial wealth, it seems reasonable to suggest that all other recorded and unrecorded investments to Constantinople were 12.35 times bigger than those entered on the pages of his cartulary.

The crucial question is whether the ratio 1:12.35 can be applied elsewhere. In 1161 Scriba drew up numerous contracts to other places, such as Alexandria, the Crusading States, Sicily, North Africa, etc. Would it be permissible to assume that the total investments to these areas were also 12.35 times bigger than those registered by Scriba? Admittedly, this is the weakest part of the entire argument and even a novice in the field of Genoese economic history

could point to numerous pitfalls. But precision cannot be the goal
of medieval statistics; the question is whether some figures, obviously
approximate, are better than none. All that can be said in favor of
following computations is that they are based on actual data which
had been subsequently augmented by a reasonable multiplier. The
left column below represents investments in Genoese pounds as
they were recorded for 1161 by Giovanni Scriba. To the right are
the projected totals, also in Genoese pounds, which are arrived at
via multiplication of Scriba's figures by 12.35.

Alexandria	1,610 pounds	19,884 pounds
Crusading States (*ultramare*)	1,767	21,822
Constantinople	1,024	12,646[37]
Romania	47	580
N. Africa	725	8,954
Provence and Spain	1,005	12,412
S. Italy, Sicily and Sardinia	1,261	15,573
"To any place"	900	11,115
Total	8,339[38]	102,986

Actually neither of these totals has to be accepted on faith alone.
Scriba's figure for the year 1161 is somewhat lower than a true total
would have been, because several minutes specified only quantities
of merchandise taken overseas.[39] No attempt was made to assess
their monetary value. A certain control is further provided by jux-
taposing 8,339 pounds to totals of other years.

Year	Export in pounds	Number of minutes	Remarks
1155	867	33	Scriba works intermittently
1156	6,262	117	
1157	7,762	168	
1158	7,626	196	
1159	2,031	76	Threat by Frederick I
1160	12,640	195	
1161	8,339	143	
1162	968	84	War with Psia. Jan.–April missing
1163	3,399	134	Jan., June, and Nov.–Dec. missing
1164	5,477	157	Most of Jan. missing, ends Aug. 23

The export figures from 1156 to 1161 indicate a steady growth in
spite of a temporary threat to Genoa by Emperor Frederick Barbarossa.[40] Missing folios in the cartulary do not affect 1161 or the
preceding years, and except for 1155, 1159, and 1162 there is no in-

dication that Giovanni Scriba was out of town or assigned to special tasks.[41] In the decade represented above, 1161 was certainly a good but by no means an exceptional year.

To check the grand total of approximately 100,000 pounds is much more difficult. A crude test can be conducted with pound values of ship cargoes, our only guide to the "capacity" of vessels in the twelfth century.[42] Considering the variety in sizes of water conveyances, references would have to be restricted to "big ships" (*magnae naves*) found in Genoese and Pisan annals. In 1136 Genoese galleys captured "a big and rich Saracen ship" the cargo of which was valued at 8,400 pounds.[43] "Two big and rich" Genoese ships, one returning from Syria, another from Constantinople, and an unspecified vessel coming from Sicily were captured by the Pisans in 1162 when the war between the two communes broke out. Their combined cargo is said to have amounted to more than 20,000 pounds. Occasionally the booty was smaller. In the same war, four years later, the Pisans detained three Genoese galliots and a "big ship" on its home voyage from Morocco. The value of the catch "exceeded" only 5,000 pounds.[44]

The very source that proved so helpful in previous calculations, the 1174 directive to Grimaldi, supplies valuable figures on Genoese merchantmen. The ambassador had orders to seek restitution in five cases of damage to Genoese cargoes. While four ships were small or middle-sized, the *navis* of Villano Gauxano must have been big, for eighty persons lost their investments when its cargo fell prey to looters. The losses were set up in two parallel columns, one in Genoese pounds, the other in bezants. In the manuscripts only the latter was added up, showing a figure of 23,216 bezants. Because of fluctuating exchange rates, which can be read off from justaposed numbers, an independent addition of the pound column is a surer way to a precise total, in this case 8,658 pounds.[45] The figure comes surprisingly close to the data furnished above by the annals.

In assuming that a *magna navis* carries approximately 8,500 pounds worth of cargo, it would be necessary to concede that some twelve of such ships could have expedited the entire export of 1161. Needless to say, such a conclusion is at variance with reality. Genoa's merchant fleet may have had three or four big ships, the rest would have been smaller. Grimaldi's instructions reveal that of the four smaller crafts three carried cargoes worth one-fifth and one a cargo worth one-tenth of Gauxano's *navis*.[46] While this breakdown is accidental, it can serve as a basis for a little play of numbers. For example, four "big ships" could have conveyed 36,000 pounds, thirty-three "middle-sized" 56,100 pounds, and ten "small" 8,500 pounds. For all we know, small crafts may have shunned Byzantine waters. Certainly, closer to home they would have been much more numerous.[47] What matters is not the distribution of ships but the feeling that 100,000 pounds for a year's export has the marks of a realistic figure, well in agreement with other sparse data of the period.

Before 100,000 pounds can be arranged along the figures gathered by Heinrich Sieveking and John Day, a brief explanation of the latter's nature is in order. Extraordinary expenditures during the war with Pisa and subsequent colonial adventures made the consuls of Genoa seek revenues commensurable with the fiscal drain.[48] By the second decade of the thirteenth century the so-called *collecta maris* (later known as *denarii maris*) must have become one of the main sources of communal revenues. In 1214, to take a specific case, the consuls decreed that for the duration of six years 4 den. per pound be collected from the export-import trade by sea.[49] The commune farmed out the tax for 38,050 pounds, counting thus on a sure income of 6,342 pounds per year. Since 4 den. constitute one-sixtieth of each pound assessed, the farmers of the tax must have anticipated a minimum taxable figure of 380,520 pounds. To be able to make profit, they hoped of course for a still larger amount. Given the provenance of 380,520 pounds one may well suspect that, all possible irregularities of collection apart, it is lower than the true figure would have been.

The 100,000 pounds of export in 1161 cannot match the other numbers, unless one can project the return cargo bought by the above sum. Of course, the value of the import will include the gain realized in the preceding sale. Since nothing is known about the method of assessment, one could suppose that the return cargo was valued at the prices current in Genoa. From a few notarial minutes of Scriba it seems as if forty per cent profit on commercial contracts was the average.[50] This would make the export-import for 1161 roughly equivalent to 240,000 pounds.

Ten selected figures from 1161–1406 should give some idea of the rate of growth, occasional lows, and the downhill trend toward the end of the period.[51]

1161	240,000	1361	1,756,440
1214	380,520	1371	2,388,960
1274	720,000	1372	2,105,040
1341	1,403,400	1399	1,171,200
1345	993,840	1406	1,173,600

As so often, numbers do not tell the complete story. The growth from 1161 to 1371 was not tenfold, as the figures may indicate. The intervening centuries experienced a substantial debasement of coinage and a concomitant rise of prices. To cite but one example, a hundredweight (*centenarium*) of pepper cost in Genoa close to 4 pounds 6 sol. in 1160–62, 12 pounds 15 sol. in 1291, and 24 pounds in 1377.[52]

It would take a much broader and longer study to set the figures quoted above into proper perspective. Such an endeavor may also find the percentages indicative of tax-farmers' profits. Another line of inquiry could concentrate on the period around 1161 which is marked by Frederick Barbarossa's effort to capitalize on the commercial and industrial wealth of Italian cities. How does, for example, the figure of his anticipated revenue from the reacquisition of the regalia compare with Genoa's export? More daring would be to explore the decades prior to 1161. Perhaps a judicious application of the rate of growth since 1161 could allow some cautious estimates as to when the commercial revolution must have become a recognizable factor. Whatever the potentials, a reasonably accurate figure for Genoa's maritime export in 1161 is a marked advance over the older fragmentary evidence built exclusively out of sums furnished by Giovanni Scriba.

NOTES

1. John Day, *Les douanes de Gênes*, (École Pratique des Hautes Études. VIe Section. Centre de Recherches Historiques. Ports—Routes—Trafics, 17; 2 vols., Paris, 1963), I, xvi–xviii.

2. Heinrich Sieveking, *Genueser Finanzwesen mit besonderer Berücksichtigung der Casa di S. Giorgio* (2 vols., Freiburg im Breisgau, 1898–9), I, 67. Volume I has a separate title: *Genueser Finanzwesen vom 12. bis 14. Jahrhundert.*

3. For documentary evidence see Gerolamo Bertolotto, "Nuova serie di documenti sulle relazioni di Genova coll' Impero Bizantino," in *Atti della Società Ligure di Storia Patria,* XXVIII (Genoa, 1896), 339–573. Many of these sources can be consulted in a more recent edition by Cesare Imperiale di Sant' Angelo, *Codice diplomatico della Repubblica di Genova,* in *Fonti per la Storia d'Italia,* LXXVII, LXXIX, LXXXIX (3 vols., Rome, 1938–42). The Genoese annals, commonly known as *Annales Ianuenses,* are best consulted in *Annali Genovesi di Caffaro e de' suoi continuatori,* ed. Luigi Tomasso Belgrano and Cesare Imperiale di Sant' Angelo, in *Fonti per la Storia d'Italia,* XI–XIV bis (5 vols., Rome, 1890–1929). Hereafter these basic sources will be cited as Bertolotto, *Cod. dipl.,* and *Ann. Ian.* The series of *Atti* will be referred to as *ASL.*

Among the secondary accounts basic is still Camillo Manfroni's "Le relazioni fra Genova, l'Impero Bizantino e i Turchi," *ASL,* XXVIII

(Genoa, 1896), 577–787. See also the classic Wilhelm Heyd, *Histoire du commerce du Levant au moyen-âge,* tr. Furcy Raynaud (2 vols., Leipzig, 1885–6), I, 198–212, and Adolf Schaube, *Handelsgeschichte der romanischen Völker des Mittelmeergebiets bis zum Ende der Kreuzzüge* (Munich and Berlin, 1906), pp. 228–234. A good summary is found in G. I. Bratianu's *Recherches sur le commerce génois dans la Mer Noire au* XIIIe *siècle* (Paris, 1929), pp. 61–89. These four studies will be cited as Manfroni, Heyd, Schaube, and Bratianu.

For the opening of diplomatic relations between Genoa and Byzantium see Bertolotto and Manfroni, 343–5; 596–602 and *Ann. Ian.,* I, 41-2.

4. On *emboloi* in Constantinople see Robert Mayer, *Byzantion, Konstantinopolis, Istanbul. Eine genetische Stadtgeographie,* in *Denkschriften der Akademie der Wissenschaften Wien. Phil.-hist. Klasse,* LXXI, 3 (1943), 118–20. On Venice at the Bosporus consult Horatio F. Brown, "The Venetians and the Venetian Quarter in Constantinople to the close of the Twelfth Century," *Journal of Hellenic Studies,* XL (1920), 68–88; and Heyd, I, 108–20, 215–20. For Pisa see also Heyd, I, 192–8, 212-4.

5. *Il cartolare di Giovanni Scriba,* ed. Mario Chiaudano and Mattia Moresco, in *Documenti e Studi per la Storia del Commercio e del Diritto Commerciale Italiano,* I–II (2 vols., Turin, 1935). Occasionally the reader may find it necessary to consult the older edition in *Chartarum* II, in *Historiae Patriae Monumenta,* VI (Turin, 1853). In this study all references, unless otherwise stated, are to the new edition, cited as *G. S.*

On the Genoese entering the imperial navy see *G. S.,* nos. 84, 97, 219, 615, 666, 674, 676, 995, 1014–16. For a comment see Schaube, p. 230.

6. On the two embassies and the sack see *Ann. Ian.,* I, 47, 60; 67–69. Caffaro is of no help in determining the time of assault. The Pisan annals by Bernardo Maragone report under June 20, 1162 (common calendar) the sudden retaliatory attack of the Genoese against Pisa. Counting backward from this date, the dispoiled Genoese must have returned home in late May or early June. The sack occurred thus either in March or April; see *Gli 'Annales Pisani' di Bernardo Maragone,* ed. Michele Lupo Gentile, in *Rerum Italicarum Scriptores,* new ed., VI, pt. 2 (Bologna, n. d.), 27; cited hereafter as *Ann. Pis.* The months of March and April coincided with the Venetian *muda* for ships coming from Constantinople, on which see Frederic C. Lane, "Fleets and Fairs," now easily accessible in *Venice and History. The Collected Papers of Frederic C. Lane* (Baltimore, 1966), 131.

On the location of Genoa's oldest quarter Manfroni first quoted Cornelio Desimoni's reasoning by which *apud Constantinopolim* (Bertolotto, 391, 393–5) "seems to indicate rather outside than inside" the city, but later in his text he admitted that "L'embolo di Santa Croce era assai probabilmente dentro la città," 607, 612. Desimoni's view has been accepted by Bratianu, 64 and Robert S. Lopez, "Silk Industry in the Byzantine Empire," *Speculum,* XX (1945), 40. Manfroni's second thought gains ample support from the use of *apud* in the cartulary of Giovanni Scriba; see e.g., "debeo tibi apud Alexandriam bisancios centum decem . . ." or "promitto dare . . . apud Alexandriam bisancios .iii. minus quarta . . ." *G. S.,* nos. 111, 117. These payments must have been made in the city. Moreover, the notion of "outside the city" was usually rendered by *ultra* or *trans,* Manfroni, 611, 617. Finally, the failure of the Byzantines to separate the fighting parties can be explained only by their proximity to each other.

7. The literature on *fondachi*, or combinations of warehouses and hostels for merchants, is quite extensive. For an attempt to reassess the origins and the importance of this institution see my "Ecclesiae mercatorum and the Rise of Merchant Colonies," *Business History Review*, XLI (1967), 177–197.

8. The above cited annals of Genoa and Pisa are an eloquent testimony to the carnage. On Frederick's peace see *Cod. dipl.*, II, 227–31.

9. On these events consult Bertolotto and Manfroni, 347–405; 602–34, and *Cod. dipl.*, II, 99–102, 104–16, 117–23, 204–23, and many other documents indirectly connected with the war. The instructions to Grimaldi are found in Bertolotto, 368–405 and *Cod. dipl.*, II, 206–22. The general instructions to Grimaldi, without the detailed lists of losses, were first edited by Ludovico Sauli in his *Colonia dei Genovesi in Galata* (2 vols., Turin, 1831), II, 183–8, doc. no. 3.

10. Bertolotto, 370; *Cod. dipl.*, II, 208–9.

11. In Bertolotto, 393 and *Cod. dipl.*, II, 209a. "Pro filiis et nepotibus quondam Cafari" refers apparently to the annalist Caffaro who died in 1166, see *Ann. Ian.*, I, lxxxi. This would indicate that four years lapsed before the Genoese drew up the *Ratio*. The *terminus ante quem* is September 1174.

12. Identification is impossible in the case of Angelerio di Camilla's serfs, Guglielmo and Fulco, Bertolotto, 390; see also 391 under "Pro Philippo de Brasili." Occasionally names were rather nicknames, e.g., Cennamello, Ingone *ferro cincto*, Guglielmo *bucca fuira, ibid.*

Of the five agents whose names do not appear in Giovanni Scriba none could be called a non-Genoese, a Greek, or an Easterner in general.

13. In 1157 the last contract involving Constantinople was drawn up on August 27, in 1158 on August 30, in 1160 on August 27, in 1161 on September 8, in 1164 on August 21; see *G. S.*, nos. 254, 468, 752, 899, 1299. Toward the end of the century the departure was a month later; see *Oberto Scriba de Mercato* (1186), ed. Mario Chiaudano, in *Documenti e Studi per la Storia del Commercio e del Diritto Commerciale Italiano*, XVI (Turin, 1940), nos. 42, 96. The dates of these two last documents of the year 1186 are September 25 and October 8.

14. The *Ratio* has been published by Bertolotto, 389–397, where it is based on the B and A manuscript versions. The edition in *Cod. dipl.*, II, 207–11 rests exclusively on the A version.

15. Both manuscripts are located in the Archivio di Stato di Genova, Materie Politiche, mazzo 1–2720. They are designated as "due quaderni cartacei, uno di 51 facce manoscritte [B], altro di facce 49 manoscritte [A]." Versions B and A are respectively "small" and "large" not on account of number of pages, but because A contains more material, its writing being more compact.

The folios of B are unnumbered; in A they have Arabic numerals, yet what should have been f.6 was left unmarked and the number 22 was skipped altogether.

16. Although Bertolotto did collate the two manuscript versions, he was not always consistent, for he omitted the important opening entry of B

which reads as follows:

M.C.LXXIIII. Indictione sexta mense septembri. Ordinationes et memorialia data Grimaldo misso legato ad constantinopolitanum imperatorem per consules communis Januae.

This establishes B as the older instruction. The "sixth indiction" shows that its composition fell between September 1 and 24, 1174. A was written in the interval December 25-31, 1174.

17. No full list of errata can be given here. A few major mistakes are, however, worth noting. *Pro Ioanatho ferri* or *Pro Ionatha Ferri* (Bertolotto, 390, *Cod. dipl.*, II, 208a) should be *Pro Ionatha Serri;* see *G. S.*, no. 1188. The sign for pounds, i.e. *lb.*, after Cerriolo and Ogerio pedicule should be changed to a *b* crossed by a bar signifying bezants (Bertolotto, 395). The *cum tertia* or *inde terciam* should be *minus tertia* (Bertolotto, 396, Cod. dipl., II, 210b). In *Mementote petere pro Ogerio et Bonovassallo de pallo ppos cxxx* the amount "130 bezants" is omitted in the A version and therefore it does not appear in the edition of *Cod. dipl.* (Bertolotto, 397, *Cod. dipl.*, II, 211a).

18. For samples given above see Bertolotto, 391, 392, 393-4.

19. Manfroni, 605-6.

20. *G. S.*, no. 840.

21. Same is true for the Venetians who distinguished between Constantinople and Romania Bassa; see Frederic C. Lane, "Fleets and Fairs," 131.

22. *G. S.*, no. 895.

23. Bertolotto, 392.

24. See below, note 28.

25. *G. S.*, no. 899.

26. Bertolotto, 392, 395, 396. The dispersion of these claims over the *Ratio* suggests an oral inquest by which the losses were established. In other cases it is rather obvious that *cartae* served as documentary evidence.

27. Bertolotto, 395, 396. In the third case, *Item pro Adalasia* etc., observe the correction of *cum tertia* to *minus tertia*; see note 17.

28. This figure derives from a secondary agreement, a little Genoese *societas ultra societatem,* so to say, found in *G. S.*, no. 840. The agreement's date is June 18, 1161 and the destination of the investment Romania or Byzantine Empire.

The parties and figures of the principal *societas* are followed by this statement: "Ultra etiam dedit ipse Philippus [investing party] ei [Petro nepoti Bernardi, traveling party] s. xx pro quibus in Romania quo iturus est cum hac societate Petrus ponere debet .iii. perperos minus quarta et ad eos de aliis rebus quas illuc habet perperum unum et novem kart. etc." Since one bezant contains 24 karats, the matching figures are 20 sol. or 1 pound and 4 bezants, 3 karats. These sums are obviously not equal, but following the custom of Genoese *societates* one must be twice as big as the other. If 20 sol. are twice as big as 4 bezants, 3 karats, then 20 sol. equal 8 bezants, 6 karats, which in the light of available exchanges from other documents is completely unrealistic. The only alternative is to assume that 4 bezants, 3 karats are twice as big as 20 sol. This would make 20 sol. equal 2 bezants, 1½ karats or 3/48 of a bezant which in decimal fractions correspond to 2.625. Since this ratio can be the only correct one, the conclusion would be that in the *ultra societatem* the travelling party contributed twice as much as the investing party.

29. *G. S.*, no. 901

30. Bertolotto, 395. The spelling of proper names follows the Italian versions given in *G. S.*

31. Obviously some items have been skipped or misread during the addition. Since the numerals were Roman, there was no incentive to write them out in columns.

32. Bertolotto, 389–90.

33. *G. S.*, no. 941. Considering the frequent exchange rate of 1:3, 100 pounds would make precisely 300 bezants.

34. These are the names of other notaries as they are given in Latin of the original: Bonus Johannes scriba (no. 1222), Girardus notarius (no. 338), Iordanus Alinerie notarius (no. 217), Macobrius notarius (no. 40), Obertus scriba (no. 583), Ogerius scriba (no. 594), Oto notarius (II, p. 310), Philipus notarius (no. 202), Wilielmus notarius (no. 412).

35. There is no need to give the exceedingly long list of travelling agents. Among the sixty-seven contracts of 1161 only one had two travelling agents; see *G. S.*, no. 824.

36. The sum of 2,383 bezants is put together from compensations claimed in the three cases discussed above. The component parts are 97, 546, and 1740 bezants.

37. At this point it would be legitimate to ask whether 12,646 pounds correspond to the official loss of 29,443 bezants. The ratio between the two figures is 1:2.33 or 0.3 lower than the free-of-interest rate 1:2.625. Surely, the figure in pounds is higher than it should have been, because, as indicated above, not every investment destined originally for Constantinople reached the city. What was meant to be disembarked at the Bosporus could have been taken to Alexandria. Given our interests in totals, variations among the component parts are of little consequence.

38. A number of years ago Eugene H. Byrne published the annual figures of Genoese export to Syria and Alexandria. Although he did indicate that they stem from Giovanni Scriba, some of his statements were vague enough to create the impression that he was presenting totals. For his study and its criticism see "Genoese Trade with Syria in the Twelfth Century," *American Historical Review*, XXV (1919–1920), 191–219, and Frederic C. Lane, "The Merchant Marine of the Venetian Republic," in *Venice and History*, 147.

39. Five of Scriba's minutes specify export of merchandise or foreign exchange without giving their value in Genoese money, *G. S.*, nos. 832, 849, 882, 889, 894.

40. Late in January of 1159 Emperor Frederick Barbarossa subdued and destroyed the city of Crema. The Genoese, who had reached a compromise with the Emperor a year earlier, were afraid that he may press once more for the surrender of the regalia. During 1158 and 1159 the commune made every effort to extend and to strengthen its walls; see *Ann. Ian.*, I, 49–59.

41. Missing folios in Scriba's cartulary have been discussed in detail by the editors; see *G. S.*, xvi–xviii.

What kept Scriba from working steadily in 1155 is hard to tell. Perhaps he was involved in government's effort to overcome the fiscal crisis which had been brought about by Genoa's crusade against the Moors of Minorca, Almeria, and Tortosa, 1146–48, see *Ann. Ian.*, I, 33–5, 79–89. On the crisis itself consult Hilmar C. Krueger, "Post-war Collapse and Rehabilitation in Genoa, 1149–1162," in *Studi in onore di Gino Luzzatto* (4 vols., Milan, 1949), I, 117–28.

In 1159 Scriba kept books on the building of the last stretch of the municipal wall. Caffaro goes to some length to explain his task which consisted of recording days and hours spent on the work by the masons and indigent who were paid by the commune; see *Ann. Ian.*, I, 54. In 1162 Scriba was a member of an embassy which accounts for a gap in his entries from May 15 to June 13; compare *G. S.*, nos. 948 and 949, *Ann. Ian.*, I, 66.

42. The first Genoese ship with known tonnage was *Paradisus Magnus*. In 1251 a consortium of merchants chartered it to convey from Tunis to Genoa a cargo of 8,000 *cantaria*, "equivalent to 600 tons, dead cargo weight"; see Eugene H. Byrne, *Genoese Shipping in the Twelfth and Thirteenth Centuries* (Cambridge, Mass., 1930), pp. 10–1.

On cargoes and their value in later periods see the stimulating articles by Jacques Heers, "Il commercio nel Mediterraneo alla fine del sec. XIV e nei primi anni del XV," *Archivio Storico Italiano*, CXIII (1955), 157–209, and Domenico Gioffrè, "Il commercio d'importazione genovese alla luce dei registri del dazio, 1495–1537," in *Studi in onore di Amintore Fanfani* (6 vols., Milan, 1962), V, 115–242.

43. *Ann. Ian.*, I, 28.

44. *Ann. Pis.*, 27, 38–9. Galliots carried small cargoes. In 1165 the Genoese captured two Pisan galliots; together they ferried 92 merchants and were worth 1,200 pounds; see *Ann. Ian.*, I, 179.

Only once for the entire twelfth century does one find a prize valued at a higher sum. In 1129, during an earlier war between the two communes, the Genoese captured a Pisan ship carrying a "precious cargo"; they took it to Genoa, "et decem milia librarum ualens de naui habuerunt." The last phrase suggests that 10,000 pounds were realized from the ship and the cargo; see *Ann. Ian.*, I, 24.

45. Bertolotto, 378–83; *Cod. dipl.*, II, 211b–213a.

46. Bertolotto, 386, *navis de Syo*, 2,390 bezants; 387–8, *navis de Nigrampo*, 4,980 bezants; 397–8, *navis Lanfranci Grancii*, 5,365 bezants, 398–9, *navis de Rodo*, 5,200 bezants.

In two cases Grimaldi's instructions reveal prices of ships. The *navis de Nigrampo* was assessed at only 353 bezants. An empty ship burned by the Venetians at Almyro was priced at 1,856 bezants; for the latter see Bertolotto, 388–9.

47. The annalist Bernardo Maragone claims that in 1165 Pisan galleys captured forty-eight Genoese ships returning from the fair of Fréjus in Southern France; see *Ann. Pis.*, 37. Like the ships carrying grain from the same area, the majority of them must have been small crafts. Of course, we possess no knowledge of the overall number of Genoa's seagoing vessels. The closest estimate comes from Caffaro's narrative of the 1147–8 campaigns against Almeria and Tortosa when he remarks that the Genoese "set out with 63 galleys and 163 other ships." However, the number of ships

participating in separate exploits of this war was much smaller; see *Ann. Ian.*, I, 80.

48. Genoa's war with Pisa, a brief truce aside, lasted from 1162 to 1175. During ten of these thirteen years the consuls of Genoa levied a *collecta* that increased from 6 den. per pound in 1165 to 13 by 1173; see *Ann. Ian.*, I, 188–9, 200, 206, 214, 229, 241, 246, 257, 260. *Collectae* were levied in 1185 and 1196, *Ann. Ian.*, II, 20, 60. Between 1208 and 1212 the attempts of Count Enrico Pescatore to capture Crete from the Venetians and to hold it, compelled Genoa to give his native son every conceivable support. The *collecta* authorized in 1210 was to cover Enrico's expenses; see *Ann. Ian.*, II, 109–10, 114–5, and Heyd, I, 277–9. On the origins and evolution of *collecta* see Sieveking, *Finanzwesen*, I, 37–8, 67 and Day, *Douanes*, I, v–vii.

49. In his detailed survey of communal revenues the annalist Ogerio Pane did not specify that the *collecta maris* was to be levied from both export and import trade. That it must have been self-understandable to him becomes apparent from two entries in the *Annales*. While speaking of the collecta of 1210 for the benefit of Count Enrico Pescatore same Ogerio Pane said that two pennies per pound were levied "de mobilia que per mare portata uel missa fuerit." Several decades later, Iacopo d'Oria, the last of the great Genoese chroniclers, spoke of four pennies per pound collected "a nauigantibus euntibus et redeuntibus"; see *Ann. Ian.*, II, 114–5 and V, 172–3.

Strangely enough, neither of these levies is a guide to export-import figures. The first was an extraordinary assessment to help Count Enrico to keep Crete. Its two pennies, its spread over six years that would have resulted in overlapping with the levy of 1214, finally its low tax-base of 250,800 pounds, all attest to its irregular nature. The second, referring to the year 1293, is most likely exaggerated, for it presupposes an annual taxable base of 2,940,000 pounds which, as can be seen below, surpasses by far the best known to us year of the fourteenth century. Would not Iacopo d'Oria's credibility be an important factor in deciding when the economic crisis of the early Renaissance began?

50. *G. S.*, nos. 48, 640, 1224.

51. The figures for 1214 and 1274 have been given by Sieveking, *Finanzwesen*, I, 67, 196. He, incidentally, did not accept Iacopo d'Oria's sum, calling it "extraordinarily high." The remaining figures are from John Day's column of forty-six yearly amounts paid by the tax-farmers; see his *Douanes*, I, xvi–xviii.

52. On depreciation of Genoese coinage see Sieveking, *ibid.*, note 4, and Schaube, p. 812. Prices for pepper are found in *G. S.*, nos. 19 (1155), 173, 176, 319 (1157), 461 (1158), 706 (1160), 940 (1162), 1099 (1163); Archivio di Stato di Genova, Not. Angelino di Sigestro, V, fol. 74 (1291); and John Day, *Douanes*, I, xxxviii.

A short hundredweight or *centenarium*, as the word indicates, comprises one hundred pounds. Pietro Rocca in his *Pesi e misure antiche di Genova e del Genovesato* (Genoa, 1871), 110 equates the Genoese pound to 0.316750 kg. A *centenarium* would thus correspond to 31.675 kg or roughly 70 English pounds.

ITALIAN BANKERS AND
PHILIP THE FAIR

JOSEPH R. STRAYER

Princeton University

One of the many puzzles in the financial policy of Philip the Fair is his failure to take full advantage of the presence of the large and wealthy community of Italian bankers who lived in France during his reign. The Italians controlled a considerable part of France's foreign trade and could have afforded to pay fairly high taxes on their commercial transactions. Such taxes would have given Philip a substantial and, what was perhaps more important, a reasonably stable addition to his revenues. The Italians could also have mobilized large sums of capital, either to meet the financial emergencies caused by Philip's wars, or to provide working balances to smooth out fluctuations in royal income.

Philip was certainly aware of these possibilities. In 1294 he instituted regular taxes on transactions among Italians in France, the so-called "penny in the pound,"[1] and sold export licenses to Italian merchants.[2] He used the Franzesi firm, headed by Albizzo (Biche) and Musciatto (Mouche) Guidi as his bankers. In the 1290's Biche and Mouche were receivers-general, and for a while treasurers of the king.[3] Their role was particularly important in the crisis of 1294–1295 which followed the confiscation of Aquitaine. In this period they advanced money to the king against anticipated royal revenues and centralized most of the important receipts of the crown.[4] They and their agents succeeded in securing a very large loan, well over 600,000 livres tournois, from individuals and communities in all parts of France.[5] In the next crisis, caused by the Anglo-Flemish alliance of 1297, the Guidi brothers provided a loan of 200,000 l.t. from their own resources and those of other Italian bankers.[6]

Philip, however, did not pursue these policies with any enthusiasm. The taxes on sales and exports were never developed as they could have been, and never became important sources of revenue. Though Biche and Mouche remained favorites of the king, their responsibilities for royal finances declined steadily after 1297. No other Italian banking house took their place. After 1297 Philip seems to have cut back sharply on his borrowing; certainly there were no more loans on the scale of those of 1294-1295. In all these respects Philip's policies differed from those of his contemporary and rival, Edward I of England. Edward made export taxes a regular and substantial part of royal income. Throughout his reign he used loans from Italian bankers—first the Riccardi and then the Frescobaldi—as a regular part of his financial system.

Certainly the "Lombards" were disliked in France, but there is no evidence that this dislike was strong enough to keep Philip from dealing with them on a regular basis. Nor is there evidence that he himself shared this prejudice. He obviously trusted Biche and Mouche; in fact, as their financial responsibilities declined he tended to use them for delicate diplomatic missions to Germany and to Rome.[7] Mouche played an essential role in the most striking event of the reign, the attack on Boniface VIII at Anagni. To take another sensitive area, the Italian Betin Caucinel was Philip's chief agent in carrying out royal monetary policy. Betin was mintmaster at St. Quentin as early as 1278 and mintmaster at Sommières and at Paris under Philip the Fair.[8] As master of the monies[9] he kept the king's confidence in spite of an anonymous accusation against him.[10] It is true that Betin had become a permanent resident of France and that he founded a French family of some importance,[11] but this in itself shows that there was no insurmountable prejudice against Italians. Moreover, when Philip wanted to improve his gold coinage, it was again to Italians (the Peruzzi) that he turned for expert advice.[12]

The basic difficulties ran far deeper than hostility to bankers in general and Italians in particular. For one thing, it was difficult for Philip to put his relations with the Italians on a stable basis when there was no stability in his financial system as a whole. The great effort he made in the decade 1295-1305 produced only one more or less permanent addition to royal revenue. The quarrel with Boniface VIII broke the Church's resistance to taxation, and after the accession of Clement V tenths from the clergy could be counted on as an almost annual source of supply. But while a tenth produced about 260,000 l.t.,[13] this was not nearly enough to meet all the king's needs, especially as tenths sometimes had to be shared with the pope. All other innovations had proved either unrewarding or dangerous. Subventions from laymen had met increasing resistance, were practically abandoned after 1305, and caused unrest when they were reintroduced in 1313–1314. The sales-tax had proved equally unpopular.[14] Over-valuation (and a slight debasement) of the currency had been bitterly criticized; revaluation had touched off riots.[15] Export taxes had given disappointing results, partly because France had no staple, such as England's wool, for which there was a steady demand, partly because no one had worked very effectively to make the tax profitable. Export licenses were sold or granted on an *ad hoc* basis; Biche and Mouche paid nothing, while the Milanese and the Fini paid too much.[16] The reforms in the French customs administration which Pierre de Chalon was beginning to introduce were not to have their full effect until the 1320's.[17]

This lack of steady and easily collected revenues created two difficulties in Philip's relations with the Italians. On the one hand, it was difficult for him to establish normal banking relations with them because he could not furnish adequate security for a large loan, or for a continuing line of credit. On the other hand, if normal banking relations were difficult to establish, then there was less reason to avoid the abnormal expedients of partial or complete expropriation. The Italians, like the Jews and the Templars, were tempting targets for a hard-pressed king. It was safer to attack foreigners, or members of an international order, than to tax Frenchmen. It probably seemed morally preferable as well. Philip, as I have said elsewhere, wanted to be a "constitutional" king, and taxation, except in real emergencies, was hardly yet accepted as proper behavior on the part of a ruler. But Jews, Templars, and Lombards had no support in France and no powerful outside protector. They could always be accused of usury, or of dishonesty in their dealings with the government. Philip lost no popularity and had no troubles with his conscience when he squeezed these victims.

Even when Philip was using the Italians most extensively, he had been unable to resist the temptation to seize some of their wealth. Renier Accorre, who had been receiver of Champagne, was disgraced and arrested in 1293 and lost most of his property.[18] Gandulph of Arcellis had to pay a fine of 4500 l.t. in 1299–1300,[19] and on his death in 1308 the king took almost half his property. Yet Gandulph had lent money to some of the greatest men in France, including members of the royal family.[20] The "Lombards" paid a heavy tallage in 1292[21] and their large contributions to the loans of 1295 and 1297 may not have been entirely voluntary. They also paid a tallage in 1297, though at a lower rate than in 1292.[22] But the worst pressure came after 1303, culminating in the seizure of Italian goods and debts in 1311. The Italians regained their assets only by paying heavy fines.[23] Philip could hardly use the Italians as bankers if he was going to seize the capital which made banking operations possible.

It may be that the death of Biche and Mouche in 1307 removed a restraining influence on the king. Philip had worked closely with these men; no other Italians had such opportunities to influence his policies. But one may wonder whether the two brothers could have done much to help their compatriots even if they had lived. Philip had cut down their responsibilities sharply since the days when they were receivers-general for the whole kingdom and had their agents in every province. In the years just before their death they had no important administrative or financial functions. Their last general account with the king, according to Mignon, was in 1303.[24] After that date, they collected an apparently light tallage on the Lombards, and subsidies in Carcassonne and Beaucaire.[25] None of these operations involved large sums of money. On the other hand, while Biche and Mouche had imposed a heavy tallage (100,000 l.t.) on the Jews in 1291–1292[26] and must have known a good deal about the Jewish community, they were not used in the seizure of Jewish property in 1306. Perhaps they were growing old and tired, but some of their younger associates were still available if Philip had wanted to use them.[27] In any case, when Biche and Mouche died, their long and faithful service did not protect their property from the usual penalties inflicted on Italian money-lenders. Philip seized all their assets in France, on the usual excuse that they owed him money as a result of their earlier dealings with him.[28] In short, all the evidence suggests that after 1305 Philip had concluded that he no longer needed anything but incidental services from the Italians, and that he could therefore pillage them with impunity.

This decision was probably made easier by Philip's growing confidence in his own bureaucracy. The Italians had had very little to do with Normandy; Norman financial affairs had been handled by *baillis,* viscounts, and receivers who were almost all from northern France. Yet revenues from Normandy remained high, and were paid in regularly, as a glance at the Journal of the Treasury shows. Some able financiers were emerging in the Center and the South, notably the Gayte family of Clermont in Auvergne. Finally, the period after 1305 is the period in which Marigny was rising to power, and Marigny was especially competent in matters of finance. As Philip's reliance on Marigny grew, he would feel less need of the Italians.

Another factor was Philip's strong desire for complete independence, manifested in all aspects of his reign. Bankers whom he could not control completely were a threat to that independence. In the first part of his reign he could not get along without bankers, but he could protect himself by playing one group off against another. Thus the peak of Italian influence came in the 1290's when Philip was trying to find an alternative to using Templars as his principal bankers. The establishment of the Treasury of the Louvre gave Philip a third choice: he could somewhat reduce the importance of the Italians without necessarily improving the position of the Templars. When, in 1303, Philip did turn back to the Temple as his chief bank, Italian participation in French finance declined notably, without being entirely eliminated. But in the end Philip seems to have decided to avoid dependence on any private bankers. When he turned against the Templars in 1307, he turned against the Italians too, though not as brutally and abruptly. He simply accelerated the policy, already evident since 1303, of squeezing the Italians out of important positions.

This policy was especially evident in appointments to receiverships of *bailliages* and *sénéchaussées*. As Ozanam has shown, the receivership of Champagne, which had long been in the hands of Italians, was given to a French royal official in 1305 and was held by French officials for the rest of the reign.[29] The same things happened in the Center and in the South. Italian financiers, who had held most of the receiverships in their area in the 1290's almost disappeared after 1305.[30] Or, to use a broader test, I have some data on 89 Italians who worked for Philip the Fair between 1285 and 1305. Of these, only 16 retained any official connection with the government after 1305, and this figure includes Biche and Mouche, who died in 1307, and the thoroughly Gallicized Betin Caucinel. Of the great banking houses, only the Peruzzi retained any importance, and their contribution was marginal—the receivership of Carcassonne, the collection of the Flemish indemnity, and some technical assistance in the mints.[31] From 1305 to his death in 1314, Philip was in no way dependent on Italian financiers. For example, when he was raising money for a Flemish war in 1314, the Italian contribution was minimal—less than 12,000 l.t.[32]

Nationalism, even in the rudimentary form of xenophobia, had little to do with these changes. After all, the Temple was headed by a Frenchman and its banking experts in Paris were French. But the

Temple was an international order, just as the Italians belonged to international banking houses. Both groups had outside bases of power and income; Philip could not be sure that either would be entirely amenable to his wishes. He therefore replaced them with men who derived all their power from the king.

The search for sovereignty, rather than any dislike of the Italians as Italians, is the key to understanding Philip's policies. We do not have to believe that he read or understood all the theories of his legists. But he had an exalted idea of the sanctity of the French monarchy and there was no place for independent or quasi-independent groups in his political system. There could be local and subordinate powers, but in the last resort everyone had to acknowledge the supremacy of the king. Philip would attack anyone who seemed to challenge that supremacy—the pope, the bishops, the great feudal lords, and the communes. The Italians were no real threat to his power; neither, for that matter, was Bishop Bernard Saisset of Pamiers. But even the remote possibility of opposition irked Philip. As soon as the Italians were no longer indispensable he freed himself from any dependence on them.[33]

NOTES

1. *Ord.,* XI, 377; *Ord.* I, 326; Borrelli de Serres, *Recherches sur divers services publics* (Paris 1904) II, 458. Actually the rate was a little more than a penny in the pound, but the tax produced little revenue, 13000 to 16000 livres tournois (l.t.) a year; see Borrelli de Serres, *loc. cit.,* and Strayer and Taylor, *Studies in Early French Taxation* (Cambridge 1939), p. 11.

2. G. Bigwood, "La politique de la laine en France sous les règnes de Philippe le Bel et de ses fils," *Revue Belge* XV (1936), 79, 429; XVI (1937) 95; Strayer and Taylor, pp. 14–16; B.N., Coll. doat no. 155, fol. 196; no. 156, fol. 20; no. 165 fol. 12.

3. A.N., J 474, no. 31, the Guidi are called receivers of the king by September 1290. This remained their usual title, but for a brief period in 1295 they acted as and were called treasurers of the king; see *Inventaire d'anciens comptes royaux dressé par Robert Mignon* (hereafter cited as Mignon), ed. Ch. V. Langlois (Paris 1899) no. 2065; *Ord.* I, 326; Borrelli de Serres, *Recherches* III, 15–17.

4. For example, Mignon, nos. 2055–2057, in 1295 they advanced money for military expenses for which they were later repaid. See also *Archives anciennes de la ville de St. Quentin,* ed. E. Lemaire, (St. Quentin 1888) p. 140, no. 153, where the *bailli* of Vermandois is told to turn over all receipts, ordinary and extraordinary, to agents of the Guidi, royal treasurers, July 1295. The extraordinary receipts included tenths on the

Church, the subvention of 1/100 for war, tallages, fines, loans, and levies on the Jews.

5. For the loan, see Mignon, nos. 1106–1163, and E. Boutaric, "Documents inédits relatifs à l'histoire de France sous Philippe le Bel," in *Notices et extraits* XX, part II (1862), 128. Both sources give a total of about 630,-000 l.t., but this is incomplete. For other activities of the Guidi at this time see Mignon, nos. 703–706, 2058, 2084–2112.

6. Boutaric, *loc. cit.*, p. 127, Biche and Mouche lent about 200,000 l.t. "de leur deniers et qu'ils enpruntèrent sus euls aus foires de Champagne et à Paris."

7. J. Viard, *Les journaux du trésor dePhilippe IV le Bel* (Paris, 1940), nos. 2443, 2985. For other embassies to Rome and to Germany see nos. 912, 1550, 3797, 4176, 4366 and the references given in the footnote to no. 397.

8. C. Piton, *Les Lombards en France et à Paris* (Paris 1892), pp. 114–119; Brussel, *Nouvel examen de l'usage général des fiefs* (Paris 1727) I, 471 (for St. Quentin); B.N., ms. fr. 20683 fol. 2 (Sommières); Viard, *Journaux*, nos. 35, 58, 65 etc. (Paris). He held this last post until just before his death in 1312.

9. Viard, *Journaux*, no. 635 and footnote; he had this title at least as early as 1296.

10. Ch. V. Langlois, "Notices et documents relatifs à l'histoire de France au temps de Philippe le Bel," *Revue historique* LX (1896), 327, an anonymous letter to the king accusing Betin of rendering false accounts.

11. Piton, *Les Lombards,* pp. 114–115.

12. *Ord.* I, 434, the new gold coins are to be struck by agents of the Peruzzi, July 1305. A.N., J J 36, nos. 236, 237, the Peruzzi, who were striking gold coins, were to have all the profits of the mints of Paris, Troyes, Tournai, and Sommières, July 1305. Both earlier, in 1291–1293, (B.N., ms. lat. 9018, no. 31) and later, in 1311 (*Ord.* I, 478), Betin struck gold coins.

13. Borrelli de Serres, *Recherches,* II, 465 ff.; *Recueil des historiens des Gaules et de la France* XXI, 545, 560.

14. Strayer and Taylor, pp. 43–77, 81–88, 12–13.

15. Borrelli de Serres, *Les variations monétaires sous Philippe le Bel* (extract from the *Gazette numismatique française* 1902) pp. 309–345; E. Boutaric, *La France sous Philippe le Bel,* (Paris 1861) pp. 313–316.

16. Strayer and Taylor, pp. 15–17.

17. J. R. Strayer, "Pierre de Chalon and the Origins of the French Customs Service," *Festschrift Percy Ernst Schramm* (Wiesbaden 1964), pp. 334–339.

18. For Renier see D. Ozanam, "Les receveurs de Champagne," *Recueil* . . . Clovis Brunel, (Paris 1955) II, 343 and the works cited there. R. Fawtier, *Comptes royaux 1285–1314* (Paris 1954) II, nos. 15281, 15299, Renier was in prison in 1293 and 1294 and paid 15,000 l.t. for his release.

19. Viard, *Journaux,* nos. 2146, 4241.

20. Piton, *Les Lombards,* pp. 99–101, 157–173; Mignon, nos. 2038–2047, 2049. A.N., JJ48, fol. 7, no. 6, in the end the king took one-half of five-sixths of Gandulph's property.

21. Mignon, nos. 2073, 2076. The first estimates the value of the tallage at 141, 484 l. t., the second at 152,000 l.p. or 221,000 l.t.

22. *Notices et extraits*, XX, part 2, p. 129, "de la taille des Lombars singuliers et de la finance de la compagnie des Richars de Luques, environ 65,000 livres tournois."

23. Mignon, no. 2053, the Italians paid a fine to a royal agent in 1303–1304. *Olim*, III, 172, they were tallaged by Biche and Mouche shortly before 1306. Mignon, no. 2050, another fine was paid in 1309–1310. A.N., JJ45, fol. 64, no. 93, in 1310 the merchants of Milan were exempted from penalties imposed on other Italians and from the jurisdiction of the superintendents of the Lombard affair, which suggests that fines were being imposed with some regularity. *Ord.* I, 489–491, 494, the goods and debts of Italians living in France were seized by royal officials in 1311, and heavy fines were paid to redeem them. B.N., ms. Clairembault 71, no. 183 shows how thoroughly the operation was carried out. The *gens des comptes* were indignant because "Estreille Macet" of Macon escaped paying a fine; they said nothing would please the king more than his arrest. "Estreille" may be the "Eschaque" or "Escaille" of Florence who was receiver of the county of Burgundy in 1303 and 1306; see Mignon, no. 110 and Borrelli de Serres, *Recherches* II, 31.

24. Mignon, no. 2071.

25. Mignon, nos. 2059, 2063; *Comptes royaux*, II, no. 21401; *Olim*, III, 172.

26. Mignon, no. 2113. No. 2114, Biche and Mouche imposed new tallages on the Jews in the period 1293–1296.

27. For example, "Thotus" and "Vanna" Guidi, nephews of Biche and Mouche were active from 1307 on in collecting the indemnity owed by Flanders; see Limburg-Stirum, *Codex Diplomaticus Flandriae* (Bruges 1879) II, 61; Mignon, nos. 1979, 1981, 1982. *Comptes royaux* II, 27533, 27555, 27560, they also acted as assayers for the mints of Troyes and Tournai in 1309–1310. But they had to work with the Peruzzi and they had little to do with the main elements of French finance. Piton, *Les Lombards*, p. 135, the relationship to Biche and Mouche is shown in the Paris tallage of 1298: "Vane, neveu messire Mouche,—Estoude, son frère . . . "

28. *Histoire de Languedoc* X col. 469, a royal order to seize the goods of Biche and Mouche dated 30 November 1307. See also A.N., JJ40, fol. 13, no. 32, and Mignon, ms. 2116–2118. A.N., JJ45, fol. 45, no. 81 seems to show that Biche and Mouche died shortly before 8 March 1307.

29. Ozanam, "Les receveurs," *Recueil Clovis Brunel*, II, 344–345.

30. Auvergne: Gerard Chauchat, 1296, 1298, 1299, 1306, 1308, 13ll (*Comptes royaux*, nos. 30109, 10695, Viard, *Journaux*, no. 5890; Mignon no. 97.)

Beaucaire: Betin Caucinel, who was almost French by this time, was receiver in 1308 (Mignon, no. 106). However, in 1309 the joint treasurers were Ricobonus Aycardi and Hugo Beti (A. D., Lozère G256, J. Roucaute et M. Saché, *Lettres de Philippe le Bel relatifs au pays de Gévaudan*, (Mende 1896), no. 18). Ricobonus was probably Italian; Hugo certainly was, see *Comptes royaux* no. 21451.

Carcassonne: Probably remained in Italian hands, see Mignon, no. 103. Tancred Benchaveni, treasurer of Carcassonne in 1305 and 1310 was an agent of the Peruzzi (A. D., Tarn, J54/246, *Comptes royaux*, no. 22553, A.N., JJ46, fol. 2, no. 3, A.N., JJ49, fol. 84, no. 196). Loterius Blanchi, treasurer in 1314, was probably an Italian (A.D., Aude, H358).

Périgord-Quercy: Gerard Baleine 1296 (Mignon no. 99, no. 107) Pierre Baleine 1302, 1304 (A.N., JJ38, fol. 53v, no. 105, A.N., JJ45, fols. 56v-58, no. 86); Arnaud de Proboleno, burgess of Cahors 1309, 1310, 1311 (Mignon, no. 99, A.N., JJ38, fol. 99v, JJ50, fol. 10v, no. 8, JJ46, nos. 70, 88, fols. 57, 65v.).

Saintonge: Pierre de Souplessano, 1302–1303, 1305–1306, 1310(?) (Mignon, no. 97, *Comptes royaux*, no. 16134); Gerard Tronquière 1311, 1312, 1313, 1314 (Mignon, no. 97; A.N., JJ48, fol. 106, no. 183, JJ49, fols. 32, 81v, nos. 68, 190).

Rouergue: Geoffroi Coquatrix of Paris, 1300, Nicolas de Ermenonville 1302, Arnaud de Proboleno 1305 (Mignon, no. 101); Nicolas de Ermenonville with Raimon Bernart as his deputy 1307 (A.N., JJ44, fols. 37v–39, no. 66); Raimon Bernart (as deputy?), 1307–1308, (*Cart. de Bonneral*, ed. P.A. Verlaquet and J.L. Rigal, Jr. 281; A.D., Areyron, G472). Rouergue seems to have been financially subordinate to Toulouse at this time.

Toulouse: Geoffroi Coquatrix, 1299, 1301, 1303 (*C.R.* no. 12078, Viard, *Journaux*, no. 5808; Mignon, no. 100); Nicolas de Ermenonville 1302–1315 (Mignon, no. 100; Viard, *Journaux*, no. 5891; A.N., JJ40, fol. 87, no. 168, JJ45, no. 134).

31. Mignon, no. 103, under Carcassonne has "a XXII Aprilis MCCCVI, societas Perruchiorum." For Flanders, see F. Funck-Brentano, *Philippe le Bel en Flandre* (Paris 1897) p. 522 and Limburg-Stirum, *Codex Diplomaticus*, II, 61. For Peruzzi advice on coinage see above, notes 12 and 27.

32. Viard, *Journaux*, nos. 6037, 6041, 6042, 6043, 6048, 6058. Even this figure assumes that the finances mentioned in no. 6041 were one-third of what was eventually paid—an assumption based on the fact that so many payments end in 6s. 8d. Thus the Scali, who made the biggest contribution, paid 743 l. 6s. 8d., which, multiplied by three, would give 2200 l.t. The Bardi and the Peruzzi paid 488 l. 6s. 8d each, or probably a total of 1765 l.t. apiece. No other companies paid as much. Cf. nos. 6038, 6060, 6061, Philippe de Marigny, archibishop of Sens provided 10,000 l.t.; the archibishop of Rouen did the same; the Chauchat family, well-to-do financiers of Auvergne but scarcely the equals of the Peruzzi, furnished 3000 l.t.

33. This article was in press when John Henneman published "Taxation of Italians by the French Crown (1311–1363)," *Mediaeval Studies*, XXXI (1969), pp. 15–43. Henneman gives some additional details on the seizure of Lombard property in 1311.

SOME INDUSTRIAL PRICE MOVEMENTS IN MEDIEVAL GENOA (1155-1255)*

WILLIAM N. BONDS
San Francisco State College

Studies of medieval European industrial prices are rare; in fact, one might easily conclude that they do not exist at all.[1] The reason for such a dearth is not lack of interest in the subject, but rather the absence of sufficient data and the difficulty of interpreting those which are available. In this article an attempt will be made to provide some industrial price data for the late twelfth and early thirteenth centuries, to explain the limitations of their use, and to draw a few tentative conclusions.

The price data which follow were obtained from microfilms of the notarial records preserved in the Archivio di Stato at Genoa, Italy.[2] As a source for price studies the business contracts contained in these records have a definite utility: They exist in large quantities (by medievalists' standards, that is); they were drawn up by a variety of public officials who had no vested interest in falsifying the prices quoted;[3] and they were all drafted in the same place—at Genoa, one of medieval Europe's most important commercial crossroads. The prices quoted are almost entirely at the same rate—the wholesale rate; they were probably determined by the market, and they are all expressed in a single monetary unit—the money of account based upon Genoa's denaro.[4]

However, such advantages, important as they are, cannot disguise the fact that serious problems of methodology do confront the price historian anxious to use these valuable records. Is an interest charge concealed within the price quoted in a given contract? If so, what role does it play in price determination? Are there likely to be unrecorded qualitative differences in the commodities examined, either within a single year or over time? Are the units of measurement constant over time, or do they vary considerably? And if the latter is the case, to what degree is the price of a commodity influenced by such quantitative changes?

Obtaining satisfactory answers to these questions is not now possible—and may never be. However, some thought has been given to the problems of an interest rate, qualitative change, and quantitative change, and tentative working-hypotheses have been adopted.

Interest is probably concealed in the prices quoted, for delivery dates and payment dates are often a week, a month, six months, even a year apart.[5] However, it is not possible to equate time with money in any precise way, for too many other variables seem to exist.[6] Nor is there any evidence that interest rates changed markedly or steadily during the century under examination.[7] Consequently, no effort has been made to deflate—or inflate—given prices by some arbitrary interest charge. Thus, the prices yielded are less valuable for short-run than for long-run studies, and for absolute rather than relative price comparisons.

Like interest charges, unrecorded qualitative and quantitative variations probably do exist, which doubtless account for some of the wide price ranges in a given year.[8] Thus the five bales of fustian cloth sold in 1186 may be quite dissimilar, and all may differ markedly from the one sold in 1248. However, in the absence of independent evidence, only the most elementary steps can be taken to reduce the impact of such differences upon the validity of a price study. Products can be and have been segregated by place of manufacture and, where possible, by color or texture or other identifiable characteristic. But what has been assumed is that the measures and the manufacturing standards for a given area have remained constant over time, and that the commodities sold have met those standards.

Of the many manufactured goods mentioned in the Genoese records, only a small fraction appear often enough with adequate descriptions to be considered in a price study. Nonetheless, as a sample they are not entirely unrepresentative: Several are products from medieval Europe's largest industry; one from what must have been her smallest. Some were for domestic use; others for export. A number were made in northwestern Europe, some in Italy, a few even in Genoa itself.

Although some consideration will be given to the price of gold thread and body armor, important industrial exports of medieval Europe, most attention will be focused upon that of textiles. For it was through the medium of the textile industry more than any other that Western Europeans changed their homeland from an "under-developed" area to a "developed" one; and it is textiles, more than any other manufactured good, that appear frequently in Genoa's

TABLE 1.

FUSTIAN CLOTH: MEDIAN PRICE PER BALE (IN *SOLIDI*)

Year	Median Price	Year	Median Price
1179	330/ 0[1]*	1220	495/ 0[47]
1180	300/ 0[1]	1224	502/ 0[1]
1186	320/ 0[5]	1225	540/ 6[3]
1191	393/ 0[4]	1228	464/ 0[4]
1192	370/ 0[10]	1233	480/ 0[1]
1197	467/ 0[2]	1236	440/ 0[5]
1198	442/ 0[1]	1237	540/ 0[1]
1200	440/ 0[15]	1239	560/ 0[3]
1201	436/ 0[32]	1241	552/ 8[3]
1203	417/ 6[14]	1248	560/ 0[1]
1205	510/ 0[73]	1250	506/ 0[3]
1206	525/ 0[22]	1251	485/ 6[8]
1210	468/ 0[11]	1252	560/ 0[3]
1212	455/ 0[1]	1253	581/ 9[2]
1213	450/ 0[3]	1254	560/ 0[3]
1214	550/ 0[3]	1255	553/ 0[1]
1216	540/ 0[1]		

*The superscribed numerals in this and other tables indicate the number of prices from which the recorded median was compiled.

records. Made of cotton, wool, linen, and silk, in England, northern France, Flanders, Germany and Italy, these cloths found their way to Genoa, and record of them entered into her notarial cartularies. From Genoa they were exported—shipped west to Provence and Spain, south to Sicily and North Africa, east to Egypt, Byzantium, the Latin Kingdom, and beyond.

The most popular by far of the cloths recorded was fustian, an inexpensive fabric produced in Lombardy from imported cotton and linen.[9] After manufacture it was hauled across the Apennines to Genoa, where it was sold to local merchants. These men then exported what they did not sell at home to almost every region bordering the Mediterranean.

Sales of fustian were most frequently by the bale (*balla*) or half-bale (*verrubius*), sometimes by the piece (*pecia*) and, on a few occasions, by the cane (*canna*).[10] Depending upon their size and weight, a bale could contain as few as thirty-six or as many as forty pieces. How many canes there were to a piece is not disclosed.

Sales of fustian by the piece and cane are few, are widely spaced over a long period, and vary substantially in price from one year to the next. Consequently, they are not of great utility for determining

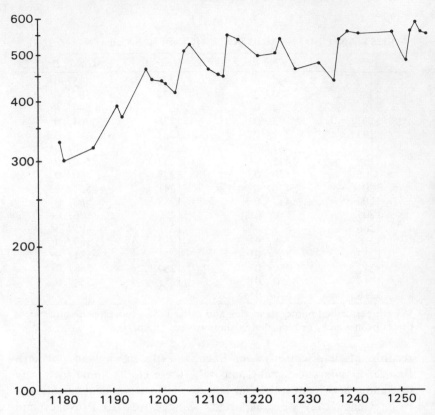

Fig. 1.   Fustian Cloth: Median Price per Bale (in *Solidi*)

a price trend. Sales by the bale and half-bale, however, are recorded for thirty-three separate years extending over the last three-quarters of the century under study. For a number of these years there is a satisfactory sample of price quotations.[11] And, although sometimes the sample price range is wide, it is never so wide that the general trend is obscured.[12]

The price of fustian cloth rose steadily in the last years of the twelfth century and the first of the thirteenth. Table 1 and Figure 1 reveal this clearly.[13] The median price per bale for 1206, 26/5/0 pounds, was some sixty per cent above that for 1179. But during the next half century (1206–1255) the rise in price was at best a moderate one. The median price per bale in the 1250's, 26/10/0 pounds, was less than one per cent above that for 1206. And there were, in addition, several long periods, especially in the late 1220's and '30's, when the median price of fustian fell noticeably below that for 1206.

Whatever the woolen cloth of northern Europe may have lacked in popularity and sales volume when compared with Lombard fustians, they made up in prestige and price. When fustians sold for eleven solidi apiece, some of these cloths brought eleven libre.[14] Manufactured in England or, more commonly, in Flanders and Artois, many of these expensive fabrics were sold at the Champagne fairs, then carried overland across the Alps to Genoa, whence they were shipped all over the Mediterranean world.[15]

The most famous of these fine cloths was stanfort.[16] Whether or not its name was derived from Stamford, England; Steenvoorde, Flanders; or *stamen forte* (strong fibre), cannot be solved here; nor will it be possible to establish what distinguished it from other cloths. To know these facts, to know exactly what stanfort was, would be a great advantage; but not to know in no way prevents a study of its price. What matters is that the merchants who bought and sold stanfort could make a definite identification, which, in fact, they did.

The men who dealt in stanfort were often careful to specify in their contracts the source of the cloth involved, for where it was produced made a difference in the price. When English stanfort sold for 19/4/0 pounds, Artesian was only 10/18/0 and Lombard a mere 5.[17] Sometimes they recorded the color, especially if it were red, dyed with kermes (*grana*), since this too affected the price.[18] Thus, there was not one but several stanforts, whose prices must be kept distinct.

Table 2 and Figure 2 denote the median price of four general categories of stanfort cloth: English, Artesian, kermes-dyed, and "continental." In the first category are all stanforts with the sobriquet, *de Anglia*. In the next are stanforts of Arras, regardless of color or additional description. The third small group contains pieces noted as *de grana*, possibly of English manufacture, but not so indicated. The last, the "continental," includes all the rest.[19]

Taken individually, each category of stanfort has too few price entries to demand much attention; but viewed together they necessitate consideration, for all show the same price trends. In the few years between 1197 and 1210 the price of stanfort rose at a fantastic rate—in most cases more than 75 per cent. English stanfort, selling per piece in 1197 at a median price of 12/3/0 pounds, in 1210 cost 21/16/3; Artesian more than doubled, increasing from 7/9/11 to 16/5/0; even the "continental" group of stanforts followed suit, rising from 8/11/0 to 15/0/0 by 1210, and to 15/10/0 by 1213. But then, perhaps shortly after 1213, the price dropped off.[20]

How much stanfort fell is difficult to estimate, as is the exact

TABLE 2

STANFORT CLOTH: MEDIAN PRICE PER PIECE (IN *SOLIDI*)

Year	English	Artesian	Kermes-Dyed	Continental
1197	243/0^{3}	149/11^{2}	—	171/ 0^{9}
1198	—	—	—	182/ 6^{1}
1200	310/ 0^{10}	209/ 0^{7}	—	201/ 0^{3}
1201	—	195/ 0^{1}	—	—
1203	—	—	396/ 8^{2}	120/ 1^{1}
1205	332/ 6^{2}	—	—	243/ 0^{10}
1206	400/ 0^{1}	226/ 8^{1}	—	210/ 0^{1}
1210	436/ 3^{1}	325/ 0^{4}	—	300/ 0^{1}
1213	—	—	—	310/ 0^{7}
1214	—	—	—	270/ 0^{3}
1216	—	—	—	223/ 8^{2}
1220	—	—	—	222/ 0^{5}
1224	—	228/ 5^{2}	—	232/10^{2}
1225	—	—	—	242/ 4^{1}
1228	—	—	—	208/ 6^{1}
1229	—	—	400/ 0^{1}	—
1234	—	—	380/ 0^{1}	—
1236	—	180/10^{2}	—	229/ 4^{2}
1239	—	—	360/ 0^{1}	230/ 0^{1}
1241	—	200/ 0^{2}	—	—
1248	355/ 6^{4}	214/ 0^{15}	—	—
1251	348/ 6^{2}	200/ 0^{5}	—	—
1252	—	210/ 6^{7}	—	—
1253	384/ 0^{1}	218/10^{8}	—	222/ 0^{1}
1254	—	229/ 3^{5}	—	—

timing of the occurrence. Sufficient data do not exist. But on no occasion before the mid-thirteenth century did its median price decline to the 1197 low;[21] and at no time did it rise again to the 1210–1213 high. Unlike that of fustian cloth, its median price in the mid-1250's—though on a similar upward swing—was well below that of 1210–1213. The English stanfort which sold for 19/4/0 pounds in 1253 cost some 12 per cent less than that marketed some four decades earlier; the Artesian traded in 1254 was 29 per cent below that sold in 1210; and the "continental" stanfort, 28 per cent below that of 1213.

Stanfort was just one of many fine woolen cloths sent to Genoa from northern Europe. There were blue-dyed fabrics (*blavi*) from Châlons and Ypres; brown cloths (*brunete*) from Abbeville, Ypres, and Ghent; and green-tinted ones (*virides*) made at Cambrai and Châlons. Serge (*saia*) was brought from Tournai, *virgati* from Pro-

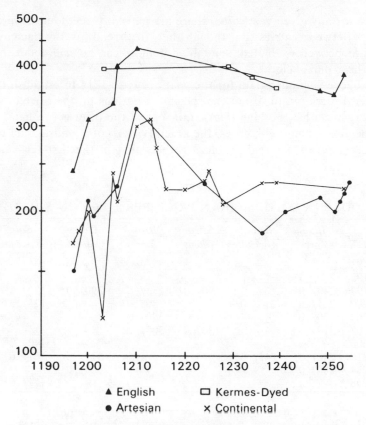

▲ English   □ Kermes-Dyed
● Artesian   × Continental

Fig. 2.   Stanfort Cloth: Median Price per Piece (in *Solidi*)

vins and Ypres, and *biffa* from several different towns.[22] And these are but a few.

As with stanfort cloth, two factors seem important in establishing their price: the specific type of cloth (*blavus*, *viridis*, *saia*) and the town of manufacture. From the former the merchant knew not only the color (its lustre and durability) but also the quality of the wool, for particular dyes were used with specific grades of wool. From the latter he knew the weave and the size of the piece procured, for these were regulated by the separate towns.[23] Unfortunately, as with stanfort, contracts specifying both these factors are few indeed.

For two brief periods only of the century under study is there much documentation on the prices of these fine cloths—the years between 1191 and 1214, and those from 1236 to 1255—and even then the evidence for a single cloth is limited: Frequently there is but one price for any given year; often there are gaps of three, four, or more years between entries. But though the price trend for any one cloth cannot be well evaluated, something definite can be said about that for the group of cloths.

There is enough data for the years 1191 to 1214 to establish the general direction of, if not the specific variations in, the price of six different cloths: the blue (*blavus*) of Ypres; the browns (*brunete*) of Abbeville, Ghent, and Ypres; the green (*viridis*) of Cambrai; and the serge (*saia*) of Tournai. Table 3 reveals that in the first ten years

TABLE 3

WOOLEN CLOTH: MEDIAN PRICE PER PIECE (IN *SOLIDI*)

Year	Blue Ypres	Brown Abbeville	Brown Ghent	Brown Ypres	Green Cambrai	Saia Tournai
1191	—	—	—	—	—	106/ 0^1
1192	219/ 3^1	—	—	—	—	—
1197	240/ 0^8	—	160/ 0^1	275/ 0^{14}	290/ 0^2	122/ 6^{10}
1200	247/ 6^8	236/ 0^1	—	280/ 0^3	—	135/ 0^{15}
1203	270/ 0^5	—	—	320/ 0^2	—	—
1205	220/ 0^2	—	180/ 0^1	300/ 0^1	—	—
1206	—	—	—	—	—	140/ 0^3
1210	246/ 8^1	248/ 0^1	—	—	373/ 0^3	167/ 6^2
1214	209/ 0^1	—	—	—	360/ 0^1	—
1248	—	—	—	—	—	177/ 6^2

(1191–1200) there was a significant rise in the price of these fine woolen cloths, if the blue of Ypres and the serge of Tournai are representative. In the next decade (1201–1210), too, the price increased.[24] Then, between 1211 and 1214, there appears to have been a slight price fall, though evidence of this is limited.[25]

For the last two decades under study (1236–1255), one must examine price trends for five other woolen cloths: *biffa*, Châlons' blue and green, and the *virgati* of Provins and Ypres. Although the limitations of the sample, indicated by Table 4, are obvious, there is evident a general trend. From the mid–1230's until the early '40's there was a price decline;[26] then, sometime in the 1240's, the price of northern woolens began to rise, continuing to do so through 1254.[27]

During neither of these two periods can one judge with confidence the degree of the price changes; even less can he establish about the intervening years. But suggestions, if not definite statements, can be made: The rise in prices in the late twelfth and early thirteenth

TABLE 4

WOOLEN CLOTH: MEDIAN PRICE PER PIECE (IN *SOLIDI*)

Year	Biffa	Blue Châlons	Green Châlons	Virgati Provins	Virgati Ypres
1197	—	234/ 0[1]	—	—	—
1216	—	—	314/ 7[1]	—	—
1234	—	—	—	127/ 4[1]	—
1236	244/ 0[1]	—	—	—	—
1237	—	204/10[1]	—	—	—
1239	206/ 8[1]	—	—	—	—
1241	—	210/ 0[1]	228/ 7[2]	117/ 9[1]	—
1244	—	217/ 2[4]	—	130/ 8[1]	—
1248	244/ 0[7]	215/ 6[15]	282/ 7[9]	128/ 9[5]	200/ 0[1]
1250	—	208/ 0[2]	—	138/11[1]	—
1251	232/ 0[1]	—	241/ 0[1]	—	—
1252	291/ 1[1]	—	242/ 6[2]	—	197/10[1]
1253	289/ 6[1]	230/ 7[4]	290/ 0[9]	148/ 7[4]	207/11[2]
1254	278/11[1]	257/ 1[1]	250/ 0[1]	131/ 7[2]	210/ 0[1]

centuries appears to have been more modest for these woolens than for stanfort, never exceeding 36 per cent.[28] The price increases in the 1250's, however, did parallel those for stanfort cloth and fustian. And during the years between, woolen cloth prices seem to have declined or, at best, remained steady.[29]

Not all of high medieval Europe's industrial plant was geared to the production of such staple items as textiles. Human needs other than the very basic ones had to be satisfied too. One product appearing quite frequently in the notarial contracts fulfilled such a need, the need for opulent display. That product was gold thread (*aurum filatum*), a highly desirable commodity which became one of Genoa's specialties.[30]

During the thirteenth century gold thread was sold by the spool (*canon*), from a few to several hundred spools (*canones*) at a time. The spool was measured by the number of canes (*canne*) of gold thread it contained. Sometimes there were eighty, but more often there were ninety canes per spool, each between two and three meters in length.[31] The median price of a spool of gold thread, tabulated for twenty separate years from 1205 to 1255, appears in Table 5 and Figure 3.[32]

The trend in the price of gold thread is undoubted. For fifty years, from its initial appearance in 1205 until the mid–1250's, gold thread's price declined steadily. The sharpest drop occurred between

TABLE 5

GOLD THREAD: MEDIAN PRICE PER SPOOL (IN *SOLIDI*)

Year	Median Price	Year	Median Price
1205	12/ 0[1]	1239	5/ 8[2]
1213	11/ 0[5]	1240	5/ 0[1]
1214	10/ 0[1]	1241	5/ 2[1]
1224	10/ 2[1]	1242	4/ 8[1]
1226	8/ 7[3]	1244	4/ 0[3]
1227	7/ 0[1]	1245	3/11[1]
1233	6/ 0[9]	1248	3/ 7[9]
1234	5/ 0[4]	1250	4/ 1[5]
1236	5/ 7[3]	1251	5/ 0[3]
1237	5/ 3[4]	1253	4/ 0[9]

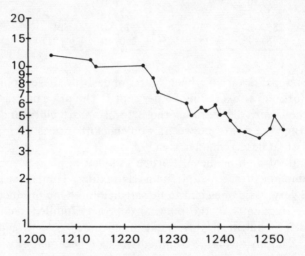

Fig. 3.   Gold Thread: Median Price per Spool (in *Solidi*)

1224 and 1227, more than 30 per cent, in fact; but the price decline neither began nor ended at that time. Except for the brief period between 1250 and 1253, there is no evidence of any recovery, and even then the median price of 0/4/1 pounds per spool remained far below that of earlier years, barely 37 per cent of that before 1224.

The men who marketed gold thread and textiles of every sort took grave risks each time they made a voyage. Not only the sea, but their fellow men often posed a serious threat. To alleviate some dangers of the merchant expedition the business men rented protective body armor. The coif (*barberia*), the hauberk (*osbergum*), the cuirass (*corellus*), and the *panceria* were among the most popular items.[33] In the contracts drawn up between the owner of the armor and the prospective traveller, a clause was included, normally requiring the lessee to pay the full value of the piece should it be lost. It is from such statements of full value that the prices for these manufactured items have been drawn.[34]

The price trends exhibited by body armor are difficult to establish. Data for the coif and hauberk are very few; data for the cuirass and its companion piece (the *panceria*), while more abundant, reveal wide price ranges for almost every year.[35] The most that can be judged from the median prices recorded in Table 6 is that for none of the armor pieces did a significant increase occur during the four decades prior to 1255.

TABLE 6

BODY ARMOR: INDIVIDUALLY PRICED (IN *SOLIDI*)

Year	Coif	Hauberk	Cuirass	Panceria
1182	—	—	—	65/ 0[1]
1191	—	—	—	48/ 4[2]
1192	—	152/ 0[1]	—	—
1203	—	—	—	30/ 0[1]
1211	32/ 0[1]	—	—	—
1213	27/ 0[1]	—	—	—
1216	—	123/ 0[1]	—	—
1220	—	—	—	64/ 0[2]
1222	—	—	50/ 0[1]	80/ 0[1]
1224	20/ 6[2]	—	46/ 0[1]	50/ 0[4]
1225	—	—	58/ 0[1]	45/ 0[2]
1226	—	—	46/ 0[2]	—
1228	—	—	—	65/ 0[1]
1238	16/ 0[1]	—	—	—
1239	—	120/ 0[1]	50/ 0[5]	60/ 0[2]
1240?	—	—	60/ 0[1]	60/ 0[3]
1241	—	—	60/ 0[4]	60/ 0[3]
1242	—	—	50/ 0[2]	60/ 0[1]
1243	—	—	60/ 0[2]	—
1244	—	—	50/ 0[3]	—
1248	—	—	45/ 0[4]	60/ 0[2]
1249	—	—	60/ 0[2]	—
1250	—	—	60/ 0[6]	40/ 0[1]
1251	20/ 0[1]	—	60/ 0[5]	—
1252	—	—	45/ 0[4]	—
1253	—	133/ 4[1]	58/ 9[4]	—
1254	—	120/ 0[1]	—	50/ 0[1]

The prices of the industrial goods sampled from Genoa's notarial records have, then, despite individual variations of some magnitude, followed a general cyclical pattern: They rose markedly in the late twelfth and early thirteenth centuries. Then for several decades they leveled off or, in some cases, dropped significantly. Only in the late 1240's and early 1250's was there a general tendency for them to rise again.[36]

What caused these industrial price movements? Are the trends observed merely reflections of local monetary activity? Or are they, instead, the result of other, more general, economic conditions? On the basis of present research no definite conclusions can be reached; but some tentative suggestions may be warranted.

The debasement of Genoa's specie in the late twelfth and early thirteenth centuries may account for some of the inflationary price movements noted for that period. However, it is not a sufficient explanation for the total price increase, for by no estimate did the denaro depreciate by more than 10 per cent during those years.[37] Nor does Genoa's monetary policy explain the leveling of prices after 1216, for the denaro continued to be debased.[38] Consequently, industrial prices ceased to rise in the 1220's and 1230's in spite of (not because of) specie changes.

If Genoa's monetary policies do not satisfactorily account for these price movements, what does? One possible explanation is suggested by the studies of medieval England's agricultural prices.[39] During the last decades of the twelfth century and the first of the thirteenth, the price of English grain rose as markedly as did that of the textiles noted in this study. Then in the 1230's and early '40's the grain price seemed to level off—and in some years to decline. Only in the late 1240's and early '50's were there again years of high grain prices.[40]

The correlation between price movements in these two sectors—agricultural and industrial—seems too close to be merely coincidental; a causal relationship is suggested. If, as has been advanced, the *cyclical* grain price fluctuations were due to variations in the harvests, then movements in the agricultural sector were probably primary;[41] and the prices of industrial goods merely followed suit in the classic pattern of a cost inflation.[42] Before the cause(s) of the *secular* price rise can be established, however, more data are needed. What there are suggest it was primarily a demand inflation;[43] but only when there is additional evidence for demographic trends, agricultural and industrial output, and specie circulation can a definite statement be made as to the exact type of demand inflation. Until that time, it is hoped that the Genoese data on industrial price movements from 1155 to 1255 will provide a basis for fruitful speculation.

NOTES

* The research for this article was completed at the University of Wisconsin between 1964 and 1965. The article itself is part of a more general study on monetary and price movements accomplished at the University of Wisconsin as part of the requirement for the Ph.D. in history. The study was begun under the direction of Professor Robert L. Reynolds, but, since Professor Reynolds' death, has been under that of Professor David Herlihy. To both these men the writer is greatly indebted.

The historically arbitrary terminal dates appearing in the title are those of the Genoese notarial records upon which this article is based. The earliest extant cartulary, that of Giovanni Scriba, dates from 1155, thus providing a point of departure. The Genoese records do not cease to exist after 1255—in fact, they become more abundant—but those available on microfilm at Madison decrease sharply in number after that date and their contents (wills, dowry settlements, land transactions) are less suitable for an industrial price study.

1. Cf. Michael Postan, "The Trade of Medieval Europe: The North," *Cambridge Economic History* (3 vols., Cambridge, 1941–1952), II, 167.

2. The original notarial cartularies are preserved at the Archivio di Stato, Genoa, Italy. Microfilms and photostats for most of the twelfth and early thirteenth century notaries are available at the University of Wisconsin's Memorial Library. Published editions of several appear in the series, *Documenti e studi per la storia del commercio e del diritto commerciale Italiano.*

3. Unlike, for example, the accounts examined by Eleanora M. Carus-Wilson, "The Aulnage Accounts: A Criticism," *Economic History Review*, Series 1, II (1929), 114–23.

4. The major interpretive studies of medieval Genoa's monetary system are Pier F. Casaretto, "La moneta genovese in confronto con le altre valute mediterranee nei secoli XII e XIII," *Atti della Società Ligure di Storia Patria*, LV (Genoa, 1928); Cornelio Desimoni, "Le prime monete d'argento della zecca di Genova ed il loro valore (1139–1493)," *Atti della Società Ligure di Storia Patria*, XIX (Genoa, 1887), 179–223; Robert S. Lopez, "Back to Gold, 1252," *Economic History Review*, Series 2, IX, 2 (1956), 219–40; and the same author's "Settecento anni fa: Il ritorno all' oro nell' occidente duecentesco," *Rivista Storica Italiana*, LXV (1953), 19–55. A more recent but less thorough essay is Mario Chiaudano's, "La moneta di Genova nel secolo XII," *Studi in onore di Armando Sapori* (2 vols., Milan, 1957), I, 187–214.

5. This holds true for purchases on credit, one type of contract which yields industrial price data. It does not hold for the *commenda* contract, for in that transaction a specific time interval is not indicated, and interest—in the modern sense—probably does not exist. For descriptions of these

contracts see the excellent study by Robert S. Lopez and Irving W. Raymond, *Medieval Trade in the Mediterranean World* (New York, 1955), 156–235.

6. For example, in 1203 several bales of fustian were sold on credit, payment for them due in the future. There is little correspondence between the price of the fustian and the time interval lapsing before payment was due.

Quantity Sold	Price per Bale	Time Interval
1 bale	Pounds 20/ 0/0	54 days
½ "	20/ 0/0	28 "
1 "	20/15/0	39 "
1 "	20/15/0	35 "
1 "	21/ 0/0	66 "
1 "	21/ 0/0	22 "
1 "	22/ 0/0	27 "
1 "	22/ 0/0	20 "
1 "	23/ 0/0	96 "
1 "	23/11/0	19 "
1 "	24/12/0	20 "

7. In fact, Sidney Homer, *A History of Interest Rates* (New Brunswick, N.J., 1963), 94–95, stresses the stability of interest rates during this period.

8. Although the price range for fustian sold in 1203 is not especially wide (see note 6, above), whatever spread there is can be attributed partially to qualitative and quantitative variables.

9. On fustian manufacture see the following studies: Franco Borlandi, " 'Futainiers' et futaines dans l'Italie du moyen âge," *Éventail de l'histoire vivante: Hommage à Lucien Febvre* (2 vols., Paris, 1953), **II**, 133–40; E. Motta, "Per la storia dell'arte dei fustagni nel secolo XIV," *Archivio Storico Lombardo*, series 2, VII (1890), 140–45; H. Wescher, "Cotton and the Cotton Trade in the Middle Ages," *Ciba Review*, VI, 64 (February, 1948), 2322–60.

10. The identification of the *verrubius* as a half-bale is based solely on the evidence of its price. For a discussion of this see John W. Culver, Prices in Genoa, 1150–1250 (Unpublished Ph.D. thesis, University of Wisconsin, 1938), pp. 49–53. The cane (*canna*) of Genoa has been variously estimated. Pietro Rocca, *Pesi e misure antiche di Genova e del Genovesato* (Genoa, 1871), p. 106, considered it to be 2.97 meters; Adolf Schaube, *Handelsgeschichte der romanischen Völker des Mittelmeergebiets bis zum Ende der Kreuzzüge* (Munich and Berlin, 1906), p. 814, identified it as a length of 2.23 meters.

11. See the superscribed numerals in Table 1 for the number of price quotations which make up each computed median.

12. For example, in 1200 the difference between the minimum and maximum price of fustian (the price range) was 13/10/4 pounds. But in that year the sample was large. Normally the price range was much smaller.

13. The prices listed in Table 1 are quoted in solidi and denari. The

denaro was a real coin; the solido, the imaginary equivalent of twelve denari. Twenty solidi, of course, made up the equally imaginary libra.

Figure 1 portrays on a semi-logarithmic scale the price data of Table 1. This particular scale has been chosen for it best indicates degrees of change.

14. Compare, for example, the price of a piece of fustian in the year 1200 (between 0/10/8 and 0/11/5 pounds) with the price of English and Artesian stanforts (Table 2) or of other woolen cloths (Table 3) for that same year.

15. Among the general works on wool cloth production and distribution in the Middle Ages the following are of especial importance: Felix Bourquelot, *Études sur les foires de Champagne* (2 vols., Paris, 1865); Eleanora M. Carus-Wilson, "The Woollen Industry," *Cambridge Economic History* (Cambridge, 1952), **II**, 355–428; Georges Espinas, *La draperie dans la Flandre française au moyen âge* (2 vols., Paris, 1923); Henri Laurent, *La draperie des Pays-Bas en France et dans les pays méditerranéens, XII -XV^esiècle* (Paris, 1935). A valuable article is Robert L. Reynolds, "The Market for Northern Textiles in Genoa, 1179–1200," *Revue belge de philologie e d'histoire*, VIII, 3 (1929), 831–52. A recent and most useful discussion of terminology and production techniques is Guy de Poerck, *La draperie médiévale en Flandre et en Artois: Technique et terminologie* (Bruges, 1951).

16. On stanfort see Bourquelot, I, 227–31; Carus-Wilson, "The Woollen Industry," pp. 374–75; Poerck, I, 214–16; and Reynolds, "The Market for Northern Textiles," p. 840, note 4.

17. This was in the year 1253. See Table 2 for the first two varieties. Stanfort of Lombardy has not been considered in this study.

18. For a detailed discussion of kermes production see Wolfgang Born, "Scarlet," *Ciba Review*, I, 7 (March, 1938), 206–27. See also the remarks of Poerck, I, 181.

19. Some of these may have come from Arras and are merely unidentified, but others definitely did not: They were produced at Lille or Châlons, at Regensburg or Ypres or another place. Some are black or white, others red or green; no distinction has been made. Only Lombard stanforts have been excluded, a small lot, much cheaper than the rest. It's doubtful, too, that any English or kermes-dyed fabrics appear, for their high price would certainly stand out.

20. This timing is suggested by the data on "continental" stanfort.

21. Ignored by this statement is the erratic "continental" entry for 1203, which is inexplicable.

22. The works cited in note 15, above, contain information on these cloths too.

23. Unfortunately, all is not as simple as the text above might seem. For any one town there were several different lengths for a "piece" of cloth, each of them "official." There could also be some "unofficial" piece lengths if the rules were not enforced. The merchant, of course, knew the length of the piece he was purchasing, but did not see any need to record it in his contract. Thus, the modern scholar does not know if all pieces were of the same length, even if they came from the same town. But, as stated earlier in the text, it must be assumed in this study that for a given town "a piece is a

piece is a piece." For some official lengths see Poerck, *La draperie*, pp. 233–300.

24. Although the price of Ypres' blue, despite its fluctuations, did not noticeably alter, that of all other cloths in Table 3 did.

25. The only data for these years are for two cloths—Ypres' blue and Cambrai's green.

26. The basis for this statement is the data on *biffa* and the *virgatus* of Provins.

27. The basis for this statement is the data on *biffa*, Châlons' blue and green and the *virgati* of Provins and Ypres.

28. Most of the price increases were far lower than 36 per cent. Only Tournai's *saia* rose by this much.

29. Tournai's *saia* was higher in 1248 than it had been before 1210, but only slightly so—some 6 per cent, in fact; Châlons' blue and green were lower in that year than they had been four and five decades earlier, the latter never reaching its high of 1216.

30. On gold thread production see the following studies: William N. Bonds, "Genoese Noblewomen and Gold Thread Manufacturing," *Medievalia et Humanistica*, XVII (1966), 79–81; M. Braun-Ronsdorf, "Gold and Silver Fabrics from Medieval to Modern Times," *Ciba Review*, no. 3 (1961), 2–16; and Wilhelm Heyd, *Histoire du commerce du Levant au moyen âge*, II (Leipzig, 1923), 667.

31. Rocca, p. 106; Schaube, p. 814.

32. The median prices for gold thread were derived from *commenda* contracts only, and they are estimates made at the end of the production process, on the eve of export. Other contracts yield the price of thread at an intermediate production stage, the stage at which the actual worker, to whom the thread had been "put-out," returned it to the merchant entrepreneur. These contracts have been eliminated from consideration.

33. On armor and the medieval armorer see the following studies: Aldo M. Aroldi, *Armi e armature Italiane fino al XVIII secolo* (Milan, 1961); Charles H. Ashdown, *Armour and Weapons in the Middle Ages* (London, 1925); Samuel E. Ellacott, *Armour and Blade* (London, 1962); C. F. Ffoulkes, "European Arms and Armour," *Social Life in Early England*, ed. Geoffrey Barraclough (London, 1960), pp. 124–38; Henrietta M. Larson, "The Armor Business in the Middle Ages," *Business History Review*, XIV, 4 (Oct., 1940), 49–64.

34. This statement does not hold true for the hauberk, whose price was derived from *commenda* contracts.

35. The price range for armor is probably wide because of the small number of pieces (usually only one) involved in a transaction. In such cases, qualitative differences play a great role and have a real impact upon prices.

36. A cursory examination of fustian cloth prices after 1255 reveals that this tendency to increase is sustained for several decades. Gold thread prices, while they do not rise significantly, do hold steady.

37. Desimoni, "Le prime monete," p. 198, estimated the silver content of twelve Genoese denari (one *solido*) at gr. 4.176 in 1172 and at gr. 3.947 in 1201. Volkert Pfaff, "Die Einnahmen der römischen Kurie am Ende des

12. Jahr-hunderts," *Vierteljahrschrift für Sozial- und Wirtschaftsgeschichte*, XL (1953), 101, determined a similar modest debasement. The studies of Casaretto and Chiaudano are not in basic disagreement on this point.

38. Desimoni, "Le prime monete," p. 198.

39. See D. L. Farmer, "Some Price Fluctuations in Angevin England," *Economic History Review*, Series 2, IX (1956), 34–43; the same author's "Some Grain Price Movements in Thirteenth-Century England," *Economic History Review*, Series 2, X (1957), 207–20; and Lord Beveridge's table of English Wheat Prices, 1160–1339, cited by Michael Postan, "The Trade of Medieval Europe: The North," *Cambridge Economic History* (Cambridge, 1952), II, 166.

40. The annual price fluctuations for agricultural commodities are naturally more severe than are those for industrial products, but this general pattern is evident.

41. Farmer, "Some Price Fluctuations," p. 38; and the same author's "Some Grain Price Movements," p. 216. Of course, the sheer magnitude of the medieval European agricultural sector, when compared with the industrial, would immediately suggest this.

42. A cost inflation exists when the costs of production increase at a rate faster than does productivity. In this case, it is probable that rising food costs simultaneously raised labor costs and reduced real profits. To compensate for this rising cost of labor and to preserve real profits, industry had to increase productivity or raise prices or do both. On the general question of inflation in underdeveloped countries see Geoffrey Maynard, *Economic Development and the Price Level* (London, 1962), pp. 43–60.

43. For a brief summary of the explanations for demand inflations see Maynard, *Economic Development*, pp. 1–8.

A VENETIAN NAVAL EXPEDITION OF 1224

LOUISE BUENGER ROBBERT

Texas Tech University

The Republic of Venice sent a force of two large armed ships down the Adriatic coast in the spring of 1224. The details of this expedition reveal much about the organization of Venetian naval expeditions, their personnel, and the financial methods of the Venetian Republic at this early date.

The source of the information is the *Liber Plegiorum*,[1] a collection of decrees, judgments, and other official documents from 1223 to 1226 issued by the Minor Council of Venice. This body, later known as the Senate, advised the doge and included certain executive officers of the Venetian state. Although the records refer to an enormous number of topics, it has its limitation as a source because it has not yet been carefully edited and very few other Venetian governmental records have survived from the first half of the thirteenth century. Knowledge of the naval expedition of 1224 thus comes from an isolated source, and the expedition itself was mentioned only once in this source. This monograph will attempt to reconstruct the expedition from the available data.

The document names Blasio Simiteculo as the commander-in-chief (*capitaneus*) of the expedition. He also bore another title, captain of the galley (*comitus*). Holding these two titles, Blasio held full responsibility for preparing the expedition as directed by the Venetian Republic. He also personally commanded the larger vessel, as its galley-master.[2] His duties occupied him for three months, whereas the other men on the expedition were engaged for two months only. Blasio directly commanded the 157 Venetians on the galley. Blasio also had to provide arms for himself and many of the men, a responsibility that Venice did not delegate to any other member of the expedition. Probably the arms of the rowers consisted of helmet, shield, broad sword, dagger, and two lances or long lances, which the law decreed for mariners on Venetian merchantmen at this time.[3] His prestige and duties as commander-in-chief were further enhanced when the Commune (the government of the Republic of Venice) gave him a personal servant or attendant. In addition, Blasio was the agent for the state in paying wages to all the men on the galley. The Commune of Venice reimbursed him handsomely. He received not only an amount for his personal use (*pro sua persona*), but also a *salario*, which is the Venetian dialect term for the reimbursement given by princes to gentlemen of breeding and substance. As will be seen later, his daily wage was much greater than that for any other man on the expedition.

Blasio was a member of the Venetian ruling oligarchy; he was educated and had some previous business experience. While no trade documents of Venice survive involving Blasio directly, two other members of the Simiteculo family made foreign trade contracts in 1224, the same year as this naval expedition. Matteo Simiteculo, living in the Venetian parish of San Cassiano, contracted to travel with 60 Venetian pounds of his neighbor, for the purpose of profitable investment.[4] Blasio Simiteculo, who bore a name similar to the commander-in-chief, contracted to receive 20 ounces of gold sent from Messina.[5] Only one other document mentioned the commander-in-chief himself. In August, 1199, he witnessed a loan contracted by a widow and her son.[6] This document reveals both that Blasio was literate (he signed his own name) and that he was at least in his forties when he was named commander-in-chief (he would have been no younger than 20 when he witnessed the loan in 1199).

The two ships of the expedition commanded by Blasio Simiteculo were of different types—one was a galley, the other, a galleon. The galley, the larger ship, carried the commander-in-chief and 157 men. Galleys commonly served as warships in the thirteenth century. Oars propelled galleys and they had one or two masts with sails for occasional assistance in travel. They were known as long ships, being lower, narrower, and faster than merchantmen, and designed with a beak for ramming the enemy and a castle in the poop for the captain.[7] Because Venetian galleys before 1290 had two men to a bench, each plying his oar, they were known technically as biremes.[8] The size of this galley can be estimated from the number of men on board; those men on board who could row numbered 139 men (*homines*). The honor guard (*honorantia*) of 13 men could probably row if necessary. By simple arithmetic, this gives a galley with 34 benches of oars on each side, one bench of oars with one man each, and a coxswain. This is a large vessel—larger than any of the Genoese ships of 1248 described by Byrne.[9]

In addition to the rowers and the *honorantia*, the galley also carried 4 crossbowmen (who probably did not row), the commander-in-chief, and his servant. All these 158 men were freemen, even the rowers.[10] The servant (*serviens* not *servus*) would attend the admiral, and possibly was a youth from a good Venetian family on his first voyage.[11] The ship carried, in addition to the men and their arms, the personal effects of each mariner. On the merchant vessels, each rower was allowed 1 *begoncia* of water, a sea chest, a mattress of a certain size, and 2 *begonciae* of wine for three men.[12] The mariners on this galley were probably allowed similar privileges. No indication is given of the way the men were fed.

The galleon cannot be identified so exactly. It was not the type of great galleon built in the Renaissance, but rather a smaller vessel of unknown construction with both oars and sails.[13] This galleon carried a crew of 101 *homines*, an *honorantia* (honor guard) of 11 men, 3 crossbowmen, and the captain. Again, if only the *homines* did the rowing and if the galleon was a bireme, it should have had 25 benches of oars on each side, plus a coxswain. This would make it roughly equivalent in size to the light galleys of Renaissance Venice.[14] It was not so large as the galley commanded by Blasio Simiteculo.

The galleon carried a crew very similar to that of the galley. In addition to the rowers, and the *honorantia*, the galleon had one less crossbowman than the galley. If their duties paralleled those of Renaissance bowmen aboard Venetian galleys, they might travel between the rowers and in time of danger stand between the rowers or on the stern or the prow to discharge their quarrels at the enemy.[15] Later Venetian galleys also carried different kinds of catapults for hurling burning projectiles. If the galleon and the galley carried these machines of war, they were kept in the castle on the poop and possibly manned by the crossbowmen.[16]

The principal officer of the galleon (*comitus de galiono*) was Giovanni di Vicenza (*Johannes de Vicentia*). Probably not a Venetian citizen but a resident of nearby Vicenza,[17] Giovanni did not enjoy as much responsibility or trust as did Blasio Simiteculo. He was paid for only two months, unlike the three-month term of Blasio. He received a smaller sum than did Blasio and only for his person (*pro sua persona*). He received no *salario* and the Commune did not provide him with a servant. Although the galleon under his command carried 115 men beside himself, the Commune of Venice trusted him to pay only 110 rowers from funds of the Commune. At the time the document was recorded, the crossbowmen and two additional armed rowers had already received their wages from the Venetian state.

The details concerning the wages paid to the members of this expedition are given in precise detail by the document in the *Liber Plegiorum*. From these details, the daily wage for each individual can be computed.[18] The following table presents these details:

DISBURSEMENTS FOR THE 1224 EXPEDITION

to whom paid	*total wages*	*months of service*	*wages per diem*	*Allocated funds*
GALLEY				
Blasio Simiteculo		3 months		
pro sua persona	£100		£1/2/2-1/2	£170/8/
pro sua salario	(100)		—	—
139 men (*homines*)				
and 13 *honorantia*	912	2 months	2s.	841/12/
4 crossbowmen	36	2 months	3s.	41/-/
the servant	3	2 months	1s.	
	£1051			1054
GALLEON				
Giovanni di Vicenza		2 months		
pro sua persona	28		8s. 4d.	120/-/
99 men and 11				
honorantia	660	2 months	2s.	568/-/
3 crossbowmen	(27)	2 months	3s.	prepaid
2 armed oarsmen	(12)	2 months	2s.	prepaid
	£688			£688

In total, the Venetian state spent 1878 *libre* on this expedition which lasted for two months.

The text mentions three different sources from which the Commune of Venice drew funds to reimburse the members of the expedition of 1224. First, the Commune drew on its reserves in the Grain Office to pay a portion of the wages of the captains and the rowers. The Grain Office, a typical medieval Italian municipal office, purchased grain to supply Venice in time of scarcity. Even in the thirteenth century the islands of Venice did not produce enough grain to feed the city. Grain was regularly imported to Venice by sea and from the mainland. In time of scarcity the city government took extraordinary measures.[19] The Grain Office maintained a permanent reserve of funds which could be lent to the state or to private investors.[20] In the text of the 1224 expedition, the doge and council of Venice gave Blasio Simiteculo credit to 142 *staria* of grain, valued at 170 *libre*, 8 *solid*; and to Giovanni di Vicenza 100 *staria* of grain valued at 120 *libre*.[21]

Another source of government funds for the expedition of 1224 was the Salt Office. The mechanics of operation of the Salt Office in this early date are not so clear, but by the end of the century they had earned such great profits as to become one of the principal financial organs of the Venetian state. In war and in time of extraordinary need the salt office would lend money to the Commune.[22] In 1224 chamberlains of the Commune of Venice held authority over the Salt Office and they were expected to give an accounting of their receipts every four months. The chamberlains also lent money from the Salt Office to the Commune, especially for the galley expeditions sailing to Constantinople.[23] In May, 1224, Giovanni Bocasso held the office of chamberlain.[24] He was a Venetian merchant of some importance. Three surviving commercial documents, from 1203, 1215, and 1235, record his active participation in Venetian commerce with large amounts of capital.[25] He and his brother, who was his business partner, resided in the Venetian parish of San Simeone Profeta, not far from the great church of Santa Croce, which gave its name to one of the sectors of republican Venice. Either Giovanni Bocasso, the chamberlain of 1224, or his descendant represented the sector of Santa Croce in the Great Council of Venice for nine terms in the second half of the century.[26] Membership in the Great Council during this time signified that a man's descendants were members of the Venetian oligarchy after the Closing of the Golden Book in 1296. Although the text of the 1224 expedition does not name the Salt Office —or the title of chamberlain, the text does state that the doge and council of Venice authorized Giovanni Bocasso to give 42 *libre* to Blasio Simiteculo to pay the crossbowmen and the servant on the galley. It is assumed that Giovanni Bocasso paid this sum under his authority as chamberlain of Venice and supervisor of the Salt Office.

Nycolao de Axevelo was the third named source of government funds to finance the 1224 naval expedition. No other contemporary references to this man have been discovered; his name is not Venetian.[27] It is uncertain whether he provided the sums for the expedition as a private individual or as the representative of some commercial company or of some government. Nycolao de Axevelo did finance a much larger share of the expedition than either the Grain Office or the Salt Office. The doge and council of Venice instructed him to give 841 *libre*, 12 *solidi* to the galley captain to make the rest of the payments to Blasio Simiteculo and to the rowers not covered by the Grain Office. Similarly, Nycolao de Axevelo was instructed to pay 568 *libre* to the captain of the galleon.

Besides drawing on the Grain Office, the Salt Office, and Nycolao

de Axevelo, still more money was needed for the expedition, and
the doge and council of Venice did not clearly designate the source
of the remaining funds. These included 39 *libre* needed to complete
the wages due the crossbowmen and the servant on the galley, and
another 39 *libre* already paid to the crossbowmen and two of the
armed rowers aboard the galleon. It may be coincidental that 39
libre for both the galley and the galleon are obtained from unidentified government funds.

In summary, the sources of funds of the Commune of Venice for
the naval expedition of 1224 are given in tabular form as follows:

ALLOCATION OF FUNDS FOR THE 1224 NAVAL EXPEDITION

source of funds	to which ship	for whom intended	amount
Grain Office	galley	wages and salary of captain and of the rowers	£170/9/
	galleon	wages of captain and rowers	120/–/
Salt Office	galley	wages of crossbowmen	42/–/
Nycolao de Axevelo	galley	wages and salary of captain and rowers	841/12/
	galleon	wages of captain and rowers	568/–/
unidentified govt. funds	galley	wages of crossbowmen	36/–/
		wages of servant	3/–/
	galleon	wages of crossbowmen	27/–/
		wages of 2 armed rowers	12/–/

Except for the unidentified government funds, the doge and council
stipulated that the money was to be given to the captains of the
ships and distributed by them to the ships' companies.

The text of the description does not give a motive for the expedition. There are two possible theories to explain why the Commune
of Venice sent out this expedition in 1224. First, the expedition may
be the armament organized to accompany the spring *muda* to Constantinople. A *muda*, in the original sense, meant a convoy of
Venetian ships sailing together at a certain time of year to a certain
destination. In the early fourteenth century, Venice had at least two
spring *muda* each year, one leaving Venice between March 15 and
April 15 for Constantinople, and another leaving between April 15
and April 30 for the other parts of the Byzantine east, *Romania
Bassa*.[28] The Simiteculo expedition had many characteristics of
a *muda*. In the text itself, drawn up in March, 1224,[29] the doge and
council directed the ships to sail on April 1. This places the departure

date exactly in the middle of the dates established in the next century for the spring *muda* to Constantinople. The chamberlain of Venice, Giovanni Bocasso, who helped finance Simiteculo's galley, also paid the expenses of a Venetian councillor going to Constantinople for the Commune the same month.[30] Also, the expedition of 1224 included two armed vessels which were not directed at any particular enemy and which were of a type particularly suited to convoy duty. However, two objections can be made to the *muda* theory. The mariners were paid for only two months service, and it is by no means certain that a number of slow-moving Venetian merchantmen escorted by a galley and a galleon could make the trip from Venice to Constantinople in two months in 1224. Another objection is that it is by no means generally accepted that the *muda* system extended to Constantinople as early as 1224.[31]

A second possible motive for the 1224 naval expedition is that the ships sailed to patrol the Adriatic coast for two months. Venetian food, Venetian wealth, and even her very existence as an independent state depended on her trade with the east. The avenue of that trade was the Adriatic Sea. Venetian ships sailed out of the lagoons, across to Istria, and then south down the Dalmatian coast until they reached Greek waters. Although the Venetians claimed that the Adriatic Sea was their own sea, foreign or piratical ships still sailed these waters and menaced Venetian merchant ships in the first half of the thirteenth century. Complete Venetian control over the Adriatic Sea was not achieved until the fourteenth century. To keep the vital Venetian food grains and luxury trade moving, the Commune had to protect her merchant shipping on the Adriatic.

Especially menacing to Venice in the 1220's were the cities of Ferrara and Ancona.[32] The *Liber Plegiorum* records that in April, 1224, the same month that Blasio Simiteculo's expedition set out, a Venetian named Leonardo Simiteculo, traveling on the Adriatic from Ancona toward Pescara, was set upon by pirates from the Dalmatian city of Split and from *Cacicii*. The Venetian ship was run aground and its goods stolen, including cloths, iron, copper, and other small articles of sale. The Commune sent one galley commanded by Mafeo Feriolo to Split to demand satisfaction, but got none.[33] There were other examples of piracy on the Adriatic in spring, 1224.[34]

To protect her Adriatic shipping in 1224, Venice sent out not only the expedition of Blasio Simiteculo, but also another. It consisted of one small ship, a sagita which carried 4 crossbowmen armed with 200 quarrels and left Venice for a one-month term.[35]

The large, fast, well-armed ships of Blasio Simiteculo's expedition were well suited to protect Venetian shipping against such piracy. The interpretation that they were on convoy or patrol duty would fit in well with the theories of the late Gino Luzzatto. He thought that, in the twelfth century, Venetian shipping down the Adriatic had always to be protected by a convoy, that these were the original *muda*, and that voyages outside the Adriatic were free of convoy.[36] The text of the Simiteculo expedition does not speak of Constantinople, but rather of a route along the coast (*per riveram*).

The more plausible reason for the Simiteculo expedition seems to be that it was sent to patrol the Adriatic coast for two months, not that it was sent to convoy the spring *muda* to Constantinople. However, the Simiteculo expedition may have conveyed certain Venetian ships down the Adriatic in a type of Adriatic *muda*. Nothing in the text either supports or negates this view. The *muda* did exist in 1224, many documents give evidence of this. But, since the exact details of the *muda* in the early thirteenth century are not known, it seems best to call the Simiteculo expedition merely a convoy or patrol expedition down the Adriatic and not a *muda*.

In conclusion, a study of the Venetian naval expedition of April and May, 1224, reveals significant details about Venetian shipping and government finance. The expedition concerned two naval vessels, a galley and a galleon. The galley, being a bireme with 34 benches of oars on each side, carried the commander-in-chief, his servant, 4 crossbowmen, 139 rowers, and an honor guard. The galleon, a medieval ship unlike the greater galleons of later centuries, was smaller with only 25 benches of oars and a crew of 101 rowers, 11 honor guard, 3 crossbowmen, and its captain. These men were paid well for their two-month service; their daily wages are computed on the preceding tables. The expedition was financed by the Venetian Commune which drew on its accounts at the Grain Office and the Salt Office for some of the funds. The voyage was probably undertaken to patrol the Adriatic coast or to convoy Venetian merchant vessels in these waters.

NOTES

1. *Liber Plegiorum*. ASV Sala Dipl. Regina Margherita, N. 5. II. 27r. This book has a register, R. Predelli, *Il Liber Plegiorum*, (Venice, 1872). It has also been edited by Roberto Cessi, *Liber Comunis qui vulgo nuncupatur 'Plegiorum'* in *Deliberazioni del Maggior Consiglio di Venezia*, I: *Il*

Maggior Consiglio: origine ed evoluzione fino alla fine del sec. XIII. Sez. III. Parlamenti e Consigli Maggiori dei Comuni Italiani. Accademia dei Lincei (Bologna, 1950), p. 57. However, this is not a critical edition. Comparison with the manuscript reveals that Cessi omits the line, "Item secundum ei dari homines quatuor quibus fecimus dari libras XXXVI." Cessi has read *et* for *ab*, and also read *libras LXII* instead of the ms. reading of *libras XLII*. The scribe also cancelled out three phrases which Cessi does not indicate.

2. Frederic C. Lane, "Merchant Galleys, 1300–34: Private and Commercial Operation" in *Venice and History* (Baltimore, Md., 1966), p. 207 and n. 44.

3. *Gli Statuti Marittimi Veneziani fino al 1255,* ed. by R. Predelli and Adolfo Sacerdoti (Venice, 1903), pp. 54–57. These laws of 1227 govern the *nave*, the merchant ships.

4. *Documenti del Commercio Veneziano nel secoli XI–XIII,* vol. II ed. R. Morozzo della Rocca and A. Lombardo in *Documenti e Studi per la Storia del Commercio e del Diritto Commerciale Italiano,* XX (Turin, 1940), doc. 618.

5. *Ibid.,* doc. 611.

6. *Ibid.,* vol. I, doc. 445.

7. Eugene Byrne, *Genoese Shipping in the Twelfth and Thirteenth Centuries* (Cambridge, Mass., 1930), pp. 5, 9–10; and Frederic C. Lane, *Ships and Shipbuilders of the Renaissance* (Baltimore, Md., 1934) Chapter I.

8. Frederic C. Lane, "From Biremes to Triremes" in *Venice and History, op. cit.,* pp. 189–192; Michele Vocino, *La Nave del Tempo.* 3rd edition (Milan, 1950) pp. 31–32.

9. Byrne, *op. cit.,* pp. 9–10.

10. *Statuti Marittimi, op. cit.,* pp. 54–57; Lane, *Venetian Ships and Shipbuilders, op. cit.,* p. 7; and Heinrich Kretschmayr, *Greschichte von Venedig* (3 vols., Gotha 1905–34, reprinted 1964) II, p. 149.

11. This type of training for young noblemen is discussed in James C. Davis, *The Decline of the Venetian Nobility as a Ruling Class,* The Johns Hopkins Studies in Historical and Political Science, Series LXXX, No, 2, Baltimore, 1962), pp. 26–27.

12. *Statuti Marittimi, op. cit.,* pp. 48–49.

13. Lane, *Venetian Ships and Shipping, op. cit.,* p. 50 and Vocino *op. cit.,* p. 56.

14. Lane, *Venetian Ships and Shipping, op. cit.,* p. 9.

15. *Ibid.,* p. 10.

16. Vocino, *op. cit.,* p. 36.

17. Perhaps he was living in Venice, since the documents of 1224 mention many foreigners residing in Venice; e.g. Brescia, *Liber Plegiorum* ed. Cessi, p. 6; Cremona, *Ibid.,* p. 10; Germany, *Ibid.,* p. 11; Florence, *Ibid.,* p. 17; and Padua, *Ibid.,* p. 20, etc.

18. The daily wages are computed in Venetian *libre.* I cannot explain why the figures given by the document for both the total wages and the allocated funds for the galley do not balance.

19. In 1226 poor crops and an extremely cold winter put Venice desperately in need of food. The Venetian doge and council sent three ships loaded with bars of gold to Ancona to purchase grain for the city. *Liber Plegiorum*, ASV, 85r, 86r, and 86v; and *Liber Plegiorum*, ed. Cessi, pp. 178, 181, 182, 183.

20. Gino Luzzatto, *Storia Economica di Venezia dall'XI al XVI Secolo* (Venice, 1961) p. 104; and Lane, "Merchant Galleys" p. 217–218.

21. The stario or staio = 2.3 Imperial bushels, according to Lane, *Venetian Ships and Shipbuilders*, p. 246. The stario also = 82 litres or 62-½ kilograms of grain according to Maurice Aymard, *Venise, Raguse et le commerce du ble pendant la second moitié du XVIe siècle*, École Pratique des Hautes Ètudes. VIe section: Centre de Recherches Historiques. Ports, Routes, Trafics, 20 (Paris, 1966), p. 17. This gives a book value of 2/15/2-2/5 pounds = 1 Imperial bushel grain = 35.65 litres grain. The Imperial bushel is the measure for wheat legally established in Great Britain in 1826, containing 2218.192 cub. in. or 80 lb. distilled water. It differs from the standard bushel used in the United States.

22. Luzzatto, *op. cit.*, p. 51.

23. *Liber Plegiorum*, ed. Cessi, p. 63.

24. *Liber Plegiorum*, ASV, 30v; *Liber Plegiorum*, ed. Cessi, p. 62–3.

25. *Documenti del Commercio Veneziano, op. cit.*, II, doc. 562, 692; and *Nuovi Documenti del Commercio Veneto dei Sec. XI–XIII*, ed. R. Morozzo della Rocca and A. Lombardo, Deputazione di Storia Patria per le Venezia (Venice, 1953) doc. 59.

26. "Electores et Electi de Maiori Consilio ab Anno 1261 usque ad anno 1296" in *Deliberazioni del Maggior Consiglio di Venezia* ed. Roberto Cessi, I, 269–362: 1265–6, 1266–7, 1269–70, 1270–1, 1275–6, 1276–7, 1277–8, 1278–9 and 1280–1.

27. Perhaps he was a foreign merchant residing in Venice from whom the state extracted a forced loan.

28. Lane, "Fleets and Fairs" in *Venice and History, op. cit.*, pp. 128–141.

29. *Liber Plegiorum*, ASV 26v and 27r. The 1224 expedition document itself is not dated, but other texts on the same pages in the same hand give the date March, 1224. The *Liber Plegiorum* ms. is bound in a very early white vellum cover, possibly a contemporary binding.

30. *Liber Plegiorum*, ASV, 30v. and *Liber Plegiorum*, ed. Cessi, p. 62–3. See also *Urkunden zur alteren Handels- und Staatsgeschichte der Republik Venedig* ed. by G. F. Fr. Tafel and G. M. Thomas in *Fontes Rerum Austriacarum*. Historische Commission der Kaiserlichen Akademie der Wissenschaften in Wien, Abt. II. Diplomataria et Acta (3 vols., Vienna, 1856), II. doc. 269.

31. Gino Luzzatto "Navigazione di linea e navigazione libera nelle grandi città marinare del Medio Evo" in *Studi di Storia di Venezia* (Padua, 1954) p. 54; and Lane, "Fleets and Fairs" p. 140.

32. Kretschmayr, *op. cit.*, II, pp. 29–41.

33. *Liber Plegiorum*, ed. Cessi, p. 60. The relationship between Leo-

nardo Simiteculo and Blasio Simiteculo is not clear. Leonardo is mentioned only this once in the surviving documents. Leonardo, unlike the commander-in-chief Blasio, came from the Venetian parish of San Vio and sailed on a small boat (*barca*). The entire piracy incident involving Leonardo Simiteculo was completed and recorded the first week of April, 1224, including the galley expedition of Mafeo Feriolo.

34. *Liber Plegiorum*, ed. Cessi, pp. 26, 54, and 55.
35. *Ibid.*, p. 60.
36. Luzzatto, "Navigazione di linea e navigazione libera", p. 54.

NOTES ON MEDIEVAL ENGLISH WEIGHTS AND MEASURES IN FRANCESCO BALDUCCI PEGOLOTTI'S "LA PRATICA DELLA MERCATURA"

RONALD EDWARD ZUPKO

Marquette University

In his valuable handbook of fourteenth century business practices and trade items, Francesco Balducci Pegolotti discussed several English weights and measures. This short study will examine the most important of these weights and measures: the hundredweight (*centinaio, centinaia*), the fother (*ciarrea*), the sack (*sacca, sacco*) and the clove (*chiovi*).[1]

The hundredweight in medieval England was either 100, 108, 112, or 120 pounds depending on the product. Although Pegolotti correctly reported the hundredweight for "Great Wares" (tin, glass, lead, iron, copper, steel, flax, hemp, tallow, hops, cheese, butter, wool, and certain other goods) as weighing 112 pounds (1/20 of a ton of 2,240 pounds), his reference to a 104 pound hundredweight for pepper, ginger, sugar, cinnamon, and other spices is not corroborated by any evidence in the English documents.[2] Usually a hundredweight of 108 pounds applied to spices, although occasionally one of 100 pounds—the standard weight for gunpowder—was used.

The hundredweight (Cwt.) should not be confused with the hundred (C.) which was a measure of quantity for many products. The hundred generally numbered 100, but larger amounts ranging from 106 to 225 were not uncommon.[3] Graphically the hundredweight and the hundred may be compared as in Table 1.

However, there is another problem concerning the hundredweights reported by Pegolotti. In order to determine their exact weight in grains, it is necessary that one know the particular pound (mercantile or avoirdupois) employed in their construction because the avoirdupois pound contained 7,000 troy grains while the mercantile contained only 6,750. Unfortunately, Pegolotti never indicated which of these two pounds applied.[4]

TABLE 1

Hundred	Hundredweight
(1) 100 (most items including iron, sugar, spices, wax, furs, and skins)	(1) 100 (gunpowder)
(2) 106 (sheep and lambs in Roxburghshire and Selkirkshire)	(2) 104 (filberts in Kent)
(3) 120 (the "long-hundred" for herrings, stockfish, eggs, oars, faggots, tile, spars, nails, stones, pins, canvas, and linen cloth)	(3) 108 (sugar, wax, pepper, cinnamon, nutmegs, and alum)
	(4) 112 ("Great Wares" such as tin, glass, lead, iron (except at the king's scales in Cornwall), copper, steel, flax, hemp, tallow, hops, cheese, butter, wool, and many more)
(4[a]) 124 (herrings on the Isle of Man)	(5) 120 (iron at the king's scales in Cornwall)
(4[b]) 124 (saltfish, ling, cod, and haberdine)	
(5) 160 (hard fish)	
(6) 225 (onions and garlic: equal to 15 ropes of 15 heads each)	

To complicate matters, it is during the period in which Pegolotti is writing that the avoirdupois pound was slowly replacing the mercantile pound, and the English documents often do not make the proper distinction between them when discussing hundredweights and tons. Since Pegolotti never tells us which of the two systems his hundredweights were based on, their actual weights in grains could vary as follows:

TABLE 2

	Weight in Troy Grains	
Hundredweights	Avoirdupois (7,000/lb.)	Mercantile (6,750/lb.)
(1) 104 pounds =	728,000	702,000[5]
(2) 112 pounds =	784,000	756,000[6]

The variation in weight between the hundredweights in line 2 is only 4 avoirdupois pounds (28,000 divided by 7,000/lb.), but when these hundredweights were multiplied by 20 to form the ton the variations became much more pronounced:

TABLE 3

Tons	Weight in Troy Grains	
	Avoirdupois (7,000/lb.)	*Mercantile* (6,750/lb.)
(1) 2,080 pounds = (104 pounds × 20)	14,560,000	14,040,000[7]
(2) 2,240 pounds = (112 pounds × 20)	15,680,000	15,120,000[8]

The tons in line 2 vary by 80 avoirdupois pounds (560,000 grains divided by 7,000/lb.) depending on whether the avoirdupois or mercantile scales were used. And this difference amounts to more than two-thirds hundredweight in every ton.

Just as the hundredweight, the fother had a number of variations.[9] This weight for lead generally weighed 2,100 pounds, but it was formed in four different ways. It could consist of 30 fotmals[10] of 70 pounds each; of 168 stone[11] of 12.5 pounds each; of 175 stone of 12 pounds each; or, of 12 weys,[12] each wey of 175 pounds. In addition, there were two lesser known fothers of 2,184 pounds (19½ hundredweights of 112 pounds each) and 2,340 pounds (19½ hundredweights of 120 pounds each). Pegolotti refers only to the fother of 2,184 pounds, and his explanation of its composition differs from the above. He merely compares its weight to the sum of 6 sacks of wool: "Piombo vi si vende a ciarrea, e ogni ciarrea si è di peso la montanza del peso in somma di 6 sacca peso di lana, di chiovi 52 per 1 sacco e di libbre 7 per 1 chiovo."[13] Hence, 52 cloves × 7 pounds = 364 pounds (1 sack of wool) × 6 = 2,184 pounds.

Again, however, there is the problem of the exact weight in grains. The various fothers could vary in grains as follows:

TABLE 4

Fothers	Weight in Troy Grains	
	Avoirdupois (7,000/lb.)	*Mercantile* (6,750/lb.)
(1) 2,100 pounds =	14,700,000	14,175,000[14]
(2) 2,184 pounds =	15,288,000	14,742,000[15]
(3) 2,340 pounds =	16,380,000	15,795,000[16]

In the case of the fother which Pegolotti discussed (line 2), there is a difference of 78 avoirdupois pounds (546,000 grains divided by 7,000/lb.) depending on which system was used. The differences in lines 1 and 3 are 75 and 83.57 avoirdupois pounds respectively.

Wool was sold in England by the clove and the sack. The standard weight for the clove was 7 pounds, but occasionally cloves of 6½ and 8 pounds were used.[17] The latter weight was the standard in Essex and Suffolk. Pegolotti mentions the 7 pound clove which was 1/52 sack of wool.[18] The clove was more often called a "nail," and it usually appeared in medieval tabulations of weights and measures as one-half the standard stone of 14 pounds. It was also employed in weighing cheese and metals.

The sack was a capacity measure for wool and certain other goods. The sack of wool generally contained 2 weys or 13 tods[19] or 52 cloves or 26 stone, each stone of 14 pounds, and it was equal to 1/12 last[20] of wool or 364 pounds. This sack was defined by statute in 25 Edward III.[21] Prior to this there was occasional use of another wool sack weighing 350 pounds, and containing 28 stone, each stone weighing 12½ pounds.[22] In addition, the 364 pound sack was established as the standard according to the avoirdupois scale, whereas the former sack of 350 pounds used the mercantile system. Hence, the difference between them was more than 14 pounds:

TABLE 6

| | Weight in Troy Grains | |
Stone	Avoirdupois (7,000/lb.)	Mercantile (6,750/lb.)
(1) 350 pounds =	——	2,362,500[23]
(2) 364 pounds =	2,548,000	——

The difference, thus, is 26½ avoirdupois pounds (185,500 grains divided by 7,000/lb.).

NOTES

1. In addition to these four, Pegolotti mentions the bale (*balla*), seam (*quartiere, quartieri*), gallon (*gallone*), dicker (*dacra, atra, acra*), piece (*pezza, pannus*), pound (*libbra*), and ounce (*oncia*). (Detailed descriptions of these weights and measures can be found in Ronald Edward Zupko, *A Dictionary of English Weights and Measures from Anglo-Saxon Times to the Nineteenth Century* (U. of Wisconsin Press, 1968). The dictionary also includes a long bibliography which will supply the interested scholar with additional source materials on the metrological units mentioned in this paper.) Pegolotti spent the years 1317 to 1321 directing the various commercial operations of the Bardi Bank's branch office in London. He devoted his time to

authorizing private loans; accepting deposits; transferring funds; and supervising the buying, selling, and shipping of merchandise. The dating of the manuscript is somewhat difficult. Colonel Henry Yule in "Notices of the Land Route to Cathay and of Asiatic Trade in the First Half of the Fourteenth Century By Francis Balducci Pegolotti," in *Cathay and the Way Thither* (London, Hakluyt Society, 1914), 140, says that *La Pratica Della Mercatura* was probably written sometime between 1340 and 1343, but no more precise dating than this can be established.

2. Francesco Balducci Pegolotti, *La Pratica Della Mercatura*, ed. by Allan Evans (Cambridge, 1936), p. 254. The only area in which a hundredweight of 104 pounds was found was in Kent, and there it was only used to weigh filberts. Equally unique was the hundredweight of 120 pounds for it was only used as a weight for iron at the king's scales in Cornwall. The standard hundredweight for iron—as well as most other items—was 112 pounds.

3. The confusion between the hundred and the hundredweight stems partly from the fact that many of the following words were used for both of these metrological units without any distinction being made for quantity or weight: bloma, bloom, c., *cent, cental, centanarium, cente, centeine, centena, centeyne, centum,* c. wayght, c. wayte, c. weyght, c. wyte, hundredlong, *hundredus, hundreth, hundrethe, hundrid,* hundridwaight, *hundrith, kintal, kintall, quintal, quintale, quintall, quintallus* and *quintile.* The italicized words are the ones that could designate either the hundred or the hundredweight.

4. Medieval English systems of weight were based either on the barley or on the wheat grain. The pennyweight—containing a certain number of grains such as 24 barley corns in the troy system and 32 wheat grains in the tower—was the unit upon which the larger weights such as the scruple, drachm, ounce, and pound were formed. The troy pound, for example, used in weighing precious stones, gold, silk, silver, bread, electuaries, and grain, contained 5,760 grains (barley corns): 240 pennyweights of 24 grains each or 12 ounces of 480 grains, each ounce containing 20 pennyweights of 24 grains each. The tower pound, used in weighing the same items as the troy pound until it was abolished by Henry VIII in 1527, contained 5,400 troy grains. Actually this pound contained 7,680 wheat grains which were usually converted to the barley corn scale as follows: 32 wheat grains = 22.5 barley corns. Therefore, (1) 32×20 pennyweights $\times 12$ ounces = 7,680 wheat grains; or, (2) 22.5×20 pennyweights $\times 12$ ounces = 5,400 troy grains. Hence, since the number of pounds in the hundredweight varied from 100 to 120, and since these pounds varied depending on whether the mercantile or avoirdupois systems were employed, the actual number of grains in the larger units varied appreciably.

5. Or 998,400 wheat grains.

6. Or 1,075,200 wheat grains.

7. Or 19,968,000 wheat grains.

8. Or 21,504,000 wheat grains.

9. The fother will appear in the English documents as follows: car, carat, carecta, carectata, carectatum, carrat, carrata, carrect, carrecta, carrectata, carretate, carriata, cartload, carucata, char, charge, charre, char-

ret, charrus, coppia, draught, ffocher, ffother, focher, fodder, foder, fodre, foother, fothir, fothre, fothyr, foulder, fouther, fouthre, fozer, fudder, futher, lade, load, loyde, plaustrata, waggon-load, and wain-load.

10. The fotmal was a weight used for lead which always weighed 70 pounds and was equal to 1/30 fother. It was usually described in the documents as the following will show: (1) H. G. Richardson and G. O. Sayles, ed., *Fleta* (Selden Society Publication, 2; London, 1955), p. 119: "Item charrus plumbi consistit ex xxx. fotmellis et quodlibet fotmellum continet vj. petras minus duabus libris, et quelibet libra ex pondere xxv.s."; (2) Hubert Hall, ed., "Select Tracts and Table Books Relating to English Weights and Measures (1100–1742) in *Camden Miscellany* (London, 1929), p. 41, 11: "Fet asauer ke la charge de plum est de xxx fotmaux, et checun fotmal est de vi pers, ii lib. meyns; checun pere est de xii lib., et checun lib. est de xx[v] sol. de peis; la sume de lib. en le fotmal, lxx lib."

11. The stone of 14 pounds was the most common, but stone of 5, 8, 12, 12½, 13½, 15, 16, 17, 20, and 32 pounds were also used.

12. The wey of lead, wool, cheese, flax, and tallow usually weighed 182 pounds, but many lesser and greater amounts were used such as 175 pounds for lead (1/12 fother of 2,100 pounds or 30 fotmals of 70 pounds each); 180 pounds (15 stone of 12 pounds each); 224 pounds (32 cloves of 7 pounds each or 2 hundredweights of 112 pounds each) for cheese everywhere in England except in Essex, Suffolk, and Norfolk; 256 pounds for cheese in Norfolk; 256 pounds (32 cloves of 8 pounds each) or 336 pounds (42 cloves of 8 pounds each) in Essex and Suffolk. The names for the wey in the documents are these: load, pece, peisa, pensa, pensum, pesa, peysa, pisa, pise, pond, pondus, pund, vaga, waga, way, waya, waye, weigh, wettha, weya, weye, and weyght.

13. Pegolotti, *La Pratica Della Mercatura*, 255.

14. Or 20,160,000 wheat grains.

15. Or 20,966,400 wheat grains.

16. Or 22,464,000 wheat grains. Of course, the larger the fother, the wider variation there will be between the avoirdupois and mercantile scales.

17. In the English documents the clove appears under the following names: clava, clave, clavis, clavus, claw, clawe, cleaue, clou, cloue, half-stone, nagel, nail, naile, and nayle.

18. Pegolotti, *La Pratica Della Mercatura*, p. 254: (1) "Lana si vende in Londra e per tutta l'isola d'Inghilterra a sacco, di chiovi 52 pesi per l sacco, e ogni chiovo pesa libbre 7 d'Inghilterra"; p. 151: (2) "Sacca 1 di lana al peso di Londra d'Inghilterra, ch'è chiovi 52 in Londra, fae in Vinegia libbre 330 grosse"; p. 223: (3) "Sacca 1 di lana in Londra, che è chiovi 52 in Londra, fa in Bruggia sacco 1 di lana."

19. The tod (todd, todde, tood) was a weight of 28 pounds used for wool and equal to 1/13 sack or 1/26 sarpler.

20. The last was a capacity measure used for a variety of goods. A last of wool contained 12 sacks of 24 weys and weighed 4,368 pounds. The versatility of the last can be seen in Table 5.

21. Pegolotti merely describes this standard sack as containing 52 cloves, each clove weighing 7 pounds.

22. Richardson and Sayles, *Fleta*, 119: ". . . et tales xij libre et xxviij petre faciunt vnum saccum lane. . . ." Fleta also informs us that his weights were based on the mercantile system. The standard sack was described as follows: Rev. John Strachey, Rev. John Pridden and Edward Upham, ed., *Rotuli Parliamentorum* (vol. II, London, 1832), 133: "C'est assavoir, xiiii livres pur la piere, et xxvi pieres pur le sak . . ."; Hall, *Select Tracts*, 10: "Et due waye faciunt unam Saccum. Et duodecim sacci continent le last."

23. Or 3,360,000 wheat grains.

TABLE 5

Product	Contents of Last
(1) herrings	10 thousand, each thousand of 10 hundred, and each hundred of 120 (or 12,000 in all)
(2) leather or hides	20 dickers, each dicker containing 10 hides (or 200 in all)
(3) iron	12 barrels on land and 13 aboard ship
(4) flax	6 hundred bonds
(5) bowstaves	6 hundred
(6) grain	10 seams or 80 bushels
(7) gunpowder	24 barrels, each barrel weighing 1 hundredweight of 100 pounds
(8) salmon	6 pipes or 504 gallons fully packed
(9) salt	10 weys, each wey of 42 bushels (or 420 bushels in all)
(10) barrel fish	12 barrels
(11) feathers	1,700 pounds
(12) raisins	24 barrels

THE CROSSBOW IN THE NAUTICAL REVOLUTION OF THE MIDDLE AGES

FREDERIC C. LANE
Brandeis University

The weapons and body armor used by seamen are of importance in maritime history in two connections: the types of ships in use and the size of the crews were affected by the efficacy of various kinds of weapons, and the status of seamen as a class was affected by the ownership of the arms and armor they used.

A change of type within the category of round ships, that is, vessels dependent entirely on sails, occurred in the Mediterranean during the first half of the fourteenth century. The leading type of round ship at the beginning of the century had side rudders and two masts, lateen-rigged. By the second half of the century it had been replaced by the cog, a type carrying its rudder on the sternpost and with one large square sail on the main mast. The change was accompanied by a reduction in the size of the crews legally required. The single square sail required fewer hands than the large lateen sails, and this is one explanation of the smaller crews permitted.[1] But another explanation is that bowmen were becoming more important in naval warfare. The period of transition from the two-masted lateener to the cog is also the period in which the supremacy of the knight was shattered by the longbow in England and the crossbow on the continent.[2] The cog was a highsided vessel which gave more protection and more range to bowmen.[3] As their weapons were made mechanically more perfect and more persons became skilled in their use, battles between ships were to an increasing extent decided by bowmen. In naval contests there was an increasing need for men skilled in the use of the crossbow and for armor made with steel plates able to stop the arrows or bolts of the bowmen; and there was less necessity than hitherto of having a large crew armed with lances, javelins, swords, shields, and daggers ready for boarding the enemy or repelling assault. The reduction in size of crew reflected a change in military as well as nautical technology between 1250 and 1350.

The change in armor and weapons is reflected in the Venetian maritime legislation, although this source may exaggerate Venetian conservatism in adopting innovations. The code which Doge Ranier Zeno issued in 1255 is clearly prior to the transition in naval architecture. It provided that each seaman, even the lowest paid, was to be equipped with sword, shield, dagger, three lances or javelins, helmet or cap, and a battle jacket (*zupam*). The mate or anyone else who received more than 40 pounds was to have in addition a crossbow with 100 arrows (or bolts) and an additional piece of body armor.[4]

There is no reason to assume that any of the body armor was of chain mail. Leather hardened by boiling or by soaking in heated wax was extensively used and the law specified that the helmet or cap could be of either iron or leather. The battle jacket of the ordinary seaman was probably what is called "soft armor," that is, quilted fabric or leather not subjected to any hardening process. Strips or horn or metal may have been sewed into it at appropriate places, but not to such an extent as to interfere with freedom of movement.[5] Battle jackets (*zupam*) "suitable and convenient for being worn continuously" were recommended, more than a half century later, to be sure, by Sanuto Torsellinus.[6]

In addition to the arms of the crew, for which they were responsible, the code contained clauses requiring the two-decked *nave* to carry additional weapons for which the owners were responsible.[7] Presumably these weapons and armor were to be used in part by the ship captain and other owners who might be on board, in part by traveling merchants, and in part by extra capable members of the crew. These clauses make no mention of sword, dagger, or battle jacket—the most personal of weapons—but the ship-owners were required to have on board two to eight sets of extra arms, the number of sets depending on the size of the vessel. A set consisted of a hood or camail, an apron, a shield, a helmet or cap with face guard, a crossbow, and a hundred javelins. The hoods (*capirones*) may have been much like the camail of chain armor, but probably of leather, fitting over the head under the hat or helmet, or possibly attached to it, and falling loosely over the shoulders. The apron (*panzeras*) hanging from the shoulders would protect the rest of the torso.

Two kinds of crossbows were required, both made of horn. One was a "stirrup bow" (*de strevo or strepa*) bent by placing the feet against a brace called the "stirrup" at the end of the bow and pulling the cord tight with a hook; the other was drawn tight by a pulley or crank (*de torno vel de pesarola*). One hundred and fifty arrows were ordered for each stirrup bow, fifty for the other kind, presumably because it fired more slowly.[8] The number of bows required as part of the armament was modest: three on a vessel of 100 to 150 tons; eight or ten on what was for the time a very large merchantman of 400 tons.

For the smaller one-decked vessels called *tarretes* different rules were made. In the code which Zeno made especially for the *tarrete,* each was required to have eight bows, two worked by cranks and furnished with 100 arrows or bolts each and the others furnished with 300 arrows each. These vessels were also to carry 300 javelins, and two iron weapons for each owner, and the seamen were to have the same personal arms as on the two-decked nave.[9] Compared to what was required of larger vessels, Zeno's regulations seem unrealistic. In 1279, rules to provide one-decked vessels with weapons made no mention of bows. Each was to carry a case full of stones suitable for throwing by slings or by hand and they were to be kept in some place where they could be reached when needed. On each side of the vessel there were to be at least three "frames" (*spontalos*) and two in the poop. I presume these were frames or slings of some kind for throwing stones. The shipowners were also ordered to supply for each seaman a lance of ash or beechwood 15 feet long, half with long blades and half with hooks.[10]

Most of the new regulations imposed on the shipowners at the end of the century concerned body armor and weapons used in close combat. In 1291 on the advice of the enforcing officials (Ufficiales super mercantionibus Levantis) hats *(capellas)* were substituted for hoods or caps *(capirones).*[11] In 1283 when special arrangements were made with the Arsenal to supply arms for galley crews, the arsenal was ordered to immediately replenish its supply so as to have a reserve of 2500 battle axes, 2500 halbards, and 500 long lances. On this occasion the commune ordered in addition 50 iron hats, 50 surcoats *(vernachiones)* each containing 8 pounds of cotton with the symbols of St. Mark on the front and back, and 50 Slavonian surcoats or battle jackets *(clippeos)* well furnished with iron plates.[12] In 1300 (after the second Genoese war), in arming of galleys (to go to Apulia) we find different body armor. Each galley was to carry a large number of breast-plates with neck protectors and gauntlets, and a smaller number of surcoats together with hats, swords or battle axes, daggers, and shields.[13] The effect of the improved crossbows appears in the provision for more body armor composed of metal plates.

Bowmen do not appear as a separate category among the crew during the thirteenth century. Although bows are specified in 1280 among the extra arms of men receiving extra pay, and the mate was ordered to have two bows, whereas Zeno's code had only required him to have one, most of the new provisions made in 1280 about the arms which men were required to have in order to receive extra pay concerned body armor, namely breastplate and camail (*colarum*) and the relatively new type of helmet called a *bascinet*.[14] The first indication of bowmen as specialists is the requirement in 1290 that each vessel of any importance have on board a man who knew how to repair bows and their parts *(scilicet cordas, clavem, et nucem)*. He could be counted in making up the required number of seamen, and on certain vessels he was paid as much as the mate *(nauclerius)*.[15] Under this provision, specialized bowmen could be hired as part of the crew. Zeno's statute had specified that no knight or soldier *(milites)* could be counted in determining whether a vessel had on board the minimum crew required by law. Under the law of 1290 soldiers ignorant of sails and seamanship could be hired provided they were experts in the repair of bows as well as in their use, as many bowmen were.

After the second Genoese war there was clear reference to bowmen as a class of specialists. In specifying how merchant galleys were to be armed in 1302 the Senate ordered that each carry 30 bowmen out of a total crew of 180. They were to be chosen according to a system then in use in choosing bowmen for the war galleys. Delegated nobles visited the shooting butts located in various parts of Venice and picked the best shots. The skill of the bowman did not yet put him in a class distinctly superior to the oarsman. On the contrary, the ordinary bowmen were to be required to row when necessary in order to man three oars to a bench *(ad terzarolos)*.[16] Only slightly more specialization is implied in the arrangement recommended by Ramon Muntaner, a leader of the famous Catalan company of mercenaries and a participant in many naval battles. In the chronicle he wrote in 1325–1328 Muntaner advised that bowmen should not be obliged to row lest they lose their skill with the bow. "But when one of the oarsmen is tired or wants to eat or drink, the bowman can take his oar for a while."[17]

In 1331 round ships also were required to carry a certain number of bowmen, now clearly recognized as distinct. But their status with relation to the seamen was still in doubt. Whether they should eat with the sailors or at a separate mess was an open question which was left for the shipmaster and the seamen to decide.[18]

As the number of bowmen increased, the number of sailors decreased. The legally required crew was determined by the rating of size given the vessel officially, and in the thirteenth century it was ten men for each 100 milliaria. In 1331 a law was passed specifying that two out of every ten of the crew must be bowmen. The law included the clause "intelligendo esse decem quinque et a quinque supra," no doubt in order to provide for cases in which the required crew was not an exact multiple of ten. In practice it was interpreted to mean that each ship was to carry five seamen and two bowmen for each 100 milliaria of capacity. In 1362 this proportion was recognized and made legal while the number required was slightly reduced by basing it on a rating in botti instead of a rating in milliaria.[19] In 1400 only six men over 20 were required per 100 botti and one of them had to be a bowman.[20] The change in the composition of the crew was by then very considerable. In 1225 a vessel of about 250 tons was required to have five bows on board counting that of the mate and a total crew of 50, all over eighteen. In 1400 a vessel of that size required only 20 adult seamen, eight boys or apprentices, and four bowmen at least, a total of 32. The number of seamen skilled in handling sails had been cut in half, and the proportion of bowmen increased.

The change in the composition and size of crews may have occurred even before 1330, for the cog type had then been in use in the Mediterranean for about three decades and it was at Venice at least as early as 1315.[21] Moreover, the great value of crossbows in naval warfare must have been clearly established before the end of the thirteenth century. Muntaner gives vivid testimony to that effect in describing a naval battle during the war following the Sicilian vespers. The Catalan galleys were lashed together so that none might be cut out of the pack and they were well equipped with crossbows and other missile weapons. The French on their ships stood ready with sword in hand unable to do anything. After the decks of the French galleys were littered with dead and wounded, the Catalans untied their ships and attacked. Muntaner concluded. "I who have seen many battles tell you that the bowmen win many battles."[22]

Skill with crossbows was a Catalan specialty, according to Muntaner, but the Genoese bowmen were at the peak of their fame at the beginning of the fourteenth century.[23] Perhaps their losses of battles to the Genoese in the war of 1297–1299 spurred the Venetians to develop their own class of crossbowmen. Many improvements in the crossbow took place about that time,[24] and made it the most important missile weapon of naval warfare until the sixteenth century arquebus and cannon.

English and American readers about the Middle Ages have a tendency to depreciate the crossbow as an inferior weapon because they think of it in comparison with the longbow. At Crécy and Agincourt the longbow proved its superiority when in the hands of expert archers. But the expert archers needed for the longbow were found only in Britain and there only for a few generations. On shipboard, however, the longbow lost many of the advantages it enjoyed on land. Ability to place the archers in a row close together was less important on a ship. The slower fire of the crossbowmen was not so serious a disadvantage when they did not have to face charging horsemen. The weight of the crossbow could be rested on the ship's parapet, not on a clumsy stake or fork. Moreover the crossbowman could discharge his weapon while crouching and peering over the protecting side of the ship's castles or bulwark, whereas the archer had to expose himself by standing erect and at some distance from any protecting wall when he drew his bow.[25] All these characteristics made crossbowmen a particularly valuable kind of soldier to have on shipboard and especially on the slow-moving, high cogs.

Whether the members of the crew, be they bowmen or seamen, owned their own weapons affected considerably their pay and status. Indeed, in simple schemes of medieval society the upper class, namely the knights, are distinguished from the lower class, the peasants, by the knight's possession of horse and armor. Their superior arms permitted the knights to lord it over the farmers who had only their leather jerkins, axes, scythes, and flails. The status of the seamen was somewhere in between.

In the middle of the twelfth century most of the arms on board an ordinary merchantman were the personal property of seamen. Each possessed his own helmet, battle jacket, shield, sword, dagger, and javelins. What the shipowners were by law required to carry in addition was enough for only about one-tenth of the crew, even counting officers and owners as crew.[26] On sea as on land, battles were fought with weapons belonging to the men using them.[27] Between 1250 and 1350 more expensive kinds of armor became increasingly important. If the seamen could supply themselves with this armor, they could command higher pay and be less dependent on the ship captain or shipowners than would be the case if the latter became the owners of the armor and the crew sold only their labor. The government of Venice, although certainly controlled more by ship captains and shipowners than by ordinary seamen, at first legislated as if it was expected that, as more bows and more body armor became necessary, the seamen would provide them and would receive higher pay accordingly. The provisions of Zeno's code providing that seamen supply their own arms was reiterated in 1278 and reinforced by orders to the owners to withhold three pounds from the pay of each seaman who was not armed as required by law.[28] Zeno's code had distinguished between ordinary seamen receiving less than 40 pounds (for the year or voyage) and those receiving more. It required of the latter only an "apron" or breast plate and a crossbow. In 1280 added arms were required of those receiving 50 pounds or more. They were to have a cloak, breastplate, the new type of helmet called a *bascinet,* a camail or some kind of iron neck protector, as well as shield, sword, dagger, and crossbow. The higher the pay the more the arms required. A seaman receiving 90 to 100 pounds was to have in addition to all the above an apron or fauld as well as a breast plate, gauntlets, ten javelins, and two pikes each fifteen feet long. The law forbade the shipowners to pay such high wages except to men supplied with specified equipment.[29] It is doubtful that many were paid the highest rate, but that the law was not entirely an empty gesture appears from the specific amendment made to it in 1288 permitting bows of horn as well as wood and reducing the minimum number of arrows for each bow from 150 to 50.[30] Further evidence that in the 1280's the arms were the responsibility of the seamen was a provision included in some special measures taken to arm particular fleets. The Arsenal was to supply specified arms: axes, halbards, pikes, etc. They were to be kept by the treasurers of the galleys (*camerarius galearum*) in a separate room until needed. Only then they were to be given to the *galeoti* and each seaman who received arms was to give a pledge for their return and to pay rent for them to the Commune of 2 groats a month.[31] The law is important as a symptom of the seaman's responsibility for arming himself and as a symptom that he was having difficulty meeting that responsibility in view of the heavier weapons required.

Breakdown of seamen's responsibility for their own arms was avowed in a law of 1300 and much of the burden was shifted to the owners or galleymasters. It cited the responsibility of the seamen as the reason that "galleys leave devoid of arms." It provided that hereafter the galleymasters should be responsible for a long list of arms, perhaps not enough for all the crew, but sufficient for about 140 per galley, light arms as well as heavy arms. Some clauses reflect the transitional state of affairs: galley masters were not to dock the pay of crewmen who lacked arms for more than 3 groats a month (about two or three days pay), and if the galley masters did make that deduction the seamen were absolved of providing their own arms ("sint galeoti absoluti ab armis portandis"), i.e., they would not be fined by the government. If the official inspectors found that the required arms were not aboard, it was the galley master *(patronus)* who was fined. But if the seaman wanted to bring his own arms, the galley-master could not charge him freight for carrying them, i.e., could not dock his pay.[32]

The arrangement made in 1300 was considered a burden on the galley masters; in compensation they were permitted to load more cargo and sink the galley an inch deeper in the water. In 1303 there was a twofold responsibility for sidearms: the galley masters were subject to a fine of 10 pounds for each crewman they hired who lacked the stipulated arms; and the crewmen could be fined 2 groats each.[33] On these galleys, heavy body armor (cuirass with iron collars or camails, and with gauntlets) was provided for about half the crew, whereas Zeno's code had provided extra armor for only about one out of ten. Of course, Zeno's code was for merchantmen, the round ships commonly called unarmed ships, not galleys. But by 1331 more of the heavier body armor was being required on the round ships for two out of ten or two out of seven. The heavy armor was for the use of the bowmen, for these "marines," now distinct from "sailors," were required to own only their own bows.[34]

How much the lighter armor which tradition had required of all seamen—helmet or hat, battle jacket, sword, shield, and dagger—was provided by the seamen themselves after 1331 is yet to be determined. The law passed that year, renewed indefinitely, made ship captain, bowman, and crew all responsible for fines which the inspecting officials could lay on them for violations. Evidence of a general depression of the status of seamen during the first decades of the fourteenth century creates a presumption that the shipowners supplied the arms which enabled an ordinary member of the crew to pass inspection, or, if the arms came from the state arsenal, paid it the rental and deducted that amount from the seaman's wages.

Among the signs of a general decline in the status of seamen at Venice in that period is the law of 1329 imposing imprisonment as the penalty for jumping ship.[35] Even more significant are the many provisions concerning the terms on which seamen imprisoned for debts could be released from jail to earn on the galleys the wages with which to pay their debts.[36] There are more signs of that kind of debt slavery among oarsmen than among sailors, to be sure, but the changes in the maritime laws made to strengthen the disciplinary authority of the ship captains were phrased in general terms.[37]

Signs of difficulty with maritime labor in the first half of the fourteenth century and of discontent among seamen are by no means peculiar to Venice. Genoese seamen were accustomed to a discipline harsher than that on thirteenth-century Venetian ships,[38] but became unruly as the Genoese commune depended less and less on conscripting its citizens and more and more on mercenary crews. It was a sailors' revolt which made Simone Boccanegra Doge of Genoa in 1339.[39] In 1345 the bloody massacre of upper classes in Salonica by the "zealots" was led by the sailors' guild.[40] In Venice there was never any revolt of seamen. Even though there was reason for discontent among ordinary seamen as their status was lowered, the aristocracy of ship captains and merchants who ruled Venice kept unshaken control.

Many factors not here considered help to explain the deterioration between 1250 and 1350 in the legal and economic position of ordinary crew members. Transformations in the economic situation, in commercial techniques, and in the political structure of Venice were involved as well as changes in the nautical and military arts. Among the new techniques which had results affecting the other changes was the improvement in the crossbow. It created the need for heavier armor and more specialized fighting men and consequently depressed the status of such ordinary seamen as were unable to equip themselves and acquire special skills either as fighting men or as sailors and navigators.

NOTES

1. A one-sided view, ignoring the extent to which the size of crews was for most centuries before the nineteenth determined more by the needs of defense than by those of navigation, was presented in my *Venetian Ships and Shipbuilders of the Renaissance* (Baltimore, Md., 1934), pp. 35–40 and in the revised edition, *Navires et constructeurs à Venise pendant la Renaissance* (École Pratique des Hautes Études, VI Section, Oeuvres étrangères, V, Paris, S.E.V.P.E.N., 1965), pp. 33–37. For a broader view see my Discussion in *The Journal of Economic History*, XXIV, 4 (December, 1964), 465–568 on Robert S. Lopez, "Market Expansion, the Case of Genoa."

2. Piero Pieri, *Il Rinascimento e la crisi militare italiane* (Turin, 1952), pp. 217, 223, 273–5; Ferdinand Lot, *L'art militaire et les armées au moyen âge en Europe et dans la Proche Orient* (2 vols., Paris, 1946), II, 424.

3. L.G.C. Laughton, "The cog," a note in *The Mariner's Mirror*, XLVI (February, 1960), 69–70.

4. *Gli Statuti Marittimi Veneziani*, eds. Predelli e Sacerdoti (Venice, 1903) and in *Archivio Veneto*), Statuta navium del Zeno, cap. 27. The additional body armor of the mate is called "panzeram vel lamam de ferro." In

view of the fact that no breastplate is mentioned in the code otherwise, it is reasonable to suppose that this refers to an embryonic breastplate, although I have generally translated *panzeram* as "apron." Later laws refer in similar context not to *panzeram* but to *corazzam*. See below, notes 13 and 14.

5. On armor in general see Claude Blair, *European Armour* (New York, 1959), chaps. 1–3; *Enciclopedia italiana*, vol. IV (Milan, 1929), 487–98; Charles J. Ffoulkes and Sir John Fortescue, "Medieval Arms and Warfare" in J. A. Hammerton, ed., *Universal History of the World*, vol. V; Charles Ffoulkes, *Armor and Weapons* (Oxford, 1909), and John Hewitt, *Ancient-Armour and Weapons in Europe*, 3 vols. (London, 1860). Charles W. C. Oman, *The Art of War in the Middle Ages*, 378–1515 (2 vols., London and New York, 1924), II, 3–9.

6. Marinus Sanutus Torsellus, *Liber Secretorum Fidelium Crucis super Terrae Sanctae recuperatione et conservatione (Gesta Dei per Francos sive orientalium expeditionem*, Hanover, 1611), p. 59.

7. *Gli Statuti*, eds. Predelli e Sacerdoti, cap. 29.

8. *Ibid.;* Hewitt, II, 276; C. J. Ffoulkes in *Univ. Hist.*, V, 2931; and Henri Stein, *Archers d'autrefois; archers d'aujourd'hui* (Paris, 1925), p. 57.

9. *Gli statuti*, Statuta tarretarum (16), (18).

10. *Deliberazioni del Maggior Consiglio di Venezia*, ed. Roberto Cessi (Accademia dei Lincei, Commissione per gli Atti delle Assemblee Costituzionali Italiane, serie 3, sezione 1), vol. II (Bologna, 1931), p. 218. Some aid in its interpretation comes from ASV, Capitolare dei Consoli dei Mercanti, caps. 39, 93.

11. *Deliberazioni del Maggior Consiglio*, ed. Cessi, III, 301.

12. *Ibid.*, III, 17.

13. ASV, Avogaria Comunis, Deliberazioni del Maggior Consiglio, Magnus, f. 1; Senato Misti, Reg. 1, f. 186–7.

14. *Delib. M.C.*, ed. Cessi, II, 70; III, 210. None of this legislation seems to have been effective. See below notes 29–31.

15. *Ibid.*, III, 262.

16. *Capitolare dei Signore di Notte*, ed. F. Nani-Mocenigo (Venice, 1877), Item no. 125, Nov. 3, 1303; ASV, Senato Misti, reg. 1, ff. 186–7. Camillo Manfroni, *Storia della marina italiana dal trattato di Ninfeo alla caduta di Costantinopoli* (1261–1453), Pt. 1 (Livorno, 1902), p. 214, n. 3, says that the Venetians attributed their defeat at Curzola to their lack of bowmen and took the measures of 1301–1303 as a result in an effort to develop a corps of Venetian bowmen. On the *bersalia* in each *sestieri* of Venice see, Pompeo Molmenti, *La storia di Venezia nella vita privata* (3 vols., Bergamo, 1927), I, 170–173.

17. Ramon Muntaner, *Chronicle*, chap. 130. The translation by Lady Goodenough, Hakluyt Society, series II, vol. 47 (1920) seems questionable in some places, e.g., p. 346, when compared with that of J. A. Buchon in vols. 5 and 6 of *Collection des chroniques nationales francaises.*

18. ASV, Maggior Consiglio, Deliberazioni, Spiritus, copia, f. 97 v.

19. *Ibid*, Novella, f. 53.

20. Senato Misti, reg. 45, f. 43. In the ASV, Capitolare dei Consoli dei Mercanti, cap. 115, there dated 1300, is really a copy of this law of 1400, which then appears over again as cap. 247.

21. The first mention of a "cocha" I have found in Venetian records is in 1315. See Maggior Consiglio, Deliberazioni, Clericus Civicus, copia, f. 21 t.

22. Muntaner's chronicle as cited, cap. 130.

23. Pieri, as cited, p. 223, 217, 273–5.

24. Ffoulkes, in *Univ. Hist.*, V, 2931; Stein, *Archers*, p. 70.

25. Stein, *Archers*, p. 57.

26. *Gli Statuti marittimi*, Zeno's statuta navium, ca. XXVII, XXVIII, and XXX. These are entered also in the capitolare of the Capitolare dei Levanti, ASV, Codice Brera, 263 ff. 36–37.

27. Although the statuta navium did not apply to the galleys, the main warships, the law of 1300 cited below in note 32 clearly implies that the seamen on galleys were also required to have their own weapons. Of course battleships carried many extra fighting men, including knights owning their own arms.

28. *Delib. M.C.*, ed. Cessi, II, 69–70.

29. *Ibid.*, II, p. 70. The *capirones* and *pancieras* in the statuta, whatever their precise meaning, certainly seem to refer to armor giving more protection than the *zupam* required for the ordinary seaman.

30. *Ibid.*, III, 210.

31. *Ibid.*, III, 17. In 1278 also, crews obtained some at least of their arms by renting them from the Arsenal. *Ibid.* II, 244.

32. ASV, Maggior Consiglio, Deliberazioni, Magnus, copia, f. 32, and in Avogaria Comunis, Magnus, f. 1 dated Dec. 18, 1300.

33. Senato Misti, reg. 1, ff. 186–7.

34. Maggior Consiglio, Deliberazione, Spiritus, ff. 44–5; Novella, f. 53. Cod. Brera, 263, f. 35; Capitolare des Consoli dei Mercanti, busta 1.

35. *Ibid.*, f. 37. This provision was then included as chap. 69 on Book VI of the Venetian Statuti.

36. For example, in the *Capitolare dei Signori di Notte*, above cited, Items nos. 266, 272.

37. Chaps. 69, 71, 76 of Libro VI of the *Statuti Veneziani*

38. A Lattes, *Il diritto marittimo privato nelle carte ligure dei secoli xii e xiii* (Rome, 1939), pp. 40–41.

39. Roberto S. Lopez, *Storia delle colonie genovesi nel Mediterraneo* (Bologna, 1938), p. 329; Vito Vitale, *Brevario della storia di Genova* (2 vols., Genoa, 1955), I, 102–3.

40. Ernest Barker, *Social and Political Thought in Byzantium* (Oxford, 1957), p. 186.

FAMILY SOLIDARITY IN
MEDIEVAL ITALIAN HISTORY*

DAVID HERLIHY

University of Wisconsin

This paper is an attempt to describe, in rather breathless fashion, some few of the changes which seem to have occurred in the structure, the cohesiveness, the solidarity of the Italian family in the course of the Middle Ages until the fifteenth century. This is a large task for a brief space, and I am well aware of the embarrassing inadequacies of the finished product. We must leave untouched major aspects of family history, and must support some affirmations with what will seem to many anemic data and skinny arguments. Still, by way of apologizing for this effort, it seems that there is value in attempting to bring our scattered information concerning the medieval Italian family into a composite picture, however partial, preliminary, and short-lived that picture may be. For one major difficulty in studying the Italian medieval family—we might have said the family everywhere in Europe—is the paucity of broad interpretations, of syntheses, of ideas really, concerning its character and development. It benefits the researcher to have some sort of synthesis, some frame of reference, some ideas even if faulty, which he can set against his own discoveries, and which he can reinforce, repair, or discard at his will.

To understand the difficulties confronting the historian of the Italian family is first to say a word about the peculiar intractability of the sources. The problem, unusual in medieval history, is not really a dearth of documents. Italy in the Middle Ages loved, as she still loves, the written record. Almost any document which tells us something about economic and social history can tell us something about the family. If we know only what a man was called, we know at least what his parents thought a good name for their child, and even that is something. Roman, Lombard, and ecclesiastical laws, and numerous communal statutes, tell us much about the family, and the status, rights, and responsibilities of its members.[1] To illuminate the family in its daily affairs, we have a rich series of private acts, chiefly land conveyances, which begins from about the middle eighth century and which with time grows ever more abundant.[2] These documents show us, to be sure, what we might call the public life of the family, and tell us very little about relationships formed or sentiments felt within the privacy of the home. Then, from the late thirteenth century, light penetrates into the heart of the Italian households. Of the many sources which cast this light, perhaps the most remarkable are the family *Ricordi*—recordances, memoirs, or domestic chronicles— which were usually composed by the paterfamilias for the private instruction of his descendants.[3] They were typically meant for their eyes only, and the historian is never more favored than when he can read documents he was never supposed to see. These *Ricordi* have survived by the hundreds; the best of them are in essence transcribed family archives, in which the father dutifully recorded the lands and animals, partners and profits, sons or daughters, he gained or lost. Many of the authors felt compelled to include sententious moralizations along with citing the price of properties. The good advice may or may not have profited their sons and heirs, but it certainly profits historians.

The real problem is, therefore, not a shortage of sources. Rather it is finding in this large and heterogenous mass of data a sound basis for generalization. The historian of the medieval family finds it too easy to adduce support for his ideas, but he finds it very hard to be sure that what he thinks he sees really represents the central trend in family history, and not the incidental, accidental, or the freakish. Our data, in my opinion, must be subject to some sort of statistical screening, even for the early Middle Ages, if only to save us from our own, uncontrolled impressions.

We have said that few ideas circulate at present concerning the history of the medieval Italian family. But there is one idea, old but still pervasive in its influence. It is implicit in most studies by legal historians.[4] Marc Bloch, in the sections on the family in his *Feudal Society,* essentially respects it.[5] For want of a better title, we can call this now venerable interpretation of family history in the Middle Ages the theory of progressive nuclearization.

In its essential features, this reconstruction maintains that in the early Middle Ages, in Italy and everywhere in Europe, the dominant type of household was very large, including many "nuclei" or constituent families—married sons, married brothers, in-laws and more distant relatives, and servants. In the Latin sources of the early Middle Ages, this enlarged household is encountered as the *fara, generatio, genealogia,* or *linea*; in later vernacular sources, it appears usually as the *consorteria* or *legnaggio.*[6] Sociologists would probably call this great household a "corporate" or "combined" family.[7] Both moral and material ties reinforced the cohesiveness of the corporate household of the early Middle Ages. Each member had a heavy ethical obligation to protect and aid his fellows. If a family member was injured or killed, his relatives would demand vengeance for him. The code of the vendetta, very strong in Italy, thus reflects the great moral solidarity of this supposedly primitive household. In property matters, sons would often preserve the integrity of their patrimony, and manage it as a single, undivided economic unity. This common ownership of property made the great household a *consorteria*, a word hard to render into English, but which we shall call the consortial family.

Still according to this theory of progressive nuclearization, at a certain point in medieval history, identified by Bloch and others as the thirteenth century, the solidarity of the great household began to weaken, and its constituent families gradually acquired a new measure of independence. By the end of the Middle Ages, the dominant type of family was not yet the "autonomous nuclear family" of most modern societies, but it had become something similar to it. The end product of this evolution, again to use a sociological term, would probably be best called the "bilateral extended family." Husband and wife lived alone with their children, but they still retained close ties with their blood relatives, and hence the family was "extended" on the sides of both spouses. This type of family, supposedly the product of the late medieval or Renaissance periods, remains characteristic of and perhaps dominant in Italian society today.

This notion of progressive nuclearization of family structure in the late Middle Ages is simple, clear, and undoubtedly has much of value in it. But there are difficulties too. It is very hard to trace this evolution in contemporary documents. Even Marc Bloch had to resort to rather confused chronological citations, in order to illustrate what he took to be the central movement of medieval family history. For example, to show the great solidarity of the family in the first feudal age, which supposedly ends about 1100, he cited the last testament of a rich Florentine, Velluto di Buonchristiano.[8] Wounded and dying, Velluto was so committed to the code of the vendetta that he offered a special bequest to whoever would avenge him. But the will is dated 1310, and there is evident incongruity in taking an example from the fourteenth century to illustrate the family *mores* of the early Middle Ages, or from the society of a great commercial capital to show the behavior of the warrior, rural classes.

Perhaps the most evident weakness with the concept of progressive nuclearization is the assumption that this movement toward nuclear families really was, or had to be, progressive. The same mistaken notion—that medieval social change always moved in one direction, and that positions once obtained were never lost—has for years made it difficult for historians to accept, for example, the existence of an economic depression or reversal in the late Middle Ages, particularly one that lasted for a century.[9] The history of the Italian family in the Middle Ages, I submit, must also be reconstructed, without prejudicing our conclusions from the start by assuming that the movement towards smaller households was unidirectional and irreversible. We should be open to the possibilities that in family history, as in other areas of social history, there may be flux and reflux, consolidation and nuclearization, with neither characteristic winning a final victory.

Let us look again at the history of the medieval Italian family. To measure its cohesiveness even in the early Middle Ages, we have one kind of data which does allow some sort of statistical screening: the rich series of land conveyances already described. In identifying a piece of property, the charters will usually name the owners of land contiguous to it—churches, monasteries, individual lords and, important for our purposes, consortial families. Some 90,000 such references can be extracted from published documents antedating the year 1200, and hence our statistical sample is reasonably sound.[10]

Consortial families are easily identifiable especially in Tuscan and central-Italian sources. Their lands are named with a peculiar terminology: *terra Gherardinga, terra Chunimandinga,* and the like. Here is the surprising point. Who searches among our thousands of Tuscan and central-Italian landlords for such households in the eighth and ninth, and through most of the tenth centuries, searches in vain. To find in our catalogue of owners our first certain references to property owned by a *consorteria,* we must wait until the last quarter of the tenth century, and only in the eleventh century do these references become common. The list on the following page shows the first reference to consortial property from some of the major documentary collections of Tuscany and central Italy.[11]

It may be, of course, that before the late tenth century, the large, corporate or consortial household was identified with such phrases as the "sons of N." or the "heirs of N." But we can also inspect our inventory of owners to see how common a practice it was for

	Year		Source
Lucca	975	terra Ciscanise (?)	*Memorie e documenti per servire all'istoria di Lucca*, IV, 2 (Lucca, 1836), no. 1458
	983	terra Gherardinga	*Ibid.* no. 1589.
	993	terra Fralminga	*Ibid.* no. 1689.
	999	terra Rolandinga terra Chunimandinga	*Ibid.* no. 1742.
	1009	terra Gherardinga	*Regesto del capitolo di Lucca* ed. Guidi & Parenti, no. 75.
Pisa	988	terra Martiscana	*Regestum pisanum*, ed. Caturegli, no. 78.
Pistoia	1038	terra Taibertinga	*Libro croce*, ed. Santoli, no. 90
Populonia	1079	terra Tedicinga terra Ubertinga	*Archivio Storico Italiano*, XVIII (1873), pp. 209–224, no. 18.
Coltibuono	1024	terra Recinise	*Regesto di Coltibuono*, ed. Pagliai, no. 20.
Farfa	1030??	terra Adelmarisca	*Regesto di Farfa*, ed. Giorgi and Balzani, no. 733.

such heirs to keep their patrimony undivided. References to unnamed sons and heirs as joint property owners are, again, quite rare in the early Middle Ages. For Italy as a whole, the number of sons or heirs who appear among the contiguous owners was only 7 percent in the eighth century (21 out of 308), 10 per cent in the ninth century (179 out of 1753) and still 10 per cent in the first three quarters of the tenth century (555 out of 5385).[12] From that time, however, the numbers increase, as shown in the following table:

	Lay Owners (Total)	Consortial Owners	Percent
976–1000	3575	556	15
1001–1025	4724	891	21
1026–1050	5134	1012	19
1051–1075	4099	853	21
1076–1100	4640	1007	22

Source: *Traditio*, XVIII (1962), pp. 116–20.

By the end of the eleventh century, in other words, at least by this measure, it was three times more common for sons to leave their inheritance undivided than it had been in the eighth century.[13] We find, in other words, not a progressive nuclearization, but a progressive consolidation, of the family in the eleventh century. The great households, which play so large a role in Italian history in the central Middle Ages, do not seem, in other words, to represent survivals from much distant times. This may sound surprising, but it is not inconsistent with what we know of the eleventh century, and of the profound reorganizations then affecting Italian social life at every level. Rural lords—*seniores, domini,* or *langobardi*—gathered into groups or associations, which functioned like collective seigneuries.[14] Above all, this age witnessed the birth of the urban communes. Amid the coalescence of many new societies, the family too seems to have gained, or perhaps regained, an enhanced solidarity.[15] The new cohesiveness seems to have been rooted, partially at least, in an effort to limit the excessive partitioning of the family patrimonies, which threatened the social position particularly of small landed households. The corporate or consortial family, holding its lands undivided, was better able than the nuclear household to defend its wealth and status in a changing and challenging world.

The evidence thus points to an increase in family solidarity in the eleventh century, but here an important qualification must be added. The combined or consortial family was very much a characteristic of the middle and upper levels of Italy's social hierarchy, and seems to have been strongest among the minor feudal nobility—the *valvassores, langobardi, capitanei,* or, in a slightly later term, the magnates. These were men, in other words, with property to defend, and this made them sensitive to the advantages of maintaining their patrimonies undivided. The poorer, humbler families, with little or no property to concern them, felt no comparable pressures.

Important as a landlord in the countryside, the corporate family was equally important in the city. The great households, often organized into "tower societies" (*societates turrium*), dominated whole neighborhoods and even quarters of the early cities.[16] Socially and even physically, the town in the eleventh century looks very much like an aggregation of great "lineages."

Family solidarity, at least among the aristocratic classes, grew in the eleventh and early twelfth centuries, but it was thereafter subject to powerful pressures, which worked to loosen its cohesiveness. These pressures made themselves felt most evidently and effectively in the city. The great families exercised a nearly unchallenged dominance in the towns until about 1150. But by then, the towns were growing, and the new men constantly entering the city soon were challenging the hegemony of the old houses. The battle reached a climax and decision in the late thirteenth century, with the emergence of the popular commune. Historians argue endlessly about the exact social composition of the Popolo, and its victory was in no sense a democratic triumph. But it did confer power upon a lower, broader and newer part of the urban social pyramid.

The popular commune took as one of its principal goals the establishment of an ordered and peaceful political life, free from the interventions of violence, to which the magnate houses were habitually inclined. In the anti-magnate legislation common to many communes in the late thirteenth century, the Popolo excluded nobles from the assemblies and principal offices of the popular commune, and subjected them to legal disabilities. They could not, for example, testify against their fellow citizens of common status. This weakened the ability of the nobles to exert influence and confer favors for the benefit of their clients. Their military power was still more rigorously curtailed. They could not take up arms nor freely assemble with their friends and factions without the people's permission. The magnates had further to post a bond for their law-abiding behavior; in case of violation, relatives were made responsible for paying the heavy fine.[17]

It should be noted that the popular commune looked askance not only at the great noble houses, but also at popular families which seemed to threaten the public peace. It characteristically imposed on all families limitations upon the right of extracting vengeance.[18] It sought also to curtail the splendor and livery with which popular households made their public appearances.[19]

The popular commune thus strove to break the cohesiveness and the power of the great, old households, and to prevent popolani families from gaining a comparable strength. Clearly, the commune and not the family was to be the first defense for the individual. In seeking to pacify communal society and to break up the solidarities of families and factions, the popular commune enjoyed a partial though not a complete success. The older houses do fade in strength. Villani, Dante, and other writers allude to the decline of many great lineages, although this was certainly not the exclusive result of anti-magnate legislation.[20] Many scions of the old magnate houses petitioned for popular status, in order to escape the disabilities imposed upon them for reason of their noble status. In this partial suppression of factional violence, the society of the free commune in the late thirteenth century appears more advanced, more modern really, than the society of the fourteenth and fifteenth centuries.

For the disasters of the late Middle Ages seem to have brought a return to older forms of social organization, and older habits of social behavior. To be sure, the consortial family, based upon the common ownership of property, never recovers. Sons in the fourteenth and fifteenth centuries keep their patrimony undivided with relative infrequency, and this for a very good reason. In troubled and uncertain economic times, the wealth of the entire household could be wiped out by the bad management, or bad luck, of a single member. The divided patrimony offered a measure of insurance against a common ruination. Urban houses in the late Middle Ages were thus very small. At Bologna, for example, in 1377, the average houschold size in the city was only 3.5 persons; at Pistoia in 1427, it was only 3.6.[21] A similar caution concerning the aggregation of money or capital in large, vulnerable funds affected business organizations as well. In contrast with such huge companies such as the Bardi and Peruzzi in the early fourteenth century, the business enterprises of the late Middle Ages tended to be smaller and more flexible, and less likely to be victimized by trouble in a single sector of their interests.[22]

Although the consortial family declines in Italian society in the late Middle Ages, the moral and cultural bonds holding relatives together grow in strength. There is a deepening sense of solidarity, which is measured simply but effectively in the spread of family names to ever lower levels in the city's social pyramid. There is a new consciousness of the importance of the family to the individual, and the need to work actively for its survival. The acute population decline meant that many once great houses had disappeared entirely, and this weighed upon the minds of men. Leon Battista Alberti wrote his *Libri della famiglia* not to show the family how to advance in wealth and influence, but how only to maintain its position, how simply to survive, in a threatening age.[23]

Consciousness of the family is further revealed by the proliferation of domestic chronicles or *Ricordi* especially after 1350. The archives of Florence have preserved more than 100 of these revealing and often entertaining records.[24] They were written usually for three purposes. They record with scrupulous detail the acquisition and sale of property and animals, and other business transactions. They often give the vital events not only of the writer's own household, but also of related and collateral lines (it was obviously important to know who were one's relatives). Frequently too, they advise the reader on how best to preserve and promote the family's interests. These domestic diaries grew out of the private account books of the thirteenth century. But by the late Middle Ages, the family, and not business enterprises, became the prime focus of their interests. This shift is itself another indication of growing solidarity in the household.

Cohesiveness seems further illustrated in the increased recognition of the cultural and spiritual content and value of the familial relationship. Families had long provided defense and aid for their members but made little evident contribution to their spiritual or cultural sustenance. To look through Dante and his predecessors for any celebration of the joys of domestic living is to search largely in vain. But after 1350, we begin to encounter fathers who play ball with their children, mothers who curl and dye the hair of their little girls, and children who dance gracefully for the entertainment of family and friends.[25] We encounter the advice of the Florentine Giovanni Morelli: "hold in enjoyment and in pleasure your family, and seek together with them the good and healthy life."[26] We do not have the space to develop this point further, but it does seem certain that the family was assuming a function it did not possess before, that of giving pleasure and contentment to its members.

It would be well perhaps to summarize the large topics we have covered, and the large conclusions we have drawn. The evolution of the Italian family towards a more nuclear structure ought not to be viewed as a continuing and irreversible movement. Rather, the great corporate households which dominate Italian society in the eleventh and twelfth centuries do not seem to have been the survivals of an ancient and distant social experience; they were themselves in large measure the product of the great reorganization of European life during the central Middle Ages. They were one of the many new social solidarities which the eleventh century produced. So also, the Italian family seems more nucleated, and in this sense at least more modern, in the society of the free commune in the late thirteenth century than later in the Middle Ages. For the troubles and upheavals of the late medieval period seem to have strengthened the family, as a chief bastion of defense for its harried members. To be sure, the consortial household, founded upon a common ownership of goods, never recovered. But if property bonds weakened, moral bonds grew. As shown by the spread of family names, a consciousness of family unity penetrated deep into Italian urban society during the late Middle Ages. As shown by the domestic chronicles, the importance of the family to the individual, and the individual to the family, were strongly felt. As shown in all sorts of literary works, the family acquired a new kind of solidarity, as a source of cultural and spiritual satisfaction, consolation, encouragement, *diletto e piacere,* for its members. The Middle Ages passed on to modern Italy not the "autonomous nuclear family" of our own society, but one strongly tied together by bonds of mutual self-interest, mutual help, and mutual appreciation.

NOTES

*A slightly different version of this paper was presented at the annual meeting of the American Historical Association, Toronto, Canada, December, 1967.

1. The sparse bibliography on the history of the medieval Italian family is largely dominated by the studies of legal historians. The best of them is probably Nino Tamassia, *La famiglia italiana nei secoli decimoquinto e decimosesto* (Milan, 1911). More technical in character are A. Marongiu, *La famiglia nell'Italia meridionale (sec. VIII–XIII)*, Biblioteca dell' Unione Cattolica per le Scienze Sociali, 9 (Milan, 1944); F. Schupfer, *Gaeta e il suo diritto,* III: *La famiglia* (Rome, 1915); and *idem, Il diritto privato dei popoli germanici con speciale riguardo all'Italia,* II: *La famiglia* (Rome and Città di Castello, 1914). The family also is given considerable attention in the standard histories of Italian law. See especially A. Pertile, *Storia del diritto italiano dalla caduta dell'Impero romano alla codificazione* (2nd ed. Turin, 1892–1902), III, pp. 274 ff., "Diretto di Famiglia."
2. Cf. the use made of these charters in my article, "Land, Family and Women in Continental Europe, 701–1200," *Traditio,* XVIII (1962), 89–120.
3. Cf. P. J. Jones, "Florentine Familes and Florentine Diaries in the Fourteenth Century," *Papers of the British School at Rome,* XXIV (1956), 183–205. V. Lugli, *I trattatisti della famiglia nel Quattrocento* (Modena, 1909). *Two Memoirs of Renaissance Florence. The Diaries of Buonaccorso Pitti and Gregorio Dati,* transl. Julia Martines and ed. Gene Brucker, (New York: Harper Torchbook, 1967), especially pp. 9–18.
4. Cf. Marongiu, *Famiglia,* p. 202, or Pertile, *Storia,* III, 274.
5. *Feudal Society,* transl. L. A. Manyon (Chicago, 1961), Chapter 9, "The Solidarity of the Kindred Group."
6. Numerous examples of the use of the Latin terms are given in Du Cange, *Glossarium mediae et infimae latinitatis* (Paris, 1884). The term "fara" also appears in several Italian and French place names.
7. The terminology is taken from Dorothy R. Blitsten, *The World of the Family. A Comparative Study of Family Organizations in Their Social and Cultural Settings* (New York, 1963).   .
8. *Feudal Society,* p. 125.
9. Cf. the comments by M. M. Postan, "The Rise of a Money Economy," *Essays in Economic History,* ed. E. M. Carus-Wilson, I (London, 1954), pp. 1–12, especially p. 8.
10. For the use of names of contiguous owners as a means of identifying patterns of property distribution, see my article, "Church Property on the European Continent, 701–1200," *Speculum,* XXXVI (1961), 81–105.

11. Compare the similar list of references to consortial ownership in Tuscany, in L. Chiappelli, "Pistoia dell' età longobarda," *Archivio Storico Italiano,* LXXIX (1921), pp. 259–66. Chiappelli too can find no references to consortial ownership before 950.

12. The figures are taken from the table in *Traditio,* XVIII (1962), pp. 116–20.

13. These figures do not include property owned by two named persons, e.g. *terra Roberti et Hugonis.* It is not always clear if these men were really joint owners, or owners of separate plots along the same boundary.

14. On these associations of rural nobles, formed from the late tenth century, see especially the old but excellent study by G. Volpe, "Lombardi e Romani nelle campagne e nelle città. Per la storia delle classi sociali della nazione e del Rinascimento italiano," *Studi Storici,* ed. A. Crivellucci, XIII (1904), 53–81; 167–82; 242–315; and 369–416.

15. In France too, in the eleventh century, there is a new emphasis upon securing the *laudatio parentum,* or agreement of relatives, in land transfers. See Georges Duby, *La societe aux XIe et XIIe siècles dans la région mâconnaise* (Paris, 1953), pp. 136–37 and 272–81.

16. See the old but informed study of P. Santini, "Società delle torri in Firenze," *Archivio Storico Italiano,* ser. 4, XX (1887), 25–58; and 178–204. One of the most remarkable examples of these great houses is the Corbolani of Lucca, the statutes of which have survived from the late thirteenth century. The association, which included more than twenty members, was governed by its own elected consul and treasurer, and imposed severe restrictions upon the rights of its constituents to alienate land. See the edition of the statutes in S. Bongi, "Statuto inedito della casa de' Corbolani," *Atti della reale Accademia lucchese di Scienze, Lettere ed Arti,* XXIV (1886), 468 ff. For consorteries elsewhere in Tuscany and Italy, see F. Niccolai, *I Consorzi nobiliari* (Bologna, 1940).

17. The character of the legislation against the magnates has most recently been reviewed by E. Cristiani, *Nobiltà e popolo nel comune di Pisa dalle origini del podestariato alla signoria dei Donoratico* (Naples, 1962), pp. 89 ff.

18. For the vendetta at Florence, see R. Davidsohn, *Firenze ai tempi di Dante,* transl. E. Dupré Theseider (Florence, 1929), pp. 677–84.

19. See, for example, the limitation to ten ladies in the processions accompanying new brides to their husbands' homes, in *Statuti della repubblica fiorentina,* I: *Statuto del capitano del popolo (1322–25),* ed. R. Caggese (Florence, 1910), V, cap. 12, p. 226, "Quia plerumque florentini cives et artifices non ad rationem sed ad similitudinem magnatum vivere volunt et sic dispendia expendia expensarum incurrunt . . ."

20. Numerous comments in Villani, *Cronica* (Florence: Magheri, 1823), I, p. 65, " . . . onde poi sono discesi molti lignaggi di nobili in Mugello e in Valdarno e in città assai, che oggi sono popolari e quasi venuti a fine." " . . . che oggi sono venuti meno . . . " "e oggi non è nullo" " . . . a' nostri di è venuto tutto quello legnaggio." See also Dante, *Paradiso,* XVI, 88–90. On these and similar references to the passing of old houses, see the recent comments by J. K. Hyde, "Italian Social Chronicles in the Middle Ages," *Bulletin of the John Rylands Library, Manchester,* XLIX (1966), 107–32.

21. Paolo Montanari, *Documenti su la popolazione di Bologna alla fine del trecento,* Fonti per la storia di Bologna, Testi, 1 (Bologna, 1966), p. 6. D. Herlihy, *Medieval and Renaissance Pistoia, 1200–1430* (New Haven, 1967), p. 75.

22. Even the Medici bank was not a single company but an aggregation of separate partnerships, which prevented the troubles of one office from ruining the entire enterprise. See Raymond de Roover, *The Rise and Decline of the Medici Bank, 1397–1494,* Harvard Studies in Business History, 21 (Cambridge, 1963), especially Chapter 5.

23. *Opere volgari,* ed. Cecil Grayson, I (Bari, 1960), p. 3, "Repetendo a memoria quanto . . . potemmo a' nostri giorni come altrove in Italia vedere non poche famiglie solere felicissime essere et gloriosissime, le quali ora sono mancate e spente . . . Ah! quante si veggono oggi famiglie cadute e rovinate!"

24. *Two Memoirs of Renaissance Florence,* p. 9.

25. Cf. Giovanni Dominici, *Regola del governo e cura familiare,* ed. Donato Salvi (Florence, 1860), p. 150, "Quanto tempo si perde in pettinargli spesso, tener biondi i capelli se son femine, e forse ancora fargli ricciuti!"

26. Giovanni di Pagolo Morelli, *Ricordi,* ed. Vittore Branca (Florence, 1956), p. 300, " . . . tieni in diletto e in piacere la tua famiglia, e fa con loro insieme buono e sana vita . . . "

PATRIAPOTESTAS, REGIA POTESTAS, AND REX IMPERATOR

GAINES POST

Princeton University

This volume of essays in commemoration of our beloved Robert L. Reynolds is rightly devoted to his great interest in Italy. My essay is not directly associated with the most important developments in the history of medieval Italy. Yet it does deal with a few Italian jurists, or with foreigners, like Johannes Teutonicus, who received their legal education in Italy, particularly at Bologna. It also deals in part with the Neapolitan jurist, Lucas de Penna, whose ideas were closely associated with the Italian Kingdom of Sicily. The ideas treated, moreover, even when they were applied to the kingdoms of France and England, were inspired by Italian jurists and theologians (St. Thomas Aquinas)—and by an African, St. Augustine of Hippo, who, of course, as a Roman citizen was also Italian in much of his education as he was in the great turning point in his life in Rome and Milan. But if my subject is not completely Italian, it is not alien to Robert L. Reynolds' deep appreciation of all medieval history, whether Italian or Anglo Saxon. I hope, therefore, that the reader will understand my striving to participate in honoring his greatness as a historian of medieval Italy and Europe.

Almost fifteen years ago I treated the legal thought of the twelfth and thirteenth centuries on the idea that the kings of England, France, and Spain were emperors in their own realms.[1] Stated as *rex imperator in regno suo*, or *rex superiorem non recognoscens*, the idea has caused considerable discussion of the question as to whether such kings and their realms were sovereign and independent, or were nonetheless subject to the Emperor of the Holy Roman Empire.

The late Francesco Calasso emphasized the analogy of the *patriapotestas* of a father as *rex* in his household to the *rex regni*, holding that just as any father could be called *rex* but was subject to a higher authority, so the king who was called emperor in his realm was nonetheless subordinate to the Emperor, and his realm was within the Empire.[2] No real sovereignty of a kingdom existed in the theories of the legists and canonists of the thirteenth century. Yet Calasso admitted that the analogy itself, with the repetition of the idea of a king as emperor, made the legists gradually if grudgingly accept, by the fourteenth century, the idea and fact of the national sovereignty of separate states.

My thesis was, and still is, that a considerable number of legists and jurists used the theme of *rex-imperator* to support the sovereignty of the king and his realm in all secular matters, for no appeal could go from the king to the Emperor of the Holy Roman Empire; the king could by himself declare a just war of defense; and the *regnum*, like the Roman Empire, was the common fatherland (*patria communis*) of all the subjects of the king within the realm. Further, as this study will show, the analogy of the *paterfamilias* as *rex* to the *rex regni* played no important rôle in the development of the *de jure* as well as *de facto* sovereignty of the kingdoms of France, England, and Spain as states by the late thirteenth century.

Yet the analogy presented by Calasso has remained a problem. In this paper I present evidence that Calasso did not go far enough into the context of the sources he consulted, and that my interpretation is supported both by the Roman and Canon law and by Thomas Aquinas and other Aristotelians of the later thirteenth century.

The arguments of Calasso start with a statement by Johannes Andreae, the great canonist of the late thirteenth and first half of the fourteenth century. "Everyone [i.e., every head of a family] is called king in his household" ("Quilibet in domo sua dicitur rex"), said Johannes in his comment on a famous decretal, the *Venerabilem*, of Pope Innocent III (*Decr. Greg. IX*, 1, 6, 34). Johannes refers to the *Decretum*, C.23 q.4, c.35 Duo ista, which is a statement by St. Augustine (*In libr. Psalm.*, Ps. 32) on the sinful nature of men that is common to kings, bishops, and heads of families. (Calasso also refers to but does not quote or analyze the text;[3] I shall do so below in order to put the analogy between king and *paterfamilias* in the proper perspective.)

After quoting Johannes Andreae, Calasso gives a statement by Lucas de Penna, the famous Neapolitan jurist of the fourteenth century, who says that "every *dominus* [lord or owner] is called king of his possessions" ("et quilibet dominus rerum suarum dicitur rex").[4]

Then Calasso turns to St. Thomas Aquinas, first quoting this statement (*Summa Theol.*, 1a 2ae, q. 90, art. 3, n.3): "sicut princeps civitatis est civitatis gubernator, ita quilibet paterfamilias est gubernator domus; sed princeps civitatis potest in civitate legem facere; ergo quilibet paterfamilias potest in sua domo legem facere."[5] Thus, according to Aquinas in this passage, the *paterfamilias* is the same kind of ruler and legislator in his household as the *princeps* is in the state. Further, as Calasso observes, in the *De regimine principum,* I, 12, Aquinas holds that a particular *regimen* of a king imitates the *regimen universale* of God, but of course is subordinate to God. By analogy, then, one can conclude that while the king may be emperor in his realm, thus imitating the *regimen* of the Empire, nonetheless king and realm are subject to the Emperor.[6]

Now is this interpretation justified by the general context of legal, political, and ethical doctrines of the thirteenth century? If we look at the sources referred to by Calasso, and to still other sources used by jurists and philosophers in the thirteenth century, we do quickly find a context that offers a very important distinction between the *potestas* of the father and the *potestas* of the king or any secular ruler of a state—a distinction that essentially rests on the principle that the *paterfamilias* enjoys a moral but not a public, political, and judicial, coercive authority.

We begin to understand this when we study not only the passage from St. Augustine which inspired Johannes Andreae to say that every head of a household is called king, but also the ideas of decretists of the late twelfth and early thirteenth century who commented on the passage (C.23 q.4, c.35 Duo ista). Now what St. Augustine said is that man is sinful, whether he is a bishop ruling (*regens*) his flock (*plebs*) a poor man ruling his *domus*, a rich man his household (*familia*), a father his offspring (*proles*), a husband his wife, a judge his province, or a king his people (*gens*). All these men, he says, have a common, sinful nature. He suggests nothing about a political nature that is common to all; nor about how the "regens domum" "regens familiam," or "regens prolem," etc., can be called a "rex regens gentem" and yet is subordinate to the *rex regni*. He is saying only that all men are equal in their sinful nature.

About 1215–1220 Johannes Teutonicus compiled the *Glossa ordinaria* to the *Decretum.* A compilation of glosses or opinions of himself and of other distinguished decretists, the *Glos. ord.* remained a standard authority during the thirteenth century in the realm of Canon law, although later canonists did not hesitate to disagree with many of the ideas of the glosses. It is important, therefore, to learn what the glosses in the *Glos. ord.* have to say about the words of St. Augustine in C.23 q.4, c.35.[7]

At once it becomes interesting that the gloss on the word *familiam* ("diviti regenti familiam suam") is a reference to the *Codex* of Justinian, 9, 15, 1, and to the *Decretum*, C.33 q.2, c.10 Placuit; and the gloss to "*marito* regenti coniugem suam" is a reference to C.7 q.1, c.39 Sicut alterius. For, since no gloss to C.23, q.4, c.35 offers a discussion of the nature of the power of rich man, husband, and king, we can judge the decretists' interpretation of St. Augustine only by looking up these references. Although the first reference is to an imperial law (*C.*9, 15, 1), let us look first at the other texts referred to in the *Decretum*, and also at the *Gloss. ord.* to these.

In the first place, C.7 q.1, c.39 Sicut alterius, compares the power of the husband over his wife with that of the bishop over his church: a wife can be judged only by her husband; as the Apostle says (St. Paul, *Rom.* 7,2), "Alligata est uxor legi viri, quandiu vir eius vivit . . ." But does this mean that a husband's power is "judicial," like the power of the bishop in his diocese? The gloss ad v. *iudicari* offers this opinion: legally, the husband cannot be the judge of his wife, for, as in the *Digest*, 2, 1, 10 Qui iurisdictioni, no one can pronounce judgment on himself or on his own wife or children; however, he can judge his wife by reforming or correcting her ("corrigenda eam"), as in C.23 q.4, c.35 Duo ista, but not by beating her ("sed non verberando eam"), as in *C.* 9, 15, 1; and he can moderately punish or restrain her ("sed temperate potest eam castigare") because she belongs to his household (*familia*), as in C.33 q.5, c.13 Hec imago.[8] Finally, the author of this gloss concludes, the husband cannot judge his wife "in forma iudicii." In a word, his opinion is that the judicial power of a man in his household is not the same as that of a true judge in public office.

The second reference to consider is to C.33 q.2, c.10 Placuit, which is a decree of a council at Toledo (*an.* 400) declaring that the clerical husband of a sinful wife shall have the power of keeping and binding her in his house, and compelling her to salutary but not fatal fasts – all such powers "praeter necem." On this the gloss ad v. *potestatem* states that the husband can be fined ("punitur in pecunia"), in ways prescribed by certain laws in the *Authentics* and the *Codex* of Justinian, if he unlawfully "eam male verberavit." Thus the power of a husband to punish his wife is so limited that his authority bears no resemblance to that of a public magistrate or judge.

One more passage from the *Decretum* is important in connection with this subject, although the glosses I have consulted do not refer to it. It is C.23 q 4, c.36 Ille gladium; this immediately follows the opinion of St. Augustine which Johannes Andreae had in mind and which started our examination of the decretists. In c.36 St. Augustine is again quoted, but on the theme (Matthew 26.52) that "they that take the sword shall perish with the sword." On the words of St. Augustine, "Ille gladium accipit, qui nulla superiori ac legitima potestate vel iubente vel concedente . . . ," the glosses explain first (v. *accipit*) that what is meant is the man who *iniuste* takes up the sword (that is, without being commanded to do so by a lawful authority); and second (v. *potestate*), that "the power of the sword is held only by the prince" ("Nam potestas gladii tantum a principe habetur").

It is interesting that this passage and the glosses to it make no mention of any right of the *paterfamilias* or husband to possess the *potestas gladii*. Nor do any glosses on the *paterfamilias* and the husband hint at their having the *potestas gladii*. The reason for this silence is obvious: in the Roman law the *merum imperium* of the ruler was, as Ulpian said (*D*. 2, 1, 3), the possession of the *potestas gladii* for the punishment of criminals. It goes without saying that no legist would attribute this full *imperium* and power of the sword to any ordinary head of a family. Nor, of course, would a canonist do so.

I have not studied the great decretists and decretalists of the later thirteenth century on the nature of the *potestas* of the *paterfamilias* in comparison with the *potestas* of the king or prince. But it is sufficient to observe that Johannes Andreae himself referred to the *Decretum*, C.23, q.4, c.35 Duo ista, when he said that "quilibet in domo sua dicitur rex." Surely he knew the glosses on the *Decretum*; and surely he meant only that, just as sinfulness is common to all men, whether heads of households or kings, so a kind of rulership is common to them. He certainly did not hold that kingship in the home is the same in quality and coercive power as the king's *imperium* or *potestas gladii* in his kingdom.

Now let us turn to the Roman law. We noted above that a gloss to C.23 q.4, c.35 refers to C.9, 15, 1. This law deals with the punishment of relatives (*De emendatione propinquorum*): *seniores* have the power of correcting *minores* in relation to the quality of the transgression (*delictum*). This power of punishing the offenses of minors shall not be boundless ("in immensum extendi"); but by paternal right ("iure patrio") the father may correct the fault of his young son ("propinqui iuvenis erratum"). If, however, the *atrocitas* of the deed goes beyond the remedy of domestic correction, the youth accused of an "enormous crime" shall be turned over to the cognizance of the magistrate or judge.

In the *Glossa ordinaria* of Accursius (*ca.* 1230) to the *Codex* of Justinian, the opinions given on this imperial law offer no dissent. On the words *iure patrio* the glossator simply remarks that this paternal authority consists in *pietas* rather than *atrocitas*.[9] On the words *atrocitas facti*, the opinion is that if the correction by the father is not adequate punishment, the *iudex* must punish. But the *atrocitas facti* can also be the father's in punishing his son: the father who kills his son "ex voluntate" "punitur de parricidio"—so in *C.*9, tit. 17 De his qui parentes vel liberos occiderunt, 1. un., Si quis, where we find that the guilty father, or son who kills his father, shall be sewn into a bag, along with vile creatures, and drowned.

Already it is evident that if power is common to rulers, judges, and fathers, there is no analogy between the kinds of power held by them. The *paterfamilias* in his power possesses no official, judicial authority, and no right to inflict such punishments as a public court can. It is clear that his *potestas* is far inferior to that of magistrate or judge, and of course to that of the king or emperor who has *merum imperium*, including the *ius gladii*.

But a few more statements in the classical Roman law and in the glosses of the legists are of interest, and they support what has been said. Let us note how the classical jurist Paulus defined *potestas* (*D.*50, 16, 215). *Potestas*, he says, means *imperium* in relation to magistrates, *patriapotestas* in relation to children, and ownership (*dominium*) in relation to slaves. That is, to interpret this passage in the context of general legal thought on *imperium*, the highest *potestas* is the *merum imperium* and *ius gladii* of the prince or emperor, while subordinate magistrates or judges have a lesser *potestas* and *imperium*, and a lesser power of *coercitio*.[10] The *potestas* of a father over his children is not associated at all with *imperium*; nor is the power of the owner over his slaves.

Another passage that offers interest is *D.*2, 1, 12, on municipal magistrates, who cannot put a slave to death, but do have the right of *modica castigatio*. The *casus* (summary of the later thirteenth century) puts it thus: the municipal magistrate does not have *merum imperium*; hence he cannot inflict the death penalty on a slave; but he can "verberare eum, vel aliter castigare legitime." A gloss on the words "castigatio eis non est deneganda" is important for the opinion that such magistrates also have the right of the *castigatio* or *coercitio* of children, and that there is no *iurisdictio* without *coercitio*.

I call attention to this because of the use of the word *coercitio*. (We shall encounter the equivalent meaning in the *potestas coactiva* in Thomas Aquinas and other scholasitc philosophers of the later thirteenth century on the subject of the coercive authority of the king.) Of course according to the legists, the supreme jurisdiction, *potestas*, or *merum imperium*, of the prince was accompanied by the supreme powers of coercion expressed in the words *ius gladii*.

Of interest, too, is the Roman imperial legislation on the *patria potestas*—in *C*.8, 47 De patria potestate. One law in particular, l.3 Si filius, is important for the legal distinction between the power of the father over his son and the power of a judge. It states that if a son who is still in his father's *potestas* has acquired property, he cannot alienate it without his father's consent. If he disobeys, his father can punish him, "castigare iure patriae potestatis." If, however, the son persists in disobeying, his father shall bring him before the governor of the province for official judgment or sentence based on the complaint brought by the father. In a word the judicial authority of a provincial governor is far superior to that of a *paterfamilias* (just as the *imperium* of the emperor is superior to the delegated *imperium* of the governor).

We can now turn to Azo for a summing up of the Roman law as interpreted by the legists of the early thirteenth century. In his *Summa Codicis*, to *C*.8, 47, he says first that the *patriapotestas* is in the Roman Empire a certain right (*ius*) of the father over his natural and legitimate sons.[11] Then he develops or elaborates the opinion of Paulus (*D*.50, 16, 215) which we gave above: the word *potestas* signifies the *dominium* of owners over their slaves, the *imperium* of magistrates, obedience in the relations of monks to abbots, and, between father and son, the bond of reverence, castigation, subjection, and *pietas*.[12] And Azo emphasizes that the *patriapotestas* cannot be *iudicium* between father and son.[13] In his *Commentarius* on the *Codex* of Justinian, to *C*.8, 47, 3 Si filius (the statement that the provincial governor's sentence should be based on the father's complaint about his son's persistent disobedience), Azo remarks that it is not absurd in this case that judgment be given according to the wishes of the plaintiff. For it is not presumed that the father wants to cut off his son's head![14] Finally, to *C*.8, 47, 4 Congruentius (that it is better that domestic quarrels be settled in the home than taken before the governor of the province), Azo makes the same statement that he made in his *Summa*: "Inter patrem autem et filium non potest esse iudicium. . ."[15]

Thus, the Roman law and the glossators clearly subordinated the private *potestas* of the father to the public *potestas* and jurisdiction of the magistrate. All the more, then, the thirteenth-century legists distinguished between the *paterfamilias* and the *merum imperium* and *potestas gladii* and supreme jurisdiction of prince or king, the ruler of the state. The canonists fully accepted this important distinction. So did two great writers of the mid- and late-thirteenth century on the common and customary laws of England and northern France. Bracton said that the king of England was under no man, but under God and the law; Beaumanoir, that the king of France was "souverains pardessus tous." I have observed nothing in their works about a kind of kingship of a man in his family. Neither suggests that the king was, although superior in his realm, subject to the emperor. To each his king was equivalent to the *rex imperator* who recognized no superior.

Given the general theories of the canonists and legists, and of Bracton and Beaumanoir, did St. Thomas Aquinas differ from them so much that, as Calasso suggests, he concluded that all kingship is subordinate to God—in ascending order from *paterfamilias* to *rex regni* to *imperator*?[16] It is true, not only in the opinions given by Calasso, but also in several others, as we shall soon see, that Thomas does like to find an analogy or *similitudo* of all kinds of secular *regimen* or *principatus*. But a close examination of his commentary on the *Politics* of Aristotle, his *Summa Theologiae*, and of his *De regimine principum*, will reveal that he makes important distinctions.

On the *Politics*, I, Lectio X, he first emphasizes the analogies. A man rules ("*principatur*") over his wife by a political rule ("politico principatu"), just as the man elected as *rector* is set over the *civitas*. (By *principatus politicus* he is simply distinguishing the rule of husband or father over wife and children, who are free, from the despotic rule of the owner over his slaves.) But a father is in command of his sons by a regal *principatus*, and this for the reason that a father has the fullness of power (*plenaria potestas*) over his sons, just as a king has in his realm, "sicut et rex in regno." He now explains how a man's "political" *principatus* over his wife differs from the father's *regalis principatus* over his children. The husband does not possess *plenaria potestas* over his wife in all things, but only in those things permitted by the *lex matrimonii;* his power is limited, just as the power of the *rector civitatis* over the citizens is limited by the laws of the city (*statuta*).[17]

Thus the "royal rule" of a man belongs to him as a father, not as a husband. The *paterfamilias*, then, is a king only in this respect; but as a king ruling his children he has a *plenaria potestas* like that of a king ruling his kingdom. (*Plenaria potestas*, by the way, was the terminology applied by St. Louis to the supreme authority of the kings of England and France. *Plenitudo potestatis* usually was attributed to the pope, but St. Thomas in another place compares the *plenitudo potestatis* of the pope with that of a king.)[18]

St. Thomas pursues the theme of the *similitudo* of father and king in his remarks on Aristotle's words, "Puerorum autem principatus regalis" (I, X §103). Aristotle, he explains, says that the *principatus* of the father is *regalis* with respect to his sons. The father rules his sons with love (*amor*), but in his prerogative of superior age lies the essential likeness to the *principatus regalis*. Yet there is some difference between the royal rule of the father and that of the king, for the king rules forever ("perpetuo"),[19] he possesses the *plenaria potestas* over all, and he differs from his subjects according to a natural magnitude of goodness, although he is human like them. Therefore it is necessary that the king differ *naturaliter* from others: if he were not better by a certain natural goodness, it would not be just for him to govern those equal to him with *plenaria potestas*. Nonetheless, it is *amor* that keeps a *principatus regalis* from being tyrannical, for the tyrant does not rule because of love for his subjects, but because of his own convenience or selfish interests.[20] Therefore, in this discussion St. Thomas seems almost to equate the *amor* involved in the *patria potestas* and royal rule of sons with the *amor* involved in the king's *plenaria potestas*.

If St. Thomas Aquinas emphasizes *similitudo* in his *Commentary* on the *Politics*, in the *Summa Theologiae* he recognizes the superiority of the office of the king as judge and legislator, thus distinguishing the royal authority from every lesser power of subjects within the kingdom. Asking whether the *virtus regnativa* belongs to the *species* of prudence, he replies that the *specialis ratio regiminis* is a *specialis ratio prudentiae*, and it exists above all in the ruler of the "perfect community of the city or kingdom." The more perfect the *regimen*, the more universal it is. Therefore, he concludes, the execution of justice which pertains to the *officium regis*, according to its use for the common good, needs the guidance of prudence. Hence the virtues of prudence and justice are especially appropriate to the king—as Jeremiah said, 23.5: "Regnabit rex, et sapiens erit et faciet iudicium et iustitiam in terra." Finally, as for the argument that the right to legislate, "leges condere," belongs not only to kings but also to other kinds of government (*principatus*), and even to the *populus* (as Isidore said, *Etymol.*, II, c.10 n.1); and as for the statement of Aristotle (*Ethics*, VI)[21] that *legispositiva* (the making of law), is not *regnative*, but a part of prudence, St. Thomas replies that what Aristotle calls *regnativa* derives from the principal business of the king, which is to make laws ("leges ponere"). Further, in so far as legislation is a function of others, it is so only because they participate in the *regimen* of the king.[22] In other words, any law-making in which other men participate is done by the authority of the king, whether the magnates of the realm consent, say in Parliament, to a new law or statue, or the people of a city within the realm draw up statutes for their local community.

This discussion and the conclusions show clearly that when St. Thomas was writing down his own opinions more fully than in a commentary on Aristotle, he clearly departed from the analogy based on a kind of kingship common to king and *paterfamilias*. The king is the supreme judicial and legislative authority in the realm; the father in his *domus* possesses no such office. Indeed, elsewhere he says that the prince and other magistrates exercise the pure or absolute justice (*simpliciter iustum*) appropriate to their offices in relation to the *communitas civitatis*; while between a husband and his wife there is only a limited kind of justice, a *iustum oeconomicum* rather than a "simpliciter politicum iustum."[23]

But the strongest statement on the public nature of the supreme authority that I have found in St. Thomas is in his discussion of the coercive power (*vis* and *potestas coactiva*) necessary for the enforcement of judicial decisions. Just as a general law should have force, so should the sentence of the judge, for otherwise justice would be without effect. "But no one has lawful possession of *potestas coactiva* in human affairs except him who holds the *potestas publica*"— "Potestatem autem coactivam non habet licite in rebus humanis nisi ille que fungitur publica potestate." And those who execute the public power are deemed superior to those over whom, as over subjects, they received this power.[24]

While St. Thomas does not mention kings at this point, it is evident that in his general thought about kingship the king's power was public and *coactiva*, and also the supreme public power. So he says, in the *De regimine principum*, the king is to his realm what the soul is to the body; and the king represents God in administering justice in the realm.[25]

In sum, St. Thomas Aquinas does make use of the analogy based on a general kind of kingship that is common to God, secular kings, and heads of families. But there is no equality in the royal powers vested in them. God as the ruler of the universe is of course the superior of all men on earth, whether they are princes or fathers of children. But if the king is subject to God, he is subject to no other human authority. As the supreme public *potestas* in his kingdom, possessing the *plenaria potestas* of legislating, judging, and enforcing the law, he is the head of the state. In general, to be sure, the king in his exercise of the supreme authority is limited (as in the standard theories of kingship in the thirteenth century) by his duty to observe law and justice, and in important matters by his duty to obtain the counsel of experts and the great men of the realm. But in his final right to interpret and enforce the law the king recognizes no superior in secular affairs.[26] The *paterfamilias*, however, does not have a supreme judicial and coercive power over his children; he is no public magistrate or judge, he is king only by a kind of similitude. Again as Bracton said, and St. Thomas would have agreed if in different terms, the *rex regni* is under no man but under God and the law. The *paterfamilias* is under the public magistrates in his community.

Is it nonetheless true that just as the *paterfamilias* is *rex* in his *domus* yet subject to the *rex regni*, so the *rex regni*, while supreme in his realm, is subject to the Emperor, and his kingdom is therefore a part of the Holy Roman Empire? Nowhere, so far as I have found, does St. Thomas discuss the meaning of *rex imperator in regno suo*, or of *rex superiorem non recognoscens*. Nonetheless, given his emphasis on *rex* rather than *imperator*, and given the general context of his theories on the powers of a king, it is safe to conclude that he does not draw the analogy between *paterfamilias* and *rex* in order to subordinate the king, of France at least, to the Emperor.

Pierre d'Auvergne, however, in his continuation of St. Thomas's *Commentary* on the *Politics*, offers a complete analogy. In the *gubernatio domus*, he says, one man rules for the utility of subjects, and is the lord of all who are in the *domus*. So in a kingdom there is one man who rules "ad utilitatem subditorum." Therefore, "sicut gubernatio patris familias est quaedam regia potestas, ita regia potestas est quaedam domestica gubernatio civitatis et gentis," whether he rules one city and people or several cities and peoples.[27] Even so it is doubtful that he would have gone so far as to say that a king is under the Emperor, thus disagreeing with his master.

Of the few discussions that I have read on this problem of kingship in the works of commentators on Aristotle in the late thirteenth

and early fourteenth centures, the best in my opinion is in an anonymous *Questiones supra librum ethycorum* written, probably, before
the end of the thirteenth century. The work exists in the MS lat.
15106, fols. 2–75, of the Bibliothèque Nationale, Paris.[28] So far as I
know it has not been published. Of interest to us here is this question,
Utrum solus rex habeat virtutem coactivam (fols. 74ᵛc.–75c.1), the
text of which (minus the author's references) I now give:

> *Utrum, etc.* Arguitur quod non, quia sicut dicit philosophus ser-
> mones paterni eodem modo se habent in domo, sicut sermones regis in
> civitatibus. Sed sermo regis in civitate est coactivus, ideo etc. . . .
> In oppositum est philosophus, dicendum quod solus rex habet
> virtutem coactivam et legem statuere, quia ille qui est superior in civi-
> tate solum habet legem statuere et virtutem coactivam. Sed solus rex est
> superior in civitate, quia quicumque alius a rege habet se superiorem.
> Ergo solus rex habet virtutem coactivam. Manifestum patet, quia quili-
> bet inferior in communitate regulatur a suo superiore. Sed ille qui ab
> aliquo superiore regulatur, non potest statuere legem, nec habere vir-
> tutem coactivam. . . .
> Dico sicut commentator dicit, quod pater non habet totalem vir-
> tutem coactivam in domo, sicut rex in regno, quia respectu filii con-
> tumacis et perversi non habet virtutem omnino coactivam, quia non
> potest ipsum cogere sicut rex potest subditum cogere. Etiam dato quod
> pater posset filium suum corrigere, sicut potest rex subditum, tamen
> propter inclinationem naturalem quam habet pater ad filium, non
> potest pati destructionem filii sicut rex potest pati destructionem sub-
> diti. Sed aliquantulum est simile de patre respectu filiorum obedien-
> tium, sicut de rege respectu subditorum [MS, subditi], quia sicut subditi
> obediunt regi, ita filii patri obediunt et mandatis eius. . . .

To paraphrase rather than translate, on the one side Aristotle
equates paternal and royal commands (*sermones*), and therewith the
coercive element in the commands of both; on the other, the author
says, Aristotle[29] states that only the king possesses a coercive
authority (*virtus coactiva*) and the power of legislating (*legem sta-
tuere*). Only the *superior* in the state holds the legislative and enforcing power. But the king alone can be the *superior* of all in the
state, for everyone else has a superior. Therefore only the king possesses the *virtus coactiva*, the supreme power of enforcing the law.
Since every inferior in the community is directed by his superior,
no inferior can legislate or have a coercive power.

A father, therefore, as the commentator says,[30] does not have
the *totalis virtus coactiva* that a king has. The reason is that his
power of enforcing commands given to a perverse and stubborn son
is not absolute (not *omnino coactiva*), while the coercive authority

of the king is. But of course, just as a king can correct a subject, so a father can correct his son. However, because of natural affection (*inclinatio*) a father cannot bear the ruin (*destructio*) of his son, while a king can endure the destruction of a subject. Nonetheless, there is a small degree of similarity between father and king: sons should obey their father and his commands just as subjects should obey their king.

Comment on this discussion can be brief. In the first place, the author leaves no doubt that in his mind there is no analogy between the *patriapotestas* and the *potestas regia* with respect to a supreme authority in jurisdiction, legislation, and coercion. The king is the supreme public, executive authority in the realm, and all fathers in the realm are subject to the king. Indeed, the king has no superior—perhaps the author reflects the opinions of the jurists, that the king *superiorem non recognoscens* is *imperator in regno suo*, although there is no mention of *rex-imperator*.In the second place—and here the author agrees fully with St. Thomas[31]—the king is the supreme lawmaker or legislator. Finally, only the king has the power to ruin or destroy—that is, to use legal terms, the *merum imperium* and *ius gladii*, the public power of inflicting capital punishment. Nevertheless, there is no suggestion that the king is inferior to the Emperor, or that the *regnum* is a part of the Empire.

Calasso, finally, drew on a few words of Lucas de Penna to support his thesis: "et quilibet dominus rerum suarum dicitur rex."[32] He should have quoted the whole sentence as supporting evidence, for Lucas says that the *nomen regis* is general, that *clerici* are called *reges*.[33] But if we read the whole of Lucas' comment, we find that he quickly abandons any comparison of such *reges* with a *rex regni*. "Strictly speaking, however," he adds, "only he is *rex* who holds the *regnum* from the Roman Church, as Hostiensis says" he refers to Henry of Susa's opinion on the decretal *Venerabilem* of Pope Innocent III (*Decr. Greg. IX,* 1, 6, 34), which deals with the papal right to control the election of the German king who would be crowned as Emperor of the Roman Empire by the pope.[34] At this point, therefore, Lucas is saying that the only real king is the King of the Germans or Roman Emperor. Yet, when we consider his treatment of the kings of France and of Sicily, we shall find that he attributes the same powers to these kings as he does to the German King-Emperor (below, to nn. 38–41). In any case, what are the powers of a king? Lucas clearly states that the king holds the public office of judging and doing justice;[35] and *potestas* is given him that he may forcibly restrain the wicked from doing evil.[36] The royal power is coercive.

Indeed, "it is the general covenant (*pactum*) of human society to obey kings," as St. Augustine said.[37] Based on a social contract, the king's power is supreme, having no superior but God—although Lucas in general accepts the traditional theory that the royal authority is limited by law and justice.

Thus, Lucas does not take analogies seriously. In fact, in another place he belittles them. The king of the French, he says, is called *magnificus* and *illustris* (by Innocent III, in the decretal *Novit, Decr. Greg. IX*, 2, 1, 13). But *illustres* and others, such as *praetores* (provincial governors) are called *magnificentissimi*. Can one then conclude that these are the equals of the French king, who recognizes no superior in temporal affairs (as Innocent III said, *Decr. Greg. IX*, 4, 17, 13 Per venerabilem)? No, Lucas concludes, for such titles as *illustris* and *magnificus* have little usefulness; because they are agreeable it has sometimes been pleasant to fill parchments (*membranae*) with them.[38] The king of France is thus superior to all others in his realm; recognizing no superior, he is *imperator in regno suo*.[39]

Yet, if this is so, does Lucas think that such a king is subject to the Emperor of the Holy Roman Empire? He does admit that ideally, in theory, all kings and kingdoms are within the Empire, and should use the Roman law and obey the Emperor. But in fact, he thinks, some kings, especially the king of France, are independent rulers of sovereign states.[40] And this *de facto* situation has become lawful, for by right of prescription (so I interpret Lucas), "some kings are exempt from the *Imperium* (*Romanum*), kings who either never acknowledged its yoke, or, having acknowledged it, threw it off." The king of France above all is free and exempt (*liber et exemptus*), because he recognizes no superior in temporal affairs. So also the king of Sicily is free (and independent).[41]

Not one of the sources mentioned by Calasso, then, seriously attributes any importance to a kingship common to *paterfamilias* or *dominus rerum* and to *reges*. Furthermore, the author of the *questio, Utrum solus rex habeat virtutem coactivam*, apparently aware of the importance of the debate, was sure that there could be no analogy of the father's kingship in his household to the kingship of the supreme public authority vested in the true *rex* who recognized no superior in his realm. The authors of these sources do not seriously consider that just as the father is subject to the king, so the king is subject to the Emperor. Nor do they indicate, any more than the early legists and Bracton and Beumanoir did, that under the influence of the analogy it was easier for them to make the transition from the idea of *rex imperator in regno suo* yet subject to the Emperor to the idea of the sovereign *rex* and *regnum*—to the idea, that is, of the sovereign state outside the Empire. No intermediate stage was needed for the canonists who, like Alanus and Vincent of Spain, as early as about 1200 to 1250, were declaring the *de jure* as well as *de facto* sovereignty of the kings of England, France, and Spain; nor for Bracton and Beaumanoir, who each in his own way said that the king recognized no superior; nor for St. Thomas Aquinas and the author of the *questio, Utrum solus rex*, who while talking about the analogy of *paterfamilias* and *rex* spoke of the *rex regni* as sovereign in authority in the kingdom; nor for Lucas de Penna, despite his hesitation.

Johannes Teutonicus himself, about 1215–1220, while arguing that all kings and kingdoms were subject to the German King-Emperor as the *dominus mundi*, made no use of the theme of kingship common to *paterfamilias* and *rex regni* in order to deduce from it that a *rex* was as inferior to the Emperor as a father was to the king. Instead, Johannes stated an opinion about the titles of *rex* and *imperator* which may have been the origin of Lucas de Penna's scorn of other titles in relation to the king of France—both Johannes and Lucas were commenting on the decretal *Venerabilem* of Innocent III (*Decr. Greg. IX*, 1, 6, 34). In the *Venerabilem* Innocent III claimed that the Apostolic See transferred the Roman *imperium* from the Greeks to the Germans, *in Germanos*. On these words Johannes said: "So, therefore, the government of the world was transferred to the Teutons . . . ; and thus it is manifest that the *imperium* is no longer in the hands of the Greeks, although broadly speaking he (the Greek ruler) may be called imperator. . . , just as a king of chessmen" (is called king).[42] Then he says that there is no *imperium* that is not recognized by or subject to the Roman Church.[43] The German King-Emperor is above all kings; all peoples are under him; and as the Roman law says, he is the prince and the lord of the world; and all secular affairs are in his power.[44]

Thus Johannes Teutonicus scorned the idea that a title in itself was important. But he was convinced that the only true Emperor was the German *Rex-Imperator* approved by the pope. Ordinary kings of France and England and Spain were subject to the Emperor and their kingdoms were mere provinces in the Empire—so also some other canonists held.[45] Yet he did not argue that, just as any *rex scaccorum* or any *paterfamilias in domo sua* may be called king, so the *rex regni* can be called emperor in his realm and is nonetheless subject to the Emperor and the Empire. He did not admit that, because Innocent III said that the king of France recognized no superior, the king could be called emperor in his realm.

To this extent, however, Calasso was right in his study of the problem of sovereignty of states apart from the Empire: although the greatest legists from Azo to Bartolus held that *de jure* even those kings who recognized no superior were within the Empire and subject to the Emperor, they perhaps gradually accepted the actual growth of sovereignty of kings and separate states because they were influenced by the idea of a kingship that was common to *paterfamilias*, *rex*, and *imperator*. On the whole, however, the Italian legists, while admitting that certain kings in fact recognized no superior, were convinced that such kings could not be true emperors or sovereign rulers of imperial, sovereign realms. Nowhere do they speak of an emperorship common to kings and the Emperor of the Holy Roman Empire.

Those canonists, however, and a few legists (French and Neapolitan), who maintained that the kings of France, England, Spain, and Sicily were *de jure* as well as *de facto* emperors who recognized no superior, make no mention of the argument from analogy, whether of kingship or of emperorship, in ascending order from fathers to the Emperor. For them the king who recognized no superior was a true emperor or sovereign ruler in a sovereign or independent realm. Furthermore, the great writers on "national" and local laws and customs, Bracton and Beaumanoir, treated the kings of England and France each as the sovereign or supreme public authority in his realm—in so far as sovereignty in the modern sense of the word can be attributed to any medieval ruler and his government. St. Thomas Aquinas and, more decisively, the author of the *questio* quoted above certainly spoke of the supreme judicial, coercive, and public power of a king as if he were under no man, not even under the Emperor. These writers accepted the sovereignty of kings and their kingdoms, of separate states, on grounds more substantial than reasoning from a lower kind of kingship or monarchy to a higher one.

NOTES

1. "Two Notes on Nationalism in the Middle Ages," in *Traditio*, IX (1953), 281–320; especially Part 2, "Rex Imperator"—revised and published in my *Studies in Medieval Legal Thought. Public Law and the State, 1100–1322* (Princeton, 1964), pp. 453–482.

2. I have used the 2nd edn. of Calasso's book, *I glossatori e la teoría della sovranitá* (Milan, 1951), pp. 173 ff. But I have also consulted the 3rd edn. (Milan, 1957), pp. 171–173. Since there are no changes on this matter in the 3rd edn., my references are to the 2nd edn., which is available to me now.

3. Calasso, *Glossatori*, p. 173.

4. *L. c.*; from Lucas' *Commentary* on the *Tres Libri* (Bks. X-XII of the *Codex* of Justinian), XI, 71 De conductor. et procurato.; in the Lyons, 1597, edn., p. 637.

5. Calasso, *Glossatori*, pp. 173 f.

6. *Ibid.*, p. 174; Calasso also refers to the *Summa contra Gentiles*, III, 76ff., and to Dante, *De Monarchia*, I, 6 f., for the same idea.

7. In what follows I refer to the *Glos. ord.* in the edition of the *Decretum* printed by Ioannes Pidaeius, Lyons, 1553.

8. St. Augustine on how man, but not woman, was made in the image of God.

9. In the Lyons, 1604, edn. of the *Corpus Iuris Civilis*; henceforth my references are to this edn.

10. The problem of *potestas* and *imperium* is difficult; I have given only a very general summary of complicated discussions by the legists on *D.* 2, 1 De iurisdictione omnium iudicium. For a general treatment of *imperium* (*merum* and *mixtum*) see Myron P. Gilmore, *Argument from Roman Law in Political Thought 1200–1600* (Cambridge, Mass., 1941), ch. 1. Of particular interest here is the gloss in the *Glos. ord.* to *D.* 2, 1, 3 Imperium, ad vv. *potestatem* and *mixtum est imperium*; also to *D.* 1, 21, 1.

11. Edn. of 1584, Venice, col. 869, no. 1.

12. *Ibid.*, no. 3: " . . . Verbum autem potestatis in dominis circa servos dominium . . . , circa magistratus imperium, circa abbates et monachos obedientiam significat, inter patrem et filium vinculum de iure civile reverentiae, et castigationis, et subiectionis, item pietatis significat . . ."

13. *Ibid.*, no. 6.

14. *Com.* (Paris, 1577), p. 662: " . . . quia non praesumitur quod pater filio vellet amputare caput." Azo adds that a father has more power over his daughter than over his wife, because the "pietas paterni nominis consilium pro liberis capit . . . "

15. *L. c.*

16. Above, to n. 6.

17. Raymundus M. Spiazzi, ed., *In libros Politicorum Aristotelis Expositio* (Turin, 1951), pp. 47 f., §152.

18. W. Stubbs, *Select Charters* (9th edn; Oxford, 1913), pp. 396 f. St. Louis declared that the king of England should have *plena potestas* and *liberum regimen* in his realm, and that he should be "in eo statu et in ea plenaria potestate," that is, he should be given the proper estate royal with *plenaria potestas*. See my *Studies in Medieval Legal Thought*, pp. 386–390. Naturally St. Louis thought that the French king should have the same *plenaria potestas* and *liberum regimen*. For the comparison of the papal *plenitudo potestatis* with that of a king see Michael Wilks, *The Problem of Sovereignty in the Later Middle Ages* (Cambridge, 1963), p. 335, and n. 4, where Wilks quotes this passage from St. Thomas, *Commentum in Senten-*

tias, IV, xx, 3 ad 3: "Papa habet plenitudinem potestatis pontificalis quasi rex in regno . . . " The words of St. Thomas surely indicate that like the pope in the Church, the king in the realm is supreme.

19. Is this a suggestion of awareness of the idea that the "public Body" or office of the king never dies? See E. H. Kantorowicz, *The King's Two Bodies* (Princeton, 1957), ch. 7.

20. Spiazzi, ed., p. 48, §154.

21. The reference apparently is to c.8 (in the Junta edn. of the Latin Aristotle, III, 86–87, with the *Com.* of Averroes).

22. *Summa Theol.*, 2a 2ae, q. 50, art. 1.

23. *Ibid.*, q. 57, art. 4.

24. *Ibid.*, q. 67, art. 1.

25. Joseph Mathis, ed., *De regimine principum* (Turin, 1924), pp. 18 f., I, c. 12. This idea is akin to that in the Roman law and the legists, that the king or prince is the *lex animata*, and that of St. Thomas, that the king is the *iustum animatum*; See Kantorowicz, *King's Two Bodies*, pp. 127–134, and my *Studies*, pp. 466 f.

26. C. H. McIlwain, *Growth of Political Thought in the West* (New York, 1932), p. 329; Brian Tierney, "Bracton on Government," *Speculum*, XXXVIII(1963), 303 f., where St. Thomas' theory is compared with Bracton's.

27. Spiazzi, ed., p.171, §486 (to the Latin text of Aristotle, III, xiii §346).

28. L. Delisle dates the MS in the thirteenth century, *Inventaire des manuscrits de l'Abbaye de Saint-Victor conservés á la Bibliothèque Impériale* (Paris, 1869), p. 73.

29. As is well known, *philosophus* usually but not always means Aristotle; probably here and at the beginning it does refer to Aristotle, but I do not find *coactiva (virtus)* or *coactivus (sermo)* in the Latin versions of the *Politics* and the *Ethics*. Of course, St. Thomas and this commentator often use their own Latin vocabulary.

30. *Commentator* usually but not always refers to Averroes; sometimes it refers to a Byzantine commentator on Aristotle, Michael of Ephesus or Eustratius of Nicaea. If Averroes wrote a commentary on the *Politics*, no Latin translation existed; and I have not found this opinion in his commentary on the *Ethics* (in vol. III of the Latin works of Aristotle, Juntas edn., Venice, 1562). Michael of Ephesus and Eustratius apparently did comment on the Nicom. *Ethics*, but not on the *Politics*.

Is it possible, then, that the *Commentator* mentioned by the author of the *Questiones* is St. Thomas Aquinas? At least St. Thomas, as we saw above, did conclude that a father did not have such *plenaria potestas* in his *domus* as a king had in his *regnum* (above, nn. 18, 22, and the text). Yet the wording used by the author of the *Questiones* is quite different from that of St. Thomas.

31. See above to n.22.

32. Above, n.4.

33. *Com.* on the *Tres Libri*, p.637, no.1; on *clerici* as *reges* Lucas refers to the *Decretum*, C. 12 q.1, c.7 Duo sunt—St. Jerome, saying that of the two kinds of Christians the *clerici* "sunt reges, id est se et alios in virtutibus regentes."

34. *Decr. Greg. IX.* 1, 6, 34. Lucas refers to Hostiensis on the words *in germanos*, i.e., Pope Innocent III's statement that the right of the German princes to elect a king who was to become the Emperor came from the Apostolic See, which transferred the Empire from the Greeks to the Germans.

35. *Com.*, p.637, no.1: "Item proprium regis est iudicium et iustitiam facere .23 .q .5 regum est" (the reference is to words of St. Jerome in the *Decretum*).

36. *L.c.*: "Potestas quippe regia constituta est ut mali coerceantur a malo."

37. *L.c.*: "Generale quoque pactum est societatis humanae regibus obtemperare"—Lucas is quoting St. Augustine (Dist. 8, c.3), who also says that disobedience to a king is against society, for just as the major *potestas* in human society is placed above lesser men to be obeyed, so God is above all other powers. See the *Glos. ord.* of Johannes Teutonicus ad v. *imo*: no *pactum* or contract of private persons can be valid against the supreme *auctoritas* in state or Church. That is, no private agreements can derogate from or injure the public welfare and the public authority. The decretist refers to *Decr. Gre. IX*, 2, 24, 19, a decretal of Innocent III declaring that an oath of the people of Todi is invalid because it injures the *ius superioris* (the pope himself in this case). The principle comes from the Roman law, *D.* 2, 14 De pactis, in general, and especially ll. 7, 38.

38. *Com.*, pp.64 f., nos. 5 and 6: "Rex quoque Francorum dicitur magnificus. de offi. leg. novit (*Decr. Greg. IX*, 2, 1, 13) . . . Sed contra: quia illustres dicuntur magnificentissimi . . . Sed hoc non multum videre obstare: quia et praetores dicuntur magnificentissimi. . . .Imperator vocatur egregius . . . Ex his licet non multum utilibus, tamen quia delectabilia sunt, interdum visum est occupare membranas."

39. See Walter Ullmann, *The Medieval Idea of Law as Represented by Lucas de Penna* (London, 1946), pp.92–104, 173, for additional ideas of Lucas on the authority of the king.

40. *Ibid.*, pp.92f.

41. *Com.*, p. 525 col.1, ad v. *imperio*, and nos.1 and 2. Of course, Lucas again refers to the famous decretal of Innocent III, the *Per venerabilem*, which was quoted over and over again both by those who sadly admitted that *de facto* the king of France recognized no superior, and by those who said that this was true also *de jure*. See my *Studies*, ch. X, Parts 2 and 3.

On the independence of the king of Sicily see also Marinus de Caramanico, quoted by Calasso, *Glossatori*, ch. IV, and pp. 194 ff.

42. In the *Apparatus* of Tancred to *Compilatio III* (decretals of Innocent III), 1, 6, 19 Venerabilem (*Decr. Greg. IX*, 1, 6, 34), the gloss of Johannes Teutonicus, ad v. *in Germanos*: "Sic ergo regimen mundi translatum est ad teutonicos –. . . ; et sic patet quod imperium non est apud grecos, licet largo nomine appelletur imperator . . . , sicut rex scaccorum . . . " I quote the gloss from the MS Can. 19, fol. 132, in the Staatsbibliothek at Bamberg.

It is amusing that *scaccorum* became *Scotorum* in some MSS and editions of the *Glos. ord.* to the *Decr. Greg. IX* in the sixteenth century; also that even J. F. von Schulte transcribed the *rex scaccorum* in the Bamberg MS as *rex francorum* ("Literaturgeschichte der Compilationes Antiquae," *Sitzungsberichte d. kais. Akad. d. Wissenschaften zu Wien, Philos.-histor. Kl.*, LXVI [1870], 130 f.).

Since Lucas knew the *Venerabilem* and, probably, the gloss of Johannes Teutonicus (for the gloss was included by Bernard of Parma in the *Glos. ord.* to the *Decr. Greg. IX*), he may have been influenced by the *rex scaccorum*. Certainly Marinus of Caramanico knew it, for he quotes the words and enlarges on them in order to indicate that he does not take seriously the terms for emperor, king, and prince; see the text in Calasso, *Glossatori*, p.192.

43. MS Can. 19, fol. 132: " . . . quoniam extra romanam ecclesiam non est imperium . . ." *Romanam* is inserted as *ro.* above *extra ecclesiam*, and may not belong originally to Johannes' gloss; but the context shows that he was speaking of the Roman Church.

44. *L.c.*: "Est autem imperator ille super omnes reges et omnes nationes sub eo sunt . . . Et dicit lex ipse enim est princeps mundi et dominus . . . Item omnia sunt in potestate imperatoris . . . " On this gloss see my *Studies*, pp. 456–459, 486–488.

45. See *Decretum*, C. 7 q.1, c.41 In apibus, and the glosses to it; also my *Studies*, p.457.

DIRECT TAXATION IN
A MEDIEVAL COMMUNE:
THE <u>DAZIO</u> IN SIENA, 1287-1355*

WILLIAM M. BOWSKY
University of California, Davis

The *dazio* or *lira*, the most important direct tax levied in Tuscan communes during the second half of the thirteenth century, was based upon an assessment of the taxpayer's wealth. In Siena as in other communes this assessment (ordinarily called the *lira*) allowed for exemptions for the basic necessities of life in amounts that varied according to one's economic and social status.[1] It is now a commonplace among historians that by the fourteenth century at the latest the wealthy landowning bourgeoisie and nobility ruling the Tuscan cities shied away from direct taxes—the *dazio* in particular. We are told that they favored levies upon the *contado*,[2] and indirect taxes that could more easily be passed on to other elements of society and would strike the affluent governing minority with proportionately less severity than the majority of the population. Historians of Florence in particular have noted that Florentine councillors sought out every other means of raising revenue before resorting to the *dazio*. After 1315 Florentine governments assiduously avoided direct taxes based on the *Estimo*, imposing *dazi* in the city only twice before mid-century—both times during the brief so-called tyrannical regimes. In 1352 and 1355 the *dazio* only reappeared because of the Visconti war and the menace of the imperial expedition of Charles IV.[3]

We are fortunate in knowing the fiscal policy of the leading Tuscan city state. But how typical was Florence of Italian or even Tuscan experience? Is a single explanation applicable to all or most towns, or are there variant patterns—and, if so, what are they? What are the causes for any divergences? These and corollary questions can only be answered through studies of the fiscal histories of numerous city states—a major undertaking. The present paper perforce is far more modest in scope: it is a preliminary analysis of the *dazio* in the commune of Siena, 1287-1355, the seven decades during which an oligarchy of wealthy bourgeoisie and nobles known as "The Nine Governors and Defenders of the Commune and People of Siena" ruled this Tuscan city state.[4]

How simple and time-saving it would be to state directly and clearly that the Sienese experience paralleled the Florentine, with perhaps some minor variations. A *prima facie* case could then be made for the theory that republican Tuscan communes had a common fiscal history. We would feel safer in generalizing broadly from our knowledge of Florence—as already is done far too extensively. The truth, however, is neither so simple nor easily attained.

Despite a statute ordering that books of assessments (*lire*) be burned once they were utilized,[5] the fires set by revolutionaries in 1355 and countless other vicissitudes over half a millenium of history,[6] sufficient documentation exists to permit the researcher to arrive at some tentative conclusions.

Eighteen *dazi*, at the very least,[7] were imposed in Siena during the regime of the Nine. They were confined to no single period. The commune levied *dazi* during the military campaigns against Arezzo in the regime's early years, during the wars against the Emperor Henry VII and their aftermath—especially immediately prior to the battle of Montecatini (August 29, 1315)—and in the closing years of the Tuscan Guelf wars against Castruccio Castracani. Still other *dazi* occurred in more peaceful times, in the closing decades of the regime as well as earlier. And, because of the sadly fragmentary nature of extant documentation, we should not make too much of those years in which *dazi* do not seem to have been imposed. Fiscal records are among the sparsest for the years 1299–1301, for example, a time when Siena warred heavily against her greatest opponents in the Maremma, the Aldobrandeschi counts. (It may be of some interest, however, that Siena imposed no *dazi* during the last great wars against the Aldobrandeschi in 1330–1331.)

Continued use of the *dazio* does not mean, of course, that this source of revenue remained constant in its importance to the communal budget—a budget that became increasingly diversified during the course of the fourteenth century.[8] On some few occasions, in fact, the government specifically ordered that its financial needs be met by other means.[9]

Evidence concerning the *dazi*, by its very omissions, often merely highlights problems of interpretation and analysis that confront the historian who wrestles with the complexities of Italian communal finance. All too often, for instance, we have no certain indication of the methods by which *dazi* were imposed, and of whether or not these varied from one imposition to the next. Little information is available concerning procedures for payment and collection. In many cases we cannot ascertain whether a *dazio* was imposed upon the entire state or upon a portion of it. Too frequently even the tax rates are unknown.

The initial impetus for imposing a *dazio* came frequently from the Nine, acting either alone or with the other three "Orders of the city—the Four *Provveditori* of the Biccherna (the highest financial magistracy), the Consuls of the Merchant Guild, and the Consuls of the Knights. Often an *ad hoc* legislative commission appointed by the City Council "to find a way to decrease expenses and increase income of the Sienese commune" recommended the imposition of a *dazio*. But even such commissions, like most others, ordinarily were appointed by the Nine and contained numerous *Noveschi* —men who had served or were eligible to serve on the Nine.

Payments were made in either of two ways: a single lump sum or several equal instalments spread over periods ranging from a month to about a year. Evidence is insufficient to establish a pattern, however, and the commune utilized both methods throughout the regime of the Nine. The arrangements made for a specific *dazio* probably depended upon the urgency of the need for cash, the size of the imposition, and what other revenue-producing measures were being employed at the same time.

Collections also were made in two ways: by officials of the Biccherna or through companies of Sienese bankers. Although the use of Biccherna officials seems to have been most common, I suspect that if the administration of the *dazi* at all paralleled that of the forced loans reliance upon the bankers increased during the closing decades of the regime—particularly following the onslaught of the Black Death in 1348 when experienced personnel were in extremely short supply.[10] On December 31, 1352, for example, the Biccherna received 2,121/17/11 pounds from a *dazio* collected by the bank of Tommuccio di Jacomo Colombini and Company.[11] Numerous questions that should be posed concerning the role of these banking companies cannot be answered on the basis of the known evidence. Did the bankers, for example, work for a fixed fee or for a percentage of the total collection, or did they "farm" the *dazi* in the manner of farmers of the gabelles—promise the government a stipulated sum and then themselves pocket all additional collections? These all are valid possibilities; for from their knowledge of the total worth of the *lire* (assessments) communal officials could estimate a *dazio's* approximate yield and set the rate so as to bring in the required sum.

A City Council deliberation of October 1, 1324 makes it clear that the government could indeed estimate the return on a direct tax and establish the rate accordingly.[12] The Council noted that an imposition (in this case, a *dazio*) that should yield 36,000 pounds had been levied on the city; another that would have garnered 18,000 pounds had been levied on the *contado*. The Council, because of increased needs, now doubled the rate of the city tax so that it would produce about 72,000 pounds in all. The *contado* ordered to pay a total of 30,000 pounds, to be distributed among the *contado* communities proportionately to each commune's share of the annual *contado* gabelle.[13] (This *contado* levy thus technically was not a *dazio* imposed by Siena itself directly upon *contado* taxpayers; rather it was to be collected as a *dazio* by the individual *contado* communes, which in turn were liable to the mother city for their shares of the 30,000 pounds). The measure of October 1 specifically enjoined the *contado* communes to take care lest any taxpayer be disproportionately or unduly burdened. Although on other occasions Siena set the rate for a *dazio* at the same time that it ordered a new assessment or *lira*, the government should have been able to anticipate the approximate yield on the basis of past experience and present economic and political conditions and by taking into account recent additions of territory to the state.

The question of the rates of the *dazi* is complex, and we are not aided by the extremely fragmentary nature of surviving data: often we do not know the rate of an individual dazio. Possibly lower rates were more common during the regime's last three decades. Nor can the existence of both very high rates (such as the 20 per cent of 1311–1312 and of 1315) and very low rates (sometimes less than 1 per cent) be explained away as having been determined solely by differing financial needs. Far more likely, variations occurred because some *dazi* were based on properties' annual income or rental value, others on estimated sale value; and because some *dazi* were based on assessments only of immovables, others on immovables and movables.[14] In May 1292, for example, it was ordered that "in the city of Siena the new *lira* of immovables (*possessioni*) must be made by itself, and the new *lira* of movables (*mobile*) by itself."[15]

A major obstacle to analysis of the tax rates is that ordinarily we do not know whether a given *dazio* was collected on the basis of a *lira* that included movables, immovables, or both. In the two cases where I have discovered the rates for a *dazio* on both, the rate for movables is 50 per cent higher than that on real property. In the fall of 1319 the rate was 3 *denari* per pound (1.25 per cent on movables and 2 *denari* per pound (.83 per cent) on immovables.[16] During the summer of 1323 "many" (*multi*) of the city, boroughs, Masse and Cortine, and others who "customarily paid" with the city were paying a *dazio* of three-fourths a *denarius* on movables and one-half a *denarius* on immovables.[17] Documentation, unhappily, does not disclose the assumptions that underlay this differential. The lower rate on immovables may reflect the greater difficulty of hiding real property and escaping taxation. It may indicate a belief that a greater certainty of income from immovables did not offset a lower yield; while the greater risks of banking and commerce nonetheless afforded higher profits. And while the Noveschi and the powerful magnates working with them in government often owned substantial amounts of real property in the city, Masse and *contado*, it was they, after all, who were the great Sienese bankers, merchants, and industrialists with widespread and extensive investments in Italy and western Europe. The higher tax rate on movables does not accord with the traditional interpretation portraying the Sienese government as a narrow, selfish oligarchy bent only on self-aggrandizement.[18] We should not, of course, have to emphasize that one cannot conclude from these two examples that such a differential always obtained in any *dazio* levied upon movables and immovables. When we further recall that the *dazio* was only one of the methods for acquiring money for the commune, it becomes evident that its rate, and the rates of its component parts, were partially determined by a consideration of what other fiscal measures were being undertaken concurrently.

Only in some cases does the documentation reveal which elements of the population were subject to any individual *dazio*. All of the known *dazi*, however, seem to have fallen upon the city, while only some applied to the *contado*—this latter was the case especially prior to the institution of the *contado* gabelle in 1291 and during the regime's closing years when it sorely needed funds. The majority of *dazi* fell upon all resident within the city (except for the Church, the impoverished, and those whose wealth was less than the minimum established for each *dazio*) and upon "those who customarily pay with the city"—several specified communities and ordinarily the Masse and the *contado* nobles. When the Masse were taxed separately and when the *contado* communities were ordered to pay *dazi*, the rates (when known) usually were either the same as those for the city, or

less—a fact that does not bespeak a conscious oppression by the city
of the rural countryside and the entire extra-urban populace. While
many *dazi* were paid by all who owned possessions sufficient to have
them recorded in the registers of the *lira,* some *dazi* were imposed
only on persons having a specified amount of wealth, for example,
those enrolled *(allirati)* for more or for less than 300 or 500 pounds.
The records of communal income in which *dazi* collections are recorded frequently indicate only the sums collected; in the absence
of the ordinances created for a specific *dazio* we cannot tell whether
or not this qualification of wealth obtained.

I have found only one *dazio* levied upon a special group based on
any classification other than residence or wealth, and that occurred
during the first year of the regime of the Nine. A *dazio* of 1287 was
levied upon the famous "Frati Gaudenti" or Jovial Brothers, those
Knights of the Glorious Virgin Mary who caused Italian communes
so much trouble in the late thirteenth century with their attempts to
evade taxes and other civic responsibilities by claiming the privileges of a religious order.[19] Derived from a brotherhood originating in Bologna in 1261, the Frati Gaudenti allegedly were dedicated
to quieting internecine strife and warring factions. But in actual fact
they were better known for their splendid banquets, and, not bound
to celibacy, they continued to live with their families, eschewing only
gold and silver ornamentation. The *dazio* of 1287 yielded less than
500 pounds, and was not repeated. Nor have I found any *dazi*
imposed upon persons engaged in specific occupations. In this the
dazio differed distinctly from the *preste,* which at least by the 1350's
were levied upon innkeepers and others doing business along the pilgrimage routes who might have been expected to profit especially
from the Jubilee Year of 1350 and upon foreign money lenders prac-
tising in Siena.[20]

One element is common to every type of *dazio* regardless of its
rate or upon whom it fell: time and again the City Council found it
necessary to impose penalties, ordinarily increased payments of one-
fourth or one-third more, upon those who failed to pay their taxes on
time. Examples can be cited from 1288,[21] 1315,[22] 1323,[23] 1330,[24]
1336,[25] 1343,[26] and 1352.[27] The regularity with which this penalty
was imposed shows clearly that the *dazio,* even on real estate, was
difficult to collect in a state that lacked the enormous and specialized
bureaucracies and means of communication and information re-
trieval of our own century.

Even these penalties proved insufficient at times. On February 5,

1323 the City Council publicly acknowledged that there "was and is a great muttering in the City of Siena" because many citizens and *contado* residents still owed *dazi* and *preste* imposed over the past twenty years. The Council imposed one-third more on all who failed to pay in full by March 5. But it also ordered far more drastic punishments: delinquents lost all rights in Sienese civil courts, and no one could work their lands or rent from them until they had paid in full—this under the penalty of a crushing 100 pound fine for each contravention. The Council commanded the Nine to select a commission of nine men whose task it would be to examine all books relating to impositions made during the past two decades and to list each of the commune's debtors and the amount he owed. If anyone did not pay within two months his name and surname and the sums that he owed were to be read aloud in the Council.[28]

Subterfuge and evasion could not be eliminated. As late as 1353 the Executors of the General Gabella (high financial officials) were ordered to proceed against citizens who evaded their taxes, especially the *dazi* on their properties in the Masse and *contado,* by telling the communities in which those holdings lay that they were Sienese citizens and hence immune from local taxation. They then defrauded Siena by entering into dishonest contracts that concealed their actual ownership of those properties.[29]

In the face of such difficulties why did not Siena, like Florence, abandon the *dazio*? That the tax could nonetheless provide substantial sums on occasion is but a part of the reason, and perhaps not the major part. The question becomes particularly intriguing when we understand that the great businessmen and landholders who controlled the Sienese government were not acting out of ignorance. They were fully aware that the *dazio* struck them with greater severity than did, for example, indirect taxes.[30] They did not act out of naiveté and did not have to wait for our own age to teach them the rudiments of economics. These medieval and early renaissance men realized clearly that different forms of taxation weighed differently upon the various components of Sienese society.

A hitherto unnoticed measure presented by a legislative commission to the City Council on May 9, 1323, is most revealing. The report began by stating that very possibly occasions would arise wherein the commune would have to act rapidly to acquire funds, and that at such times citizens might disagree strongly as to the best methods. Since this could cause great "scandal" and even danger to the city, the commission asked the councillors now to consider the various alternatives for raising money and to decide what portions of revenue should be obtained from each source. The measure then set forth five possible alternatives and the Council was asked to select its preference:

> Whether the commune of Siena ought to live and accomplish its business by means of the Table [of Possessions] or by the Table,[31] or indeed whether it should live and accomplish [its affairs] by making a *Lira* or through the *Lira*, or by means of the Gabella or through the Gabella; or if it rather please the same Council that all of the aforesaid three methods be reduced to one and the same, and then the exaction of some money that will be made in the future for the commune of Siena be exacted of the citizens in this way, namely, a third part by means of the Table, a third part, indeed, by means of the *Lira*, and a third part by means of the Gabella and through the Gabella. *And this because a greater equality will be maintained among the citizens, because if anyone is burdened in the Table he can be relieved in the Lira and in the Gabella, and so on.* Or if the said Council would rather prefer to select two from the aforesaid means, those two means which the Council wishes can similarly be combined into one, and in that case the exaction that will be made for the commune will be exacted in this way, namely, one-half by one of the two methods and the remaining half by the other method, so that if anyone is burdened in one he can be relieved in the other, as was said.[32]

It is most important that we realize that the Sienese government understood that different persons were differently burdened by each of the various means suggested for raising money, and that the commissioners stressed the need to achieve an equality of sacrifice among Sienese taxpayers in order to create a just and equitable fiscal system. This emphasis upon equality—not in the sense that each man should contribute the same amount as his fellows, but rather that each should bear his proportionate share of the burden according to his own means and tenor of life—is a traditional and well known theme in Sienese tax legislation,[33] and it recurs frequently in the opening paragraphs of money bills.[34] The theme in fact is almost ubiquitous in Sienese legislation and thought throughout the regime of the Nine, and is underscored in Ambrogio Lorenzetti's famous fresco and allegory of *Good Government* enshrined in the very council chamber of the Nine in the Sienese communal palace.

Nor can we discount this as a platitudinous wish or a mere sop to tradition. Inequality there was, to be sure, as in any society. But the rulers of Siena must have believed that this was the sort of government and the system of values expected of them. And there is no evidence that they themselves did not share this belief, but merely mouthed it as an opiate for the masses. The Nine were not Jacob Burckhardt's Constantine, and fairness and equality were more than slogans. The desire to attain them accounts in part for the continued utilization of the *dazio* in the city, a tax that weighed more heavily upon the ruling oligarchy than upon the less affluent majority of the population. This is in striking contrast with the Florentine experience. That the *dazio* remained one of the mainstays of the Sienese financial system resulted from more than its occasionally substantial returns, or from fiscal conservatism and traditionalism. The *dazio* was not discarded in part because the government wished to have as many strings as possible in its fiscal bow and never relied exclusively upon any single means for raising funds. The desire, however, for equality and fairness in taxation and the support of the state also played a significant role in the history of the *dazio* during the regime of the Nine.

APPENDIX

1287, Jan.–June

Pounds 3,775 paid by 48 *contado* communities for various old *dazi,* especially those of 100s. per 100 pounds (5 per cent), 4 per 100 pounds (4 per cent), 13d. (5.33 per cent) and 15d. (6.25 per cent) per pound Biccherna, N. 95, fol. 28r-v) [Hereafter Biccherna will be abbreviated as B.]

4,205 (approximately) paid as "datia recollecta" by about 1,700 persons in all three of the *Terzi* (major districts) of the city. The great majority of payments range from less than one pound to five pounds. (B. 95, fols. 31r–70r)

850 (approximately) paid by persons in the city as "old *dazi*" of 3 florins per 100 pounds (ca. 5.42 per cent) and 9d. per pound (3.75 per cent). (B. 95, 71r–87r)[1]

477/10/10 "datio Gaudentium," paid in a total of eleven separate entries. (B. 95, fol. 87v)

1288, July–December

Pounds 23,439/–/11 received from a *dazio* of 12/10/–pounds "per centenarium" (12.5 per cent) in all three Terzi of the city. (B. 97, fol. 55v)

12,133/18/8 received from a *dazio* of 12.5 per cent "a comunitatibus terrarum comitatus." (B. 97, fol. 55v)

1289, Jan.–June

Pounds 513/4/–from persons throughout the city "pro datiis veteribus."
(B. 99, fol. 31r)
148/17/3 "ab hominibus at personis totius comitatus pro datiis
veteribus." (B. 99, fol. 31r)
April 4, 1289: a *dazio* of 6/5/–pounds "per centenario" (6.25 per cent) "recently" imposed in the city is extended to the *contado*. (CG, N.
37, fols. 78v–80r; cf. *ibid.*, fol. 85v [April 15, 1289])

1289, July–December

Pounds 479/17/5 from a *dazio* of 15d. per pound (6.25 per cent) from persons throughout the entire city. (B. 102, fol. 38v)
173/18/6 from a *dazio* of 30d. per pound (12.5 per cent) (B. 102, fol.
38v)
4,521/17/8 from a *dazio* of 4 pounds per 100,Terzo of Città
3,349/10/7 _____, Terzo of SanMartino
4,779/15/7 _____, Terzo of Camollia
12,653/3/10 total for this *dazio* from all three Terzi (B. 102, fol.
38v and B. 101, fol. 39v)

1291 Jan.–June

Pounds 3,408/ 1/ 1 from a *dazio* of 6/5/–pounds per 100 (6.25 per cent),
Terzo of Città
2,362/12/ 4 _____, Terzo of San Martino
3,465/ 9/ 2 _____, Terzo of Camollia
9,236/ 2/ 7 total for this *dazio* from all three Terzi (B. 104, fol.
40r)
1,695/4/3 old *dazi* and *preste* in the city (B. 104, fol. 52v)
4,608/12/4 old *dazi* and *preste*, from 81 *contado* communities (B.
104, fols. 53r–54v)

1291 July–December

Pounds 384/ 4/–"residui datii sex libr. et V s. per cent. [6.25 per cent]
impositi personis et hominibus civitatis sen. de mense Junii anno
dni. millesimo CCLXXXXI Ind. IIII.," from Terzo of Città.
(B. 106, fols. 61r–76r)
281/13/ 8, for the same reason, from Terzo of San Martino
(B. 106, fols. 77r–89v) [Some folios of B. 106 are missing between fols. 89v and 90r]
292/ 1/ 6 from a *dazio* of 15d. per pound (6.25 per cent) in the
Masse (B. 106, fols. 90r–97v)

July 7, 1307

The City Council decides that a *dazio* is to be imposed in the city in order to
repay a *presta* ordered on the same day. (Statuti, Siena, N. 15,
fols. 308r–310r)

1311–1312

A *dazio* of 20 per cent, collected ca. December 1311–June 1312. (See W. Bowsky, "*Buon Governo*," 378, especially with reference to Lira, N. 10). Lira, N. 10 is not a complete record of the collections in the city and does not include the totals collected. About a third of the payments are for 1 pound or less, over three-fourths are for 5 pounds or less. It is difficult to tell from Lira, N. 10 how much this *dazio* acquired for the commune. It allowed discounts for a *presta* and probably for a *cavallata*, but some entries note that the payment is the "remainder" of one's *dazio*—e.g., fol. 2r: 41/6/10 pounds "da Incontro del Balza . . . [from San Pellegrino in Terzo of Città] i quali [denari] sono di rimanenze del suo dazio di quatro soldi per libra scontate la sua presta in libris et denariis de la cavallata." According to an unclear statement in the chronicle of Agnolo di Tura del Grasso[2] 20 per cent was the highest rate yet imposed for a *dazio* and this *dazio* yielded 27,250 pounds in the first payment in the city, and 180,000 pounds in all—including the *contado*. An anonymous chronicle reports "it was said that more than 180,000 'duchati' were collected. . . . "[3]

March 13, 1313

The City Council approved provisions to raise 12,000 gold florins with which to pay the cavalry whom King Robert of Naples "mictere debet in subsidium partis Guelfe Tuscie et omnium amicorum." (This refers, of course, to the Guelf opposition to the Emperor Henry VII in Italy.[4]) As the contents of the provisions are not included we do not know whether or not a *dazio* was intended. (CG, N. 82, fols. 99r–102r; quotation on fol. 99r)]

August 1, 1315

There began the collection of a *dazio* of 4s. per pound (20 per cent) in the city, against which a *presta* of 1315–1316 was later discounted. (Lira, N. 274, fol. 1r)

1319 Sept.–October

A *dazio* was imposed on the wealthiest persons of the city, Masse and *contado* at the rate of 2d. per pound (.83 per cent) on immovables and 3d. per pound (1.25 per cent) on movables. One half of this *dazio* was to be paid at once, and those who had paid a *presta* of 3,000 gold florins could discount that *presta* against this payment. The second half was to be collected at a time to be set by the Nine. (CG, N. 92, fols. 110v–113v, Sept. 29, 1319; fols. 120r–121r, Oct. 14, 1319.) For immovables this *dazio* was to be based on the Table of Possessions, already completed for the city and the Masse and almost completed for the *contado* (*Ibid.*, fol. 120r-v, Oct. 14, 1319)

July 9, 1323

A *dazio* of one-half d. on immovables and three-fourths d. on movables is currently being paid by many (*multi*) of the city, boroughs, Masse and Cortine and *contado* nobles and others who customarily pay with the city; it is being collected in the city by means of the Table of Possessions. (CG, N. 98, fols. 55r–56r)

1324, probably summer to Oct. 1

The City Council doubles the rate of a *dazio* recently imposed on the city, so that it will yield 72,000 pounds rather than 36,000; an imposition on the *contado* that would have raised 18,000 pounds is now set at the fixed sum of 30,000. In addition an imposition, almost certainly a *dazio*, is now ordered made on the heads of families of the Masse and Cortine, *contado* nobles, and others who customarily pay with the city. This is to be paid at the same rate as the newly doubled *dazio* for the city. (Statuti, Siena, N. 23, fols. 123r–126r; see the discussion of this measure, above p. 208.)

1325

In the city, Masse, and *contado* four payments have already been made on a "lira," some of which seem to have been *dazi*. September 16, 1325 a fifth payment, in the form of a *presta*, was ordered paid by those in the city by mid–October, those in the Masse and Cortine by mid–November, and by residents of the *contado* by Jan. 1, 1326. (CG, N. 102 fols. 48r–50r, Sept. 16, 1325).[5]]

August 20, 1328

The City Council approves a decision of the Nine, the Four Provveditori of the Biccherna, the Executors of the General Gabella and a commission of nine men (three per Terzo) appointed by the Nine. All these had examined the books of the Lira and recommended that a *dazio* of 20s. per 100 pounds (1 per cent) be collected in the city, boroughs, and suburbs from each person listed in the Lira (*allirato, allibratus*) in four equal instalments. The first payment is to be made within one month, the second within the following three months, the third in the next three months, and the final payment within the next three months—a total of ten months being allowed for the entire collection. (CG, N. 106, fols. 34r– 38r)

March 30, 1330

The City Council orders the payment of the fourth instalment of a *dazio* imposed in the city on those allirati 500 pounds or more. (CG, N. 109, fols. 83v–88r)

July 12, 1336

A *dazio* is now being paid in Siena by all who are allirati 3d. (= 300 pounds)[6] or more in the last lira. (CG, N. 119, fols. 7r–10v)

October 9, 1342

A *dazio* of 9d. per 100 pounds (.0375 per cent) is imposed in the city on the basis of a newly made *lira*, and is (?) to be paid in two equal installments (CG, N. 131, fols. 64r–65v). It is possible, however, that each of the instalments was to be paid at the rate of 9d. per 100 pounds (or, less probably, a separate *dazio* of 18d. per 100 pounds was collected in the Masse). See B. 212, fol. 93r, noting the collection by one Francesco di Neri di Giovanni of a *dazio* of 18d. per 100 pounds in the Masse.

1342

A *dazio* of 12s. 2d. per "denaro" (100 pounds), the equivalent of 2 florins per 1,000 pounds, was imposed on those in the city, the Masse, *contado* nobles, sylvan citizens[7] and a few communities that paid with the city (Mensano, Monteriggioni and Frosini). (Lira, N. 11; see also E. Fiumi, "imposta diretta," p. 353.) This *dazio*, too, was collected for the Biccherna by Francesco di Neri di Giovanni (B. 212, fol. 93r)

August 9, 1343

A *dazio* of 18d. per 100 pounds (.075 per cent) is now imposed in those *allirati* in the last *lira* who paid a *dazio* of 9d. per 100 pounds [see above, Oct. 9, 1342].[8] This new *dazio* was needed especially to pay the salaries of mercenaries, crossbowmen, and ambassadors sent recently to Florence. (CG, N. 132, fols. 131r–132v.)

October 8, 1348

An imposition of 6s. per 100 pounds (.3 per cent), almost certainly a *dazio*, was imposed on those in the city, Masse, and *contado* nobles and all others who customarily paid with the city *allirati* 1,000 pounds or less. (W. Bowsky, "Black Death," p. 22n. 117)

1349, May–June

Payments were made to the man preparing the *lira (alliratori)* of a "dazio nuovo." (B. 224, fols. 176v, 182v)

1352, July–December

Pounds 17,663/13/7 from a dazio of 12s. 6d. per 100 pounds (.625 per cent) paid in all three Terzi of the city. (B. 230, fol. 71v)/ Several

other small payments of this *dazio* are also recorded, e.g.,
7/2/6 pounds from Francesco di Gualtieri Squarcialupi (a Noveschi noble) (B. 230, fol. 72v)

2,121/17/11 from a *lira (dazio)* with one-fourth more as the penalty
for late payment, collected by Sienese bankers. (above, p. 207 n.
11)

NOTES

*A Guggenheim Fellowship and a Social Science Research Council
Fellowship helped to make possible the research upon which this paper is
based. The unpublished documents cited below are in the Archivio di Stato
of Siena.

1. The best treatment of the *dazio* and the *lira* is E. Fiumi, "L'imposta
diretta nei comuni medioevali della Toscana," *Studi in onore di Armando
Sapori,* I (Milan, 1957), 327–353. See also D. Herlihy, "Direct and Indirect
Taxation in Tuscan Urban Finance," *Finances et comptabilité urbaines du
XIIIe au XVIe siècle. Colloque international Blarkenberge 6-9-IX-1962.
Actes* (Brussels, 1964), pp. 385–405; B. Barbadoro, *Le finanze della Repub-
blica fiorentina. Imposta diretta e debito pubblico fino all'istituzione del
Monte* (Florence, 1929). Essential to an understanding of the Sienese *dazio*
are the following rubrics in A. Lisini, ed., *Il costituto del comune di Siena
volgarizzato nel MCCCIX-MCCCX,* 2 vols. (Siena, 1903): Dist. I, r. cccxli,
"Di pagare li datii; et come si constrengano coloro e'quali debono pagare."
Ibid., r. cccxlii, "Di quel medesimo." *Ibid.,* r. cccxliv, "Che neuno abia
immunità di non pagare datio." *Ibid.,* r. cccxlv, "Come si debia fare la
libra nuova." *Ibid.,* r. cccxlvi, "Che li beni di ciascuno s' invengano et
s' allibrano." *Ibid.,* r. cccxlvii, "Che ciascuno se et li sui beni faccia allibrare."
Ibid., r. cccxlix, "D' elegere li officiali per trovare coloro, e' quali non sono
allibrati," *Ibid.,* r. ccclix, "Di non servare ragione a colui el quale non
pagarà el suo datio, o vero condannagione."

2. The Sienese *contado* was that portion of the state outside of the city
(and its immediate environs—the communities of the Masse) most completely and/directly subject to Siena. I will deal with the entire problem of
Sienese *contado* taxation elsewhere, as part of a separate study of Sienese
city-*contado* fiscal relations.

3. See, e.g., G. Brucker, *Florentine Politics and Society, 1343–1378*
(Princeton, 1962), p. 93; M. Becker, "Florentine Popular Government
(1343–1348)," *Proceedings of the American Philosophical Society,* CVI
(1962), 362; cf. Herlihy, "Direct and Indirect Taxation," p. 402.

4. For an introductory study of the Nine, a bimensile magistracy, see
W. Bowsky, "The *Buon Governo* of Siena (1287–1355): A Mediaeval
Italian Oligarchy," *Speculum,* XXXVII (1962), 368–381.

5. Lisini, *Il costituto,* Dist. I, r. cccxlv; cf. Biccherna, N. 1, fols. 65v–
66r. For similar legislation in Pistoia, see D. Herlihy, *Medieval and Renaissance Pistoia* (New Haven–London, 1967), p. 185.

6. For a brief survey of the history of the Sienese archives see G. Cec-
chini, "La legislazione archivistica del Comune di Siena," *Archivio Storico*

Italiano, CXIV (1956), 224–257; cf. W. Bowsky, "The Sienese Archive and the *Pubblicazioni degli Archivi di Stato," Manuscripta,* V (1961), 67–77.

7. See the Appendix for documentation for this and other new statements of fact not specifically documented in the footnotes.

8. I will examine the large and intricate subject of the Sienese fiscal system and the roles of its individual components in a separate monograph.

9. E.g., Dec. 11, 1290: no *dazi* or *preste* (forced loans) are to be imposed in the commune of Siena (Consiglio Generale, Deliberazioni [CG], N. 40, fol. 62r); Oct. 1, 1324: a *dazio* is imposed, but in the hope that future *dazi* and *preste* will not be necessary (Statuti, Siena, N. 23, fol. 123r); cf. Statuti, Siena, N. 23, fol. 323r, July 10, 1332, although it is not completely clear that *dazi* are to be excluded.

10. See W. Bowsky, "The Impact of the Black Death upon Sienese Government and Society," *Speculum,* XXXIX (1964), 1–34; for the forced loans, cf. *idem,* "Medieval Citizenship: The Individual and the State in the Commune of Siena, 1287–1355," *Studies in Medieval and Renaissance History,* IV (1967), 232 n. 101.

11. Biccherna 230, fol. 72r: "Item a libra que exacta fuit cum quarto pluri ad banch[um] Tommuccii Iacomi [Colombini] et sotiorum. . . ." The Colombini were a Noveschi family, Bowsky, "*Buon Governo,*" 373 n. 22.

12. Statuti, Siena, N. 23, fols. 123r–126r.

13. For the *contado* gabelle, instituted in 1291, see W. Bowsky, "*Buon Governo,*" p. 375 n. 32; *idem,* "Black Death," pp. 12–13, 23.

14. Cf. E. Fiumi, "imposta diretta," [cited above, n. 1], pp. 344ff.

15. Lisini, *Il costituto,* Dist. I, r. cccxlv (see vol. I, p. 250: "Et fatto è questo capitolo in anno Domini Mcclxxxxij. Inditione v, del mese di magio."). An addition, included within the body of the rubric, "se parrà a li signori Nove, Mcclxxxxviiij. Inditione xij, del mese di magio," probably misled Fiumi into dating the entire rubric as 1289: "imposta diretta," p. 352.

16. See Appendix, p. 215.

17. See Appendix, p. 216.

18. For this traditional interpretation, see the literature cited in W. Bowsky, "*Buon Governo,*" 369 n. 3.

19. See Appendix, p. 213 for the *dazio* of 1287. On the Frati Gaudenti see, e.g., A. Hessel, *Geschichte der Stadt Bologna* (Berlin, 1910), pp. 413–414, 474; R. Davidsohn, *Geschichte von Florenz,* IV, 3 (Berlin, 1901), 57; P. Toynbee, *A Dictionary of Proper Names and Notable Matters in the Works of Dante* (Oxford, 1898), pp. 251–252.

20. See W. Bowsky, "Black Death," p. 22.

21. CG, N. 36, fol. 33v, Dec. 4, 1288: all who fail to pay in full within eight days their share of a *dazio* of 12.5 per cent imposed in the city and *contado* must pay one-third more.

22. CG, N. 86, fols. 161v–162v, Nov. 10, 1315: persons in the city failing by December 1, 1315 to pay their *dazi* on the basis of the last *lira* must pay one-fourth more.

23. CG, N. 98, fols. 55r–56r, July 9, 1323: Those failing to pay within eight days their *dazi* of one-half d. per pound on immovables and three-fourths d. per pound on movables must pay one-third more.

24. CG, N. 109, fols. 83v–88r, March 30, 1330: Those failing by Apr.

20, 1330 to pay the fourth instalment of a *dazio* imposed on persons in the city *allirati* 500 pounds or more must pay one-fourth more.

25. CG, N. 119, fols. 7r–10v, July 12, 1336: Those failing by August 1, 1336 to pay the *dazio* imposed on persons *allirati* 300 pounds or more must pay one-fourth more.

26. CG, N. 133, fol. 13v, October 10, 1343: Those who by Nov. 1, 1343 fail to pay their share of a *dazio* imposed Aug. 9, 1343 must pay one-fourth more.

27. See above, n. 11.

28. Statuti, Siena, N. 22, fols. 17r–18r. Cf. Lisini, *Il costituto*, Dist. I, r. ccclix (above, n. 1).

29. Biccherna, N. 2, fol. 63r–v, July 24, 1353.

30. See, e.g., Statuti, Siena, N. 22, fols. 11r–13v, Jan. 10, 1300.

31. For the Tables of Possessions, volumes recording the descriptions and evaluations of real property, see W. Bowsky, *"Buon Governo,"* pp. 375–377 and *idem*, "Black Death," p. 10–11, and the literature there cited, esp. I. Imberciadori, "Il catasto senese del 1316," *Archivio 'Vittorio Scialoja'*, VI (1939), 154–168. For a brief clear discussion of the Sienese, Florentine and Lucchese "Tables" see E. Fiumi, "imposta diretta," pp. 341–345.

32. Statuti, Siena, N. 23, fols. 17r–18v (quotation on fol. 17v; the italics are mine). We cannot be certain at present which method, if any, the Council selected.

33. E. Fiumi rightly emphasized this, especially in his analysis of the phrase "coequato paupere cum divite" and his refutation of assertions made in Romolo Caggese's, "La Repubblica di Siena e il suo contado nel secolo decimoterzo," *Bullettino Senese di Storia Patria*, XIII (1906), 3–120: E. Fiumi, "Sui rapporti economici tra città e contado nell'età comunale," *Archivio Storico Italiano*, CXIV (1956), 18–68, esp. 25–27.

34. See, e.g., Statuti, Siena, N. 23, fol. 28r, July 7, 1323; *Ibid.*, fol. 346r, Feb. 17, 1333, "ut inter cives senenses equalitas observetur et honera ipsius comunis tollerentur equaliter per eosdem. . . ." *Ibid.*, fol. 348r, another measure of Feb. 17, 1333, "In primis attendentes sapientes predicti, Quod equitatis debitum exigit unumquemque debere secundum sue facultatis exigentiam honere sui comunis incumbere. . . ."

NOTES TO APPENDIX

1. The florin was worth about 1/6/2 pounds; cf. B. 95, fol. 97v. Beginning with 1302 the almost daily official exchange rates between Sienese coinage and the florin (copied from entries in the Biccherna volumes) are published in C. Cipolla, "Studi di storia della moneta," *Università di Pavia. Studi nelle scienze giuridiche e sociali pubblicati dall' Istituto di Esercitazioni presso la Facoltà di Giurisprudenza*, XXIX (1948), 31–239, in Appendice III, 156ff.

2. Chronicle of Agnolo di Tura del Grasso, in *Cronache senesi*, A. Lisini and F. Iacometti, eds., *Rerum Italicarum Scriptores*, n. s., XV, Part VI (Bologna, 1931–1937), 318.

3. *Cronache senesi*, 93.

4. See W. Bowsky, *Henry VII in Italy. The Conflict of Empire and City-State, 1310–1313* (Lincoln, Nebr., 1960).

5. Cf. CG, N. 102, fols. 51v–55v, Sept. 20, 1325: the imposition of one-fourth more on those who failed to meet the deadlines established for their *presta* on September 16.

6. For the occasional usage in Siena of d. = 100 pounds, see E. Fiumi, "imposta diretta," p. 353.

7. See W. Bowsky, "*Cives Silvestres:* Sylvan Citizenship and the Sienese Commune (1287–1355)," *Bullettino Senese di Storia Patria*, LXXII (1965), 3–13.

8. This apparently is a case in which an old *lira* was reused for a new imposition, and not destroyed as demanded by statute. Cf. above, n. 1.

THE CIVIC IRRESPONSIBILITY OF
THE VENETIAN NOBILITY

DONALD E. QUELLER

University of Illinois

Romantic myth pervades the history of Venice to a remarkable degree, for few places on earth so readily capture the romantic imagination. Gina Fasoli describes a *mito bifronte*: "the myth of a Venice, magnanimous, heroic, generous, liberal, powerful; the myth of a Venice, wrteched, vile, avid, tyrannical, foolishly proud in its impotence."[1] A primary characteristic of the sanguine face of Venetian mythology is the conceit of a patriciate, guarding its monopoly of power by its selfless dedication to the welfare of the state.

Popularizers and serious scholars alike have lavished upon the Venetian aristocracy hyperbolic praise. Giuseppe Volpi, for example, transported by chauvinism, effused:

> Per servire degnamente la Repubblica non pochi "oratori" n'ebbero dissestato il patrimonio familiare. Ma nessuno venne mai meno al proprio dovere. Amanti della patria, ligi agli ordini, compresi dell' importanza e della necessità dell'ufficio, noi li troviamo sempre alacri, diligenti e premurosi attendere ad esso con tutte le forze, superando disagi, dispendi, contrarietà e difficoltà.[2]

Better scholars than Volpi have been equally profuse in their praises of the oligarchy of the lagoons. Molmenti finds a characteristic remorse for any failure to fulfill a noble's patriotic duty in the will of Giovanni Contarini, who left to the Commune fifty *pounds* in recompense for the offices and councils to which he was obligated, but which he had avoided.[3] Renouard lauds the Venetian men of affairs, preoccupied with the greatness of the city and capable of sacrificing themselves for the public welfare, who created in Venice a "masterwork of man."[4] Diehl's adulation of Venetian patriotism offends common sense. According to him, the essential rule of life of the Venetian patrician was absolute devotion to the state. For every Venetian, indeed, "the Republic is everything and the individual nothing."[5]

In official documents evidence can be found for Fasoli's *mito bifronte* under both guises. Luzzato cites a public loan of 1187 in which the Republic addresses itself to its citizens (and primarily to the patriciate), as *amatores terrae nostrae, qui possunt et consueverunt nostrae patriae necessitatis suae tempore subvenire.*[6] Three centuries later the Great Council declared that in this world above all things we are obligated to the public welfare. Reality, however, did not match this pious ideal, for the very same act was addressed to the problem of finding noblemen to fill offices, because they did not wish to do so without large salaries, "a thing harmful, shameful and perilous to our republic."[7] Another act concerned with election to office reports that "for the greater part they refuse."[8] An intended embassy to England in 1417 had to be abandoned, because the Senate could not find any noble who would accept.[9] Frantically attempting to avoid their civic duties, Venetian patricians disrupted the electoral procedure with cries of "Don't elect me! Don't see me!"[10] Sanctions even had to be imposed against refusal of membership on the highest councils of the Republic, such as the Small Council and the Council of Forty.[11] Opposed to the ideal of the selfless patriot, we see here the Venetian businessman shirking public duties in pursuit of his individual ends. Frederic Lane has pointed out that Andrea Barbarigo, after he had made what use he could of public office, never served the state after he was thirty-two, but devoted himself exclusively to commercial opportunities.[12]

The recent work of James C. Davis on *The Decline of the Venetian Nobility as a Ruling Class* argues that the Venetian patriciate became inadequate in the seventeenth and eighteenth centuries for the responsibilities it had once so nobly filled. Davis attributes this inadequacy to "the economic and demographic decline of the nobility, their loss of public spirit, their more or less conscious imitation of the customs of foreign aristocracies, and the decline in the number of patricians experienced from youth with ships and the sea."[13] Prior to about the middle of the sixteenth century he finds no great problem in recruiting nobles for public office.[14] On the contrary, however, the evidence is overwhelming that there was enormous difficulty in filling public offices reserved for the nobility from as early as the late twelfth century, as Lazzarini's article of 1936 suggested, although he only scratched the surface of the evidence.[15] Davis stresses that he is dealing mainly with the economic and demographic causes of the governmental problem, and only incidentally with others such as political apathy, and he has made his main point skillfully and convincingly, but "loss of public spirit" should be stricken from the list of causes on the grounds that the vaunted public spirit of the Venetian patriciate at the height of Venetian power from the *Dugento* through the *Quattrocento* was probably about the same as the public spirit of any other urban patriciate, neither greater nor less.[16]

Difficulty in obtaining noblemen to fill public office became serious enough even before the thirteenth century to require legislative coercion. By the earliest act on this subject known to us the Great Council in 1185 required that anyone elected to public office must accept within three days under penalty of being ineligible for all honors and offices and losing his right in the court, and in 1211 a fine of two hundred *pounds* was added for refusal of office.[17] A law of 1257 appears to weaken the coercion applied to electees, for it provided that refusal of office in itself should not be penalized, although refusal after the acceptance (even tacit) should be penalized by a fine of one hundred *pounds*.[18] Returning to a more severe attitude, the Great Council in 1263 established a penalty of ten large *soldi* and six months' exclusion from salaried office for refusing any post.[19] Ambassadors and officials who accepted, then later refused to go or to remain as ordered by the doge, fell not only under the penalty for refusal, but also exclusion from all public office for a year, according to an act of 1269.[20]

Embassies and other assignments outside Venice proved particularly costly to the individual and were the specific object of a group of acts beginning in 1272, when a penalty of twenty *grossi* was imposed for refusal of any ambassadorship.[21] The exclusion from all offices and benefices for a year was reaffirmed in 1361 for all those who accepted embassies, commands, and other missions abroad, and subsequently refused.[22] Although the principle of imposing penalties for refusal to assume public duties was long established by the fifteenth century, the problem was far from solved, for in 1454 the Great Council sought to reinforce earlier acts by forbidding elected ambassadors, provisors, and others to refuse their elections under penalty of one hundred *pounds* and exclusion from office for two years.[23] The minimum penalty was raised to three hundred *pounds* in 1479.[24] Still large numbers of Venetian nobles refused their service, as evidenced by the list of Venetian orators at Naples from 1450 to 1501 indicating many refusals of the office.[25] The anonymous French "Traité du gouvernement de Venise," written about the end of the fifteenth century, calls attention to the imposition of financial penalties and banishment to coerce patricians into service as ambassadors.[26]

A special problem arose out of the custom of assigning suitable escorts to distinguished visitors to the city. Although this does not appear to be an especially oppressive duty, "all refuse" to serve in this capacity. The Senate, therefore, imposed a penalty of loss of office and exclusion from office for a year for refusal to carry out such an assignment. Since "many when they receive such a command do not care to obey" a penalty of ten ducats was added at a later date.[27]

Since public office could not be refused without penalty, nobles went to extraordinary lengths to avoid election. From a very early time they sought to escape their obligations by avoiding notification, so that the Great Council specified that announcement of his election outside a noble's house was equivalent to a personal summons.[28] Nonetheless, one could not be elected ambassador, provisor, *tractator*, or other official serving outside of Venice unless he was in the city between the time of his election and the three days allotted for his acceptance. Nobles suspecting that they might be elected fled to Murano, remaining in that shelter until the three days had passed and escaping all penalty. The Senate, therefore, decreed that such an excuse would no longer prevail unless the electee had left Venice at least eight days before his election and could swear that he had not left the city for the purpose of escaping office.[29] Apparently considerable numbers of Venetian noblemen swore falsely as to their purpose for being out of the city, for the act was amended in 1441 to impose the penalties for refusal unless the electee should be absolved by two-thirds of the Senate upon his oath that he did not leave Venice in order to escape office.[30] Many patricians continued to use this avenue of escape, so in 1458 it was required that an electee must have left Venice fifteen days before the election under the customary oath that he had not done so for the purpose of avoiding his duty. It is interesting that this act adds ducal councillors and advocates of the commune to the more burdensome offices beyond the city which had earlier been the subject of such legislation.[31]

It was much more convenient, of course, if one could prevent his election in the first place, and vigorous campaigns *not* to be elected were conducted. When unwanted offices, such as captain, ambassador, provisor, or *tractator,* had to be filled, some nobles cried to their fellows *non me eleze* or *non me voie,* or they had those who carried the balloting urns or others say it. An act of 1427 sought to put a stop to this indecorous and harmful practice.[32] The reason for an act of 1443 requiring that nobles coming to an election of a rector, provisor, orator, or other official should promptly accept their ballots and cast them is not so clearly stated, but since disorders and inconveniences are mentioned it also was probably designed to minimize manipulations for the avoidance of election.[33] When elections of ambassadors, provisors, and others were held in the College, a small body, they could be significantly affected by the relatives of a nominee. The Great Council and the Forty therefore legislated in 1475 against fathers, sons, or brothers of a nominee voting for another candidate in the College to protect their own house against the burdens of office.[34]

The earliest coercive legislation known did allow a prospective office-holder to be excused for legitimate reason.[35] In the continuing struggle to fill its approximately one hundred important offices, however, the state found it necessary gradually to limit the acceptable excuses. Evasion of office on the grounds of a vow or an oath was outlawed at an early date.[36] From the oath of office taken by the doge's Council in 1229 it appears that some patricians were avoiding their responsibilities simply by accepting the penalty, which the councillors swore not to accept as an excuse.[37] Those who held public office employed their official duties as an excuse for refusal to serve as *tractatores* assigned to treat with visiting ambassadors, until in 1268 the Great Council decreed that they should be excused from their regular responsibilities during the period of negotiations without loss of salary. The very fact of multiplication of civic duties upon single individuals points up the shortage of qualified nobles to accept public responsibilities either willingly or under coercion.[38] According to an act of 1272 the Great Council required that an excuse for avoiding an embassy had to be supported by oath.[39] By 1286 it became necessary to specify clearly the excuses that would be accepted: the electee's own illness, or that of his father, mother, wife, child, or brother.[40] These specified excuses continued to be acceptable for centuries, although the increasing pressure to find suitable nobles to serve their country in the fifteenth century led to the qualification that excuses of old age, infirmity, and other legitimate ones could be accepted only by a two-thirds vote of the Great Council with at least one hundred twenty members present.[41] Legitimate excuses were, in fact, accepted, both before and after the act just mentioned. In 1468, for example, the Senate accepted the excuse of advanced age and in 1480 the Great Council accepted the excuse of poor health upon the oath of the electee's physician.[42]

A favorite device of the nobility for escaping civic responsibilities was to flee abroad. Lazzarini noted that the penalties imposed upon those who sought to evade their public duties in Venice were related from the time of the Fourth Crusade to the inclination of many to pursue their own profitable affairs in the colonies and to the consequent paucity in Venice of qualified candidates for public offices, embassies, and other duties.[43] Since fleeing abroad entailed considerable costs and some risks, the Great Council in 1339 decided to accept a penalty of twenty large *soldi* (unless the penalty for refusing the specific office should be greater) to free the delinquent electee from his self-imposed exile. Always aware, however, of the commercial basis for the prosperity of the Republic, the Council provided that *bona fide* merchants who went abroad in a ship or a galley for at least two months should be exempted from the penalty. Originally passed for a two year trial period, this act was put on a permanent basis in 1341.[44] Under cover of the Republic's concern for foreign commerce, many nobles, according to an act of 1376, excused themselves *pro eundo extra* and then failed to depart. It was required, therefore, that they must leave Venice within one month and remain abroad for the prescribed two months.[45] It was proposed to the Senate in 1389 that the required period of absence should be raised to four months, since many nobles simply moved to Murano for two months in order to avoid the penalty for refusing public office, but the act failed to pass.[46] Lazzarini suggests that this flight to Murano to evade civic responsibility accounts for the large number of palaces and the extraordinary number of patrician births occurring on the island of glass. The danger which the Visconti posed to the Republic of St. Mark at this very time makes this evasion of duties by the patriciate all the more reprehensible.[47] It was this *pars* of 1389, moreover, which indicated that the majority of those elected refused. An act of 1410 summarized the body of legislation just described, increasing the penalty for failure to depart within one month or for returning within two months of departure to double that for outright refusal of office.[48] Another abuse appeared when many excused themselves in order to go abroad, and then proceeded to obtain postponement after postponement. Thus the duty was not performed by anyone, the penalty for refusal was unpaid, and the electee remained ineligible for election to other offices or duties. In an effort to end this intolerable state of affairs a new act made it much more difficult to obtain such postponements.[49] So many nobles continued to spend a comfortable two months at Murano or other nearby place in order to avoid going on embassies that the Great Council yielded to the Senate, which daily deliberated concerning the sending of embassies to various courts, the authority to impose penalties just as if those penalties had been voted in the Great Council, so that those elected would have reason for fulfilling their duties. An amendment added that provisors and *tractatores* should be subject to the same penalties.

The preamble to the act indicates the great harm sustained by the Republic on account of this pernicious practice and the danger that the harm might become irremediable.[50] An act of 1479 made escape from public duties by means of self-imposed exile more difficult, for it required that the noble being excused on account of a commercial voyage must leave within fifteen days and remain abroad at least six months.[51]

Another device employed by the nobles in their efforts to evade service was to find some flaw in their election. Some evidence of this appears toward the end of the thirteenth century in a law providing that although ambassadors and *tractatores* ought to be elected one by one, their election should be valid even if elected together.[52] A question also arose concerning the election of ambassadors by the grain officials. Some sought to refuse without paying the penalty of twenty *grossi* which had been fixed by the Great Council in 1272. A senatorial decree of 1301 declared that the penalty should apply just as if they had been elected in a Council.[53] In the fifteenth century ingenious nobles had found another means for escaping onerous embassies, provisorships, and other assignments abroad by discovering a flaw in their election. A senatorial act of 1440 established that they must serve anyway or be subject to the penalty for refusal. The preface of the act deplores the "diverse pretexts and excuses" by which the nobles withdraw from their responsibilities and seek to be absolved.[54] In spite of all measures previously taken a "wicked and scandalous custom" grew up, which, if continued, could cause the greatest difficulty and peril. Nobles had discovered that they could escape election as councillors, advocates, ambassadors, and other unwanted posts under the pretext that some had taken part in their election who were excluded from doing so by acts of the Council of Ten. Thus they shirk all posts to which they are elected which are not pleasing to them. By this perverse reasoning all acts of the councils and even the sentences of criminals could be called in doubt. The Great Council in 1461, therefore, declared that any objections to those taking part in any election must be made before the balloting, specifying those made ineligible to participate by act of the Ten, so that those persons should be expelled and the balloting proceed without possibility of nullification. If prior objections were not raised the election should be valid.[55]

In their unceasing quest to shun duty Venetian patricians even had resort to becoming or appearing to be violators of the law. An act of 1254 had imposed ineligibility for salaried office as a penalty upon officials, rectors, captains, and ambassadors who failed to ac-

count for their expenses or to surrender goods belonging to the
commune within a prescribed term. Under this act it became possible
to evade civic duties by declaring previous failure to report expenses
or to return the commune's property. What had been intended as a
punishment thus became an unfair advantage to the unscrupulous
shirker. In 1302, therefore, the Great Council took measures against
such slackers, providing that if an electee revealed his delinquency
after his election, it should not be accepted as an excuse, and although
he could not undertake the office or embassy, he must pay the fine for
refusal.[56] Exclusion from office, as we have seen, was a common
penalty in acts concerning the Venetian ruling class. In 1401 the Great
Council awakened to the fact that what was intended as a severe
penalty in fact worked to the advantage of those who sought to evade
their responsibilities and to the damage of the republic. The acts
which excluded from public office those who accepted election as
captains, *supracomiti,* ambassadors, provisors, or *tractatores* and subsequently refused and those who refused office under financial penalty
and then failed to pay were reformed to prevent escape from responsibility in this way.[57] Acts of 1454, 1458, and 1468 also specified that debtors of the commune should not be absolved of their
duties on that account.[58] The necessity of finding suitable nobles to
accept embassies continued to be so great, however, that the Great
Council passed an act in 1484 declaring that even those who were
contumacious could be elected and having performed their mission
be absolved of their contumacy.[59]

Closely related to the problem of coercing noblemen to accept
missions or offices was the problem of getting them on their ways
promptly (or, indeed, at all) once they had accepted. An act of the
Great Council in 1269 imposed upon those who did not undertake their
accepted duties at the proper time and when ordered to do so by the
doge the same penalties as they would have suffered for refusal of
office.[60] An act of 1498 also refers to a rule that those elected to *regi-
mina et officia* must assume their positions immediately after their
predecessors with some specified delays permitted for distant posts.
Apparently the rule had been disobeyed, and the Great Council insisted that it should be enforced.[61]

Just as the republic had difficulty in finding patricians to accept
foreign missions and to depart upon them at the appointed time, it
also had a problem with those who returned prematurely without
license to do so. In 1269 the Great Council subjected the failure to
remain at one's post without license to return home to the same penal-

ties as refusal of the assignment in the first place.[62] The Senate later discovered an abuse in those elected by that august body who sought license to return from the Signory. The offending ambassadors and provisors were subjected to a penalty of one thousand ducats. Any councillor approving such a request also had to pay five hundred ducats.[63]

A considerable body of legislation from 1185 until the end of the fifteenth century proves that during the centuries of her greatest power Venice suffered seriously from the unwillingness of the patrician class to assume its duties. These acts were uniformly directed, however, toward the filling of a specific and limited group of offices. Ducal councillors, advocates of the commune, ambassadors, provisors, *supracomiti, tractatores,* and a few others, either unsalaried or demanding large expenditures out of the incumbent's private purse above and beyond his salary, required coercive legislation. It has long been known that the Venetian nobility was in fact a double class, one part of which was rich and powerful and monopolized the honors and the burdens of such high offices, and the other poor and struggling, though still a part of the ruling oligarchy.[64] Although the problems of the poor nobles were undoubtedly more severe in the centuries of Venetian decadence, they were dependent for their very survival upon the salaries of lesser offices well before the end of the fourteenth century.[65] Romanin indicates that the number of salaried offices increased, not only in proportion to the natural augmentation required by the increased territories of the republic, but according to the need for providing income and responsibilities for the poorer nobles.[66] They sought offices. The indictment of civic irresponsibility, therefore is lodged specifically against the wealthy and powerful patrician houses for evading governmental responsibilities which were costly in money or in time and energies diverted from more profitable pursuits.

Even so, the indictment has been iconoclastically one-sided for the purpose of bringing into balance our judgment of the Venetian patriciate and destroying the myth of its singular patriotism and self-abnegation. Admittedly the performance of these offices and missions was not so much a privilege and an advantage as a grievous financial burden.[67] And even though Luzzato has pointed out that the holding of the highest offices did not necessarily compel a Venetian patrician to abandon commerce, the public duties were beyond question a serious hindrance to his private business.[68] The risks of bodily harm or imprisonment were also inherent in many foreign missions.[69] The nobles of Venice had ample reason to wish to avoid such duties and it is not the intention of this article to portray them as worse than comparable classes elsewhere or than the common run of men. When the public interest was sufficiently compelling and apparent, Venetian noblemen were capable of great self-sacrifice. For the general run of relatively humdrum affairs, however, Venetian noblemen went to fantastic lengths to shun burdensome civic responsibilities.

NOTES

1. Gina Fasoli, "Nascita di un mito," in *Studi storici in onore di Gioacchino Volpe* (Florence, 1958), p. 449.

2. Giuseppe Volpi, *La repubblica di Venezia e i suoi ambasciatori* (Milan, 1928), pp. 45–46.

3. Pompeo Molmenti, *Venice,* trans. by Horatio F. Brown, 6 vols. in 3 parts (London, 1906–08), I, i, 83.

4. Yves Renouard, "Mercati e mercanti veneziani alla fine del Duecento," in *La civiltà veneziana del secolo di Marco Polo* (Florence, n.d.), pp. 98–100.

5. Charles Diehl, *Une république patricienne. Venise* (Paris, 1938), pp. 91, 103, 116, 118–119, 163, and 259–260. This is a romantic work, lacking bibliography and with few footnotes, guilty of perpetuating both sides of Fasoli's *mito bifronte.* The two faces of the myth are not necessarily contrary to each other: the selfless and patriotic Venetian nobility was completely ruthless and devious in its efforts to build the power and prosperity of Venice. For another example of the two parts of the myth used jointly, see Ludwig Streit, *Venedig und die Wendung des vierten Kreuzzugs gegen Konstantinopel* (Anklam, 1877), p. 28. (I owe this reference to Miss Susan Stratton, who is working with me on an historiographical study on the "deviation" of the Fourth Crusade.) For more moderate views on public responsibility of the Venetian patriciate see: Horatio Brown, *Studies in the History of Venice,* 2 vols. (London, 1907), I, 312–313; Heinrich Kretschmayr, *Geschichte von Venedig,* reprint of 1st ed., 1905–34, (3 vols., Darmstadt, 1964), II, 132; Gino Luzzatto, "Les activités économiques du patriciat vénitien (X-XIV siècles)," *Annales d'histoire économique et sociale,* IX (1937), 47–48. Reprinted in Luzzatto, *Studi di storia economica veneziana* (Padua, 1954), pp. 125–165.

6. "Le patriciat vénitien," p. 27.

7. Donald E. Queller, *Early Venetian Legislation on Ambassadors,* (Geneva, 1966), pp. 116–117.

8. Archivio di Stato di Venezia, Senato, Misti, XL, 146v (151v).

9. This was a mission of some importance. Henry V had seized three Venetian ships for his invasion of France. *Calendar of State Papers preserved in the Archives of Venice,* Rawdon Brown, ed., I (London, 1864), nos. 214–215, p. 58. Other cities, of course, also encountered aversion to accepting ill-rewarded embassies. Sergio Angelini, *La diplomazia comunale a Perugia nei secoli XIII e XIV* (Florence, 1965), p. 48.

10. Queller, *Early Venetian Legislation on Ambassdors*, no. 50, pp. 86–87.

11. Vittorio Lazzarini, "Obbligo di assumere pubblici uffici nelle antiche leggi venziane," *Archivio veneto*, XIX (1936), p. 189.

12. Frederic C. Lane, *Andrea Barbarigo: Merchant of Venice 1418–1449*, The Johns Hopkins University Studies in Historical and Political Science, Series LXII, no. 1 (Baltimore, 1944), p. 19.

13. James C. Davis, *The Decline of the Venetian Nobility as a Ruling Class*, The Johns Hopkins University Studies in Historical and Political Science, Series LXXX, no. 2 (Baltimore, 1962), p. 9.

14. *Ibid.*, pp. 32–33 and 82.

15. David was aware of Lazzarini's article (see above, n. 11), but, in my opinion, underestimated its significance, as did perhaps Lazzarini himself, who saw in the legislation a means of habituating the ruling class to that self-abnegation and patriotism which was the basis of Venetian grandeur. This educational value of the coercive legislation might be convincing if the number of acts were not so great and if the nobles' incessant quest for loopholes and the Councils' repeated efforts to close them were not so obvious. Davis, *The Decline of the Venetian Nobility as a Ruling Class*, p. 25; Lazzarini, "Obbligo di assumere pubblici uffici," p. 185.

16. Davis, *The Decline of the Venetian Nobility as a Ruling Class*, pp. 9–10. I wish to emphasize my admiration for Davis's work. It is often easy to criticize an author unfairly on matters peripheral to his main thesis and to the time with which he is chiefly concerned, and it is not my intention to do that, but to offer complementary evidence.

17. *Deliberazioni del Maggior Consiglio di Venezia*, ed. Roberto Cessi, (3 vols., Bologna, 1931–1950), I, 252–253; also in Lazzarini, "Obbligo di assumere pubblici uffici," pp. 192–194. Molmenti cites a decree of 1189 against "Jacopus Julianus de confinio Santi Juliani," according to which "nullum honorem, nullum officium de nostra curia habere debeat quod per electores fiat et insuper nulla ci ratio debeat in curia nostra tencri," apparently without being aware of the generalized legislation of 1185. *Venice*, I, i, 83.

18. *Maggior Consiglio* II, 88. Failure to respond to the announcement of election either in the Council or at home would constitute tacit acceptance. *Infra.*

19. *Maggior Consiglio*, II, 89; Lazzarini, "Obbligo di assumere pubblici uffici," pp. 195–196.

20. *Maggior Consiglio*, II, 233.

21. *Ibid.*, II, 102.

22. Queller, *Early Venetian Legislation on Ambassadors*, no. 30, pp. 72–73. In 1395 Ser Leonardus Bembo tried to get off with the penalty of exclusion under this act, avoiding the penalty of one hundred ducats, which was presumably imposed by the specific act of election. He did not succeed. ASV, Pien Collegio, Notatorio, I, 73v (88v).

23. Queller, *Early Venetian Legislation on Ambassadors*, no. 63, p. 96.

24. *Ibid.*, no. 88, pp. 116–117; Marino Sanuto, *I diarii*, Rinaldo Fulin, *et al.*, eds. (58 vols. in 59, Venice, 1879–1903), III, 1176.

25. Fausto Nicolini, "Frammenti veneto-napoletani," offprint from

Studi di storia napoletana in onore di Michelangelo Schipa (Naples, 1926), pp. 9–19.

26. "Traité du gouvernement de la cité et seigneurie de Venise," in P.-M. Perret, *Histoire des relations de la France avec Venise*, (2 vols., Paris, 1896), II, 289. Other cities had the same problem. Vedovato discusses the reasons for reluctance of Florentines to accept foreign assignments. Giuseppe Vedovato, *Note sul diritto diplomatico della repubblica fiorentina* (Florence, 1946), pp. 11–14. See also M. A. R. de Maulde La Clavière, *La Diplomatie au temps de Machiavel*, III, 428–429 and 432. In Perugia as well. Angelini, *La diplomazia comunale a Perugia*, pp. 50–51 and 54.

27. Queller, *Early Venetian Legislation on Ambassadors*, no. 62, p. 95, and no. 94, p. 123.

28. Lazzarini, "Obbligo di assumere pubblici uffici, " pp. 193–194.

29. *Ibid.*, pp. 197–198.

30. Queller, *Early Venetian Legislation on Ambassadors*, no. 55, p. 90.

31. *Ibid.*, no. 65, pp. 97–98. Davis includes ducal councillors and advocates of the commune among those offices easily filled. He is aware that coercive legislation of an earlier date applied to these offices, but his seventeenth century source says "no one recalls" a refusal. *The Decline of the Venetian Nobility as a Ruling Class*, pp. 92–93.

32. Queller, *Early Medieval Legislation on Ambassadors*, no. 50, pp. 86–87.

33. *Ibid.*, no. 60, p. 94.

34. *Ibid.*, no. 80, p. 109.

35. *Maggior Consiglio*, I, 252–253; Lazzarini, "Obbligo di assumere pubblici uffici," pp. 192–193. See also *Maggior Consiglio*, II, 89 and 102, and III, 71. The first also printed in Lazzarini, "Obbligo di assumere pubblici uffici," pp. 195–196.

36. Lazzarini, "Obbligo di assumere pubblici uffici," p. 195.

37. *Maggior Consiglio*, I, 229.

38. Queller, *Early Venetian Legislation on Ambassadors*, no. 1, p. 59.

39. *Maggior Consiglio*, Cessi, ed., II, 102.

40. *Ibid.*, I, 142–143. The brother is included because of the character of the Venetian noble family and its manner of conducting its business affairs.

41. Queller, *Early Venetian Legislation on Ambassadors*, no. 88, pp. 116–117.

42. ASV., Senato, Terra, VI, 38r (39r); Maggior Consiglio, Stella, 1r (5r). For a Florentine law`on the subject, see Maulde La Clavière, *La diplomatie au temps de Machiavel*, III, 411–412.

43. Lazzarini, "Obbligo di assumere pubblici uffici," p. 187.

44. *Ibid.*, pp. 196–197.

45. Queller, *Early Venetian Legislation on Ambassadors*, no. 35, p. 76. The interpretation given above should supplant my earlier one. *Ibid.*, p. 34.

46. Lazzarini, "Obbligo di assumere pubblici uffici," p. 197.

47. *Ibid.*, pp. 190–191.

48. Queller, *Early Venetian Legislation on Ambassadors*, no. 47, pp. 84–85.

49. *Ibid.*, no. 56, p. 91.

50. *Ibid.*, no. 61, pp. 94–95.

51. *Ibid.*, no. 88, pp. 116–117.

52. *Ibid.*, no. 7, p. 61. More than one ambassador or *tractator* was often assigned to a single task.

53. *Deliberazioni del Consiglio dei Rogati (Senato) Serie Mixtorum,* vol. I, eds. R. Cessi e P. Sambin, vol. II, eds. R. Cessi e M. Brunetti (Venice 1960–61), I, 37, no. 129.

54. Queller, *Early Venetian Legislation on Ambassadors,* no. 54, pp. 89–90.

55. *Ibid.*, nos. 68–69, pp. 99–102.

56. *Ibid.*, no. 10, p. 62. The act of 1254 is in *Maggior Consiglio,* II, 294–295.

57. Queller, *Early Venetian Legislation on Ambassadors,* no. 42, p. 81.

58. *Ibid.*, nos. 63 and 65, pp. 96 and 97–98. The act of 1468 appears to duplicate the provisons of that of 1458. ASV., Maggior Consiglio, Regina, 75v (81v)-76r (82r).

59. Queller, *Early Venetian Legislation on Ambassadors,* no. 98, p. 126.

60. *Maggior Consiglio,* II, 233. For Florentine concern with the same problem, consult Maulde La Clavière, *La diplomatie au temps de Machiavel,* III, 411 and 420–421.

61. ASV, Maggior Consiglio, Stella, 157rv (161rv).

62. *Maggior Consiglio,* II, 233. See also "Traité du gouvernement de Venise," in Perret, *Relations de la France avec Venise,* II, 289.

63. Queller, *Early Venetian Legislation on Ambassadors,* no. 92, p. 122.

64. Samuel Romanin, *Storia documentata di Venezia,* (10 vols., Venice: 1853–61), IV, 469. See also Lane, *Merchant of Venice,* pp. 14–15, and Davis, *The Decline of the Venetian Nobility as a Ruling Class,* pp. 49–50 and 77.

65. Luzzato, "Le patriciat vénitien," p. 34. Lane describes the manner in which the son and grandsons of Andrea Barbarigo sought public positions during years of economic hardship. *Merchant of Venice,* p. 39.

66. *Storia documentata di Venezia,* IV, 478.

67. Gino Luzzato, review of Vittorio Lazzarini, *Proprietá e feudi, offici, garzoni, carcerati in antiche leggi veneziane* (Rome, 1960), in *Archivio veneto,* LXVII (1960), 104–105; Andrea Da Mosto, *L'Archivio di Stato di Venezia,* (2 vols., Rome, 1937–40), II, 25. Queller, *Early Venetian Legislation on Ambassadors,* pp. 14–28, contains a treatment of the expenses of embassies.

68. *Storia economica di Venezia dall' XI at XVI secolo* (Venice, 1961), p. 135; Luzzato also reports of Guglielmo Querini in the fifteenth century that, having just been nominated for two years to the office of *auditore alle sentenze,* he did not see the possibility of being able to attend very much to commercial affairs. *Studi,* p. 173.

69. ASV, Maggior Consiglio, Novella, 83r (94r).

CIVISM AND ROMAN LAW
IN FOURTEENTH-CENTURY
ITALIAN SOCIETY*

PETER RIESENBERG
Washington University

This paper will attempt to draw some traits of the civic state of mind in fourteenth-century Italy, construct something of an urban psychology on the basis of a variety of non-humanist sources, and question existing theories on the revival of an activist ethic. Examination of archival data, *consilia*, citizenship legislation, and literature, legal and otherwise, is necessary because in theory and actuality citizenship touched every important historical development in Italy during the late Middle Ages: for example, inter-city relations, movement between town and countryside, class mobility, and public morality.

The hardest question to answer is, perhaps, who was a citizen?[1] The simplest response is that all were citizens born in a given locality or naturalized according to the locality's established practice. But this obscures the very important fact that the citizenry constituted a hierarchy of politically and legally privileged persons. The maximum citizen was a person born within the walls of citizen parents, one whose wealth permitted him to meet any property qualification for office, and who also was defended and empowered by every applicable statute. A minimum citizen was one recently admitted to some but not all the city's legal benefits, and to the political responsibilities but not privileges of citizenship. Such persons, taking the two extremes as limits of the citizenry, probably constituted the large majority in any town, but at any given moment immigrants were present who were at some stage of a naturalization procedure. What proportion of the entire population this group generally constituted, I cannot at this moment say. What I can give here, if very briefly, is a suggestion of the makeup of the immigrant group, the immigrants' motivation in coming to town or changing towns, and that of the city in accepting them. Even a casual reading of council deliberations, statutes, *consilia*, and legal commentaries reveals that there was a new co-citizens bearing the city's reputation abroad. No wonder that again and again we meet with the demand that the prospective citizen spiritually and emotionally as well as physically commit himself to his new patria.[9] It must not have been easy changing love and allegiance for it meant switching saints as well as neighbors, one set of religious and political symbols for another, hills for plains or plains for hills, one quaintly named wind for another. Even the tintinnabulation of the bells changed from town to town. But move men did, acknowledging as they did, and as the lawyers and specimen oaths demanded, their new love. One's whole new legal condition was based, I suggest, on an official recording of a change of heart, an emotional act. The narrow spaces within town walls would not allow of inimical strangers; and in their wide piazzas town authorities feared the dangerous unassimilated *straniero* whose affection might still belong to foreign prince or council, or be too easily won by native faction.

This love, patriotism, change of will, constituted the emotional basis for material commitment. Both the needs and the hope of the community were represented in this demand for political *conversio*. What constitutional theory demanded from the citizen was purposeful activity for the commune, hopefully inspired from within, yet acceptable, since necessary, if coerced a bit by legislation and civil authority.

But the city authorities could never be certain, at least immediately, of the depth and sincerity of the new citizen's conversion, and so the statutes and private bills abound with demands for purchase of property and payment of taxes before the new citizen might receive even minimum political privileges.[10] This suspicion of newcomers was reinforced by a cultural disdain, for by the fourteenth century if not earlier each town viewed itself as culturally unique, the product of a special and favored history. The city was seen by theorists and its citizens as a social and spiritual entity whose peculiar laws and customs formed a man according to a specific local ideal. So the great jurist Bartolus held that the adjective "urban" referred to more than a physical place bounded by walls. Referring to Rome and Perugia as examples, he said "urban" signified more a quality than a place.[11] Perugian history and culture, law and language, so to speak, had achieved a certain form of life its citizens enjoyed. Bartolus was not original in this approach, for even earlier the town fathers of Bologna has translated such cultural civic spirit into legislation by declaring, in the Statutes of 1288, that no one could be an ancient of the city or a consul, or in fact hold any office or be on any council, all privileges notwithstanding, who did not speak the Bolognese tongue.[12]

A strong clear statement of cultural xenophobia comes from Dante himself, and upon his verses in Canto XVI of the *Paradiso* there developed a critical tradition that spelled out and supported the poet's words.[13] Jacobus della Lana, who wrote the first commentary on Dante about 1328, notes the evil and drunken ways of those from Certaldo and Figline, in his day incorporated into the citizenry, and complains that they had corrupted the sober and peaceful life of the city. He demands good moral character as prerequisite for citizenship and worries lest the mass of new citizens ruin the old stock and the very structure of the community.[14] The *Ottimo Commento*, glossing Dante's reference to the old arms-bearing citizenry, tells us that the newcomers bring "little faith and love." Its author translates Dante's distaste for blood mixture into a socio-political criticism: the presence of the aliens does not jibe well with the single principle of order, rule of local custom—the Italian word is *reggimento*—desired for the city.[15] Pietro Alighieri, writing about 1340, asserts that every male citizen is an integral part of his city and that no one may be considered a good man unless his actions are in harmony with the public welfare. This demand, too, was in relation to Dante's phrase: "confusion delle persone."[16] Later in the century, Benvenuto da Imola reiterated these hostilities and fears.[17] Cultural as well as economic and political conformity was desired in the medieval city state.

But for all the physical, emotional, and cultural differences, it is clear that many did migrate and establish new homes. One reason they were able to do so is that, once transplanted, the new arrivals did not find themselves in a completely unfamiliar social environment. The religious scene was not different: the *duomo*, the parish church, and the multitude of ecclesiastical foundations—all that was familiar enough, as was the social structure of the community. New families were in control, to be sure, but the conventional clan alliances and hierarchy of officialdom surely was reminiscent of home. The school organization was familiar, though perhaps the folk heroes and tie with this or that ancient city or legend might be different. Nor did political assumptions or forms of institutions vary greatly, for everywhere was found the reality or fiction of representative institutions in which the citizen was called to serve.[18] We may say that the immigrant moved from one civic culture to another. Although distant from familiar faces, the newcomer was not surrounded by unfamiliar institutions. Perhaps this made his nostalgia less intense and his assimilation more certain.

So, despite the suspicion with which immigrants were viewed, many were investigated, accepted, inscribed on the roll of parish and town, granted a certificate of citizenship, and eventually integrated socially and politically into the new community. And, just as there had been a period of residence as alien prior to grant of citizenship, so now there followed a period of trial and probation, before assuming public responsibility.

Towards office holding, there was always a decided ambivalence in the medieval city. However, it is clear that men knew what was expected from them and why long before the "ideal of republican liberty and of a classical and literary culture useful for the active life of the educated statesman and businessman"[19] became a conscious ideology—that is, before the development of civic humanism in the first half of the fifteenth century. True, there was reluctance to pay taxes and to serve in military office, but it probably came as much from a desire to stay in the shop and make money as from conscious compliance with "medieval" theories on the rejection of the worldly life. In every book of municipal statutes, there is at least one chapter or run of chapters dealing with the specifications and electoral procedures for public and administrative offices. And in the glosses and commentaries of thirteenth- and fourteenth-century civilians, tax paying and personal service are almost always linked in a functional definition of citizen responsibility, without which responsibility one is not a citizen. Much as political theorists demanded a certain quality of action if the ruler was truly to merit the title *rex*, so too did the legists demand a certain performance from the individual if in law and public estimation he was to fulfil the expectations of *civis*.[20]

But if men were not always clear on the need for their service to the community, they were quite clear on what service the city might render them. What, then, were some of the benefits of citizenship? And, how did citizens grasp and use them in litigation? Citizen status was never far from one's consciousness, and if citizenship was a spiritual and emotional condition, it was also, so to speak, a congeries of tailored abilities and limitations that one was always aware of and eager to exploit as he traveled, traded, sued, and served. That this was so will be seen in a brief examination of several *consilia*, legal cases arising from contemporary experience and presented by judges for the opinion of eminent jurists. Each case reveals interrelationships between legal theory, constitutional law, and notarial or other written evidence. Amounting to hundreds if not thousands of folio volumes, the body of *consilia* literature presents us with a dynamic picture of the activities and theories of late medieval society.[21] *Consilia* handed down by jurists were cited as precedent by other jurists and by judges. As such, the *consilia* constituted one source of the so-called *diritto commune* . . . the common law of urban Italy of this period. Of all political issues in the *consilia*, the one that arises most frequently is that of citizenship. Such frequency manifests the great range of issues in which citizenship status might be involved; it also shows a vigorous growth of citizenship law.

One case discussed by Bartolus concerns the assault by a foreigner from Arezzo named Azolus upon one who claimed Florentine citizenship, a certain Petrus.[22] At issue is the amount of the recompense, since Florentine law demanded from the foreigner for the injured citizen four times what a citizen assailant would have paid. Bartolus is not interested in the facts surrounding the assault, but rather in the determination of status. This is not an inconsequential matter, he says, for the penalty depends upon the personality of the accused; and finally he determines that the burden of proof rests on Petrus who will benefit, and that Petrus must present proof of his name and of his parentage.

Throughout the citizenship literature, in the *consilia*, and repeatedly in every kind of formula in the Florentine petitions and grants, we encounter the phrase "verus et originarius civis." Time and again newly made citizens are told they will be treated as true citizens by birth with all rights thereto pertaining, all legislation to the contrary notwithstanding. Given this conflict of laws specific and general, and given too the jurists' penchant for meticulous examination of all crucial words, it is not surprising to find a small literature of cases bearing on the word "verus." One of these is a *consilium* of Baldus concerning the nature of Orlandus' citizenship. At issue is the payment of certain taxes, but Baldus uses the case to present his theory on the making of a citizen.[23]

Ser Orlandus claims the full rights of Florentine citizenship—rights of a *verus civis*—because they have been granted him by special privilege. Baldus inclines to agree that such a grant, although extraordinary, is possible and legal because citizens may bestow such full *civilitas* upon a foreigner. Their act confers upon the new man what he calls a *vera essentia*, a gift that is possible since, in general terms now, citizenship may be a matter of creation (*arte*) as well as of birth. "Civilitas est quid factibile, et non solum nascitur sed creatur. . . . " Moving from a quasi-philosophical approach, Baldus turns to more technical matters. He examines the law under which the concession was made, and he notes that Ser Orlandus was being rewarded for his services to the city. He specifies that the grant was not made gratuitously by the city but rather was won by Orlandus' merit. Exactly what Orlandus' services were we are not told; what is clear from this *consilium*, however, is the city's willingness to take special pains to reward a faithful servant, and that it must surround its action with proper legal theories and forms.

Baldus' brother Angelus presents us with another Florentine case—this one concerning the financial relations of a nobleman, Luchinus, with the commune.[24] Luchinus is a recent citizen who, like Orlandus, had been granted full citizenship privileges equal to those of a citizen by birth. As a condition of his naturalization he had promised to purchase a certain number of shares in the public debt. The *consilium* arises from his complaint that he is now being forced to take a loss on the shares, from which loss he claims to be protected by the specific wording of his grant of citizenship. Following the jurisconsult's practice, Angelus argues *pro* and *con*. What interests us here is one of the arguments he finally demolishes, namely, that Luchinus must sell as ordered, because now, a full *civis*, he must involve himself fully with the well-being of the Florentine state. However, although Angelus emphasizes the fullness of the new citizen status and the fullness of obligation that implies, he rejects this line of argument on the grounds that the charter contemplates benefit to Luchinus, not harm. I discuss this *consilium* of Angelus to show that if citizenship was treated in relation to matters of a petty fine, it was related also to principles of traditionally the greatest importance: for the previous two centuries jurists and kings had never ceased to expand the area in which "public necessity" and the "common welfare" served as a basis for action or decision.[25]

Paul de Castro reports a case forwarded to him by the judges of Venice.[26] At issue is property contested by two ecclesiastical corporations. One has legal title to the bequest, but the other has been in possession. The case is interesting since one argument is that Ser Sallatini was not a citizen of Belluno and therefore not legally competent to purchase the property in question, there existing at Belluno as elsewhere the law that only citizens might purchase landed property. Reviewing the evidence and the law, Paul declares that Ser

Sallatini eventually became a citizen, and that therefore his purchase has validity. And he is satisfied with the evidence: the presence of Sallatini's name on the old if not the new tax rolls of the city. The point of all this is to illustrate how one's legal status as citizen determined the course of legal proceedings, to say nothing of one's ability to engage fully in buying and selling. Litigants, lawyers, and judges were all sensitive to matters of personal civic status.

Interesting also is a *consilium* of Jason de Mayno concerning one Cristoforo who has lived long in Genoa and who now wishes membership in the Milanese college of judges.[27] The Milanese statute holds that no doctor may be a member of the guild unless he or his father was born in Milan. Franciscus, Cristoforo's father, although born in Milan had moved to Genoa and had lived there a long while—but always, emphasizes Jason, with the intention (*animus*) of returning to his native city. The father's condition, which must satisfy the statute if Cristoforo is to gain his request, is further clarified by the fact that in Genoa, in both his legal and mercantile affairs, he was treated by the Genoese community as a foreigner, as a Milanese. Jason strengthens his analysis and opinion by noting that the statutes of Padua and Bologna (two cities with strong legal traditions) agree with that of Milan, that Paul de Castro and Felinus have declared similarly, and that he has seen "many" cases of a similar nature decided in favor of one whose father was abroad at the time of his son's birth. Here, then, is a case which reveals a good deal about the life of foreigners in any busy city of the period. In addition to those foreigners living within the walls with an *animus* to adopt it, there were others declared in their intention to remain outsiders, subject to various forms of legal and social discrimination, who took no part in the political life of the community, and who, presumably, looked forward to the day of return to their native place.

Another case touching citizenship and guild membership is one examined by Paul de Castro that arose from the fact that Florentine guild and city statutes differed in their demands for time in residence as a citizen before one might practice the notarial art.[28] Paul's task is to evaluate the current force of the legislation and to determine, finally, which prerequisite applies. Apart from the facts and the law, we learn that Florence has special agreements with certain towns in its territory covering the approach to citizenship of their residents, that such matters are negotiable, that one constant issue between Florence and its subject towns is the ability of the *contado* folk to hold Florentine office, and that such frequently used terms as *habitator*, *civis*, *incola*, and *municeps* are subject to varying interpretation. In this *consilium* as in that of Angelus just mentioned, the concept of public welfare plays a role. Paul accepts a twenty- as opposed to a thirty-year residence requirement because the lesser will more quickly bring more people to bear community obligations and to guide the state. And like Bartolus before him, Paul speaks almost mystically of a "communem qualitatem inhaerentem civibus."

The *consilia* reveal details of the lives of those legally considered in special categories such as women, minors, and Jews; for example, the case presented to Alexander of Imola concerning the Jew, Abraham, taken in adultery with the Christian woman, Benedicta.[29] The issue is sticky. If Abraham is treated as a Jew, then he dies. But if he benefits from his status as citizen, then he pays a fine of 100 pounds. At the end of a long and involved analysis Alexander's conclusion is that although, as a Jew, Abraham is not a full citizen, he has a citizen's rights in the present instance as is clear from the language of the privilege to the Jews. The significant fact in this case is that the Jew's status as citizen prevails over his religious condition.

My examination of these cases has been very inadequate, since their analysis was not meant to bring out details of substantive law or formally develop the law of citizenship, but rather to point to the existence of such a law as part of the functioning structure of every city. The development of such a law with its basic concepts and assumptions and great variety of detail took place in a society of fundamentally similar social units, the cities, which operated upon a universally accepted spiritual principle, patriotism. The jurists' arguments showed a common intellectual background formed by reading in the Roman and canon laws together with their medieval glossators and commentators, city statutes and *consilia*--to say nothing of occasional plunges into ancient and medieval literature, philosophy, theology, and the Bible.

Most of the jurists who wrote *consilia* wrote legal commentary as well, and it is instructive to see how the views on citizenship they evidence in comments upon certain texts in the *Corpus Juris Civilis* sustain the same themes we have noted in the *consilia*. For the most part, the *leges* in the last three books of the Code, the so-called *Tres Libri*, which, principally focused on public laws as they are, were neglected by most commentators. However, among those jurists who did write on them were Azo, Accursius, Baldus, Lucas de Penna, and Bartolus, and so a body of substantial thought survives.

Azo, who lived in the first third of the thirteenth century, makes the bearing of public responsiblity the *sine qua non* of citizenship; it is this activity that distinguishes the *civis* from the mere inhabitant of a city.[30] Lucas de Penna is very thorough in his examination of key words. Along with almost every other jurist who considered citizenship theory, he asks in terms of his own experience whether one "de Napoli" is the same as a "Napoletanus." For him this was not a question of words, for real consequences flowed from the interpretation. At a higher conceptual level Lucas discusses the special quality that citizenship conferred upon a man.[31] Baldus too discussed a whole range of issues including the philosophical meaning of citizenship, taxation, reprisals, and citizenship legislation.[32] Frequent is his use of the expression *opinio communis* which tells us that this or that issue had provoked a tradition of discussion and a *de facto* doctrine. Bartolus' words on these and other issues constitute veritable short treatises on the whole range of citizenship problems.[33]

Again I have stressed that the jurists discussed a given topic, not the substance of what they wrote. Unfortunately, all one can do in a brief essay is suggest areas of widespread concern and interest, the variety of relationships between important concepts, the close relation between theory and practice (and theoreticians and practitioners who often were one and the same), and the importance of the men involved, both as intellectual authorities and as high officials. My point of course is that the whole legal-constitutional-administrative-political environment contributed to the diffusion of the notions of citizen and civic activity. Given all this legal theory, and the central position in government of men trained in the law, it should be evident how deeply the concept of active citizenship and all the practical matters related to it were worked into Italian municipal life by the thirteenth and fourteenth centuries.

If this is so, our next concern must be to examine the nature of the civic culture[34] before 1400, and to see what generalizations can be made with respect to the nature and extent of the knowledge men had of their government, their beliefs about that government, and their affection towards it. In viewing Italian urban society and political life from the mid-twelfth century to the fifteenth, one is tempted to assume much uniformity over the entire period.

With respect to civic pride, we may say, without the statistics available to modern analysts of the civic culture, that in towns and cities of every size men knew and sang the praises of their local past. In the middle of the fourteenth century Buccio di Ranallo wrote a *Cronica* to honor his liberty-loving ancestors of Aquila and to praise the beautiful town they built. His love of city is on every page—when he speaks of the unity of the citizens, their sagacious attempt to build a town handsome without peer, their sad breach of faith with Charles of Anjou, their cooperative effort in building a new aqueduct, and their conscious attempt to create something worthy and enjoyable for their citizen descendants. All this from the panegyrist of a small town in the Abruzzi.[35]

The same patriotic notes are familiar from more sophisticated environments: from Milan where Bonvicinus in the 1280's celebrated not only the size of the city's markets, the number of its hospitals, churches, and professional people, but also the valor of its citizens who rose against the two Fredericks. The sumptuous arms of the citizens as well as their strength and wisdom, fidelity and religiosity are cause for his joy. In his prologue Bonvicinus tells us that he writes not only to inform foreigners of Milan's glories but also for the moral instruction of his fellow citizens. For, once they know "what a city their *patria* is they will never again disparage or dishonor it with evil acts."[36]

Florentines too praised not only the material greatness of their city but also its beauty and the qualities of its people. In his *Guerra Pisana* Antonio Pucci writes of the deep affection Florentines have for their city and its citizen government, and commends Florence's fight for *libertade* in the war against Pisa. Characteristically joined to his love of country and its principles is his happiness that the war, with its heavy taxes, is over. Much earlier, as we have seen, Dante started his own tradition of self-praise and xenophobia that persisted throughout the fourteenth century. Dante himself was nurtured in a tradition of civic pride that already in the middle of the thirteenth century identified the city with the majesty of ancient Rome.[37]

Citizens were born and made in such atmospheres created by poetry and a civic education in which religious and political authorities cooperated. In his *Guerra Pisana* Antonio Pucci describes the funeral of the Florentine mercenary general after the defeat of Pisa. In the procession walked the hero's charger, draped in black as were his shieldbearers. Those who carried his lance and helmet and the crucifix are mentioned in the same poetic breath. Women cried as did man and boy when the body passed accompanied by the podestà, the rectors, fifty members of the Priorate, friars, priests, and other religious. After a solemn mass in S. Giovanni, the body was carried by soldiers to the old cathedral, S. Reparata, where the condottiere was buried in a marble tomb. Presumably the city paid the expenses of this religio-political spectacle as it did for others.[38]

Besides pride, pre-humanist citizens evidenced a true interest in, one should perhaps say they enjoyed, politics. From Salvemini on, modern students of Florentine politics have observed that for economic, social, or political goals members of the Florentine aristocracy, merchant class, and eventually members of the lesser guilds organized in various ways to achieve political power. Idealism and political opportunism both characterized Florentine political life in this period. Recently Hyde, in his study of Paduan politics, has emphasized the political activity of the great family associations.[39] The debates of city assemblies, the constant concern with which the entrance of new personalities and new factions into politics was watched, the search for political office and prestige, the constant re-examination and refashioning of city statutes, the care princes took not to disturb too greatly the forms of traditional parliamentary life all this testifies to interest in politics and surely enjoyment thereof. Certainly the rewards of politics were well known in terms of financial and social gain.[40]

Moreover, city dwellers were well aware of the influence of government upon day-to-day activities. Taxes, dress, working hours and procedures—all this and more was regulated by the city, alone or with the cooperation of the guild. Men were interested in government because it immediately affected their lives as rarely in history. For not only was a whole variety of legislation on the books, but there existed also—and no doubt as much to give employment as to accomplish surveillance—a substantial lesser officialdom to see to law enforcement within the crowded hence open city.

In terms of one modern analysis of civic culture, I should say that Florence and other medieval cities had a subject-participant political culture, that is, one whose citizens felt a sense of loyalty and identification, a willingness to obey the laws, and who, many of them, made demands upon government which, translated into policies, were enforced.[41] Those who were not so active and interested were subjects in a conventional sense. Numbers are hard to come by; what is important is the pervasiveness of the ideal of participation—at many levels and in many areas of self-government. The phrase "self government at royal command" is easily translatable into Italian terms of the thirteenth and fourteenth centuries. This is not to say that democracy flourished then. Hierarchical political institutions supported by an hierarchical church preaching hierarchical social and political theories also existed. It is to say that many active persons lived and valued the active political life. The structure of government had long forced men to pay taxes and perform in a multitude of city and guild offices. And for two centuries the Roman and canon lawyers had developed theories which legitimatized political activity. Personal service as well as taxation was desired and considered desirable. To the duty of the prince as taught by John of Salisbury was added the civic ideal of antiquity as revealed in the Code and Digest, to say nothing of a rhetorical tradition the full import of which is only currently being revealed.[42]

All this description and analysis is aimed somewhere: obviously at the concept of civic humanism which would have us believe that the revival of the ideal of active political life came only at the very end of the fourteenth century and then in forms influenced by classical literature and against the background of the Milanese thrust at Florentine liberty. In this cataclysm, we are to believe, modern political man appears, shrugging off the warnings of medieval clerical disapprobation.[43]

One result of my research has been to make me suspicious of the whole concept of civic humanism, or better to question the importance either of a body of literature or of a very limited historical period or event in bringing about the revival of the ideal of antique life, the ideal of the committed citizen. To be sure, about 1400, Florentines turned to certain ancient works and gained insight and inspiration in them. But was that contact and generation as crucial as Professor Baron and others have made them out to be? While some Florentines were emboldened to defense of liberty by their reading of the ancients, others were, as the deliberations in the *Provvisioni* reveal, conspiring with the Milanese tyranny.[44] They too should be in the picture. As should, too, certain ancient works in the Latin language, but not Latin literature. What is significant is that both groups, loyalists and fifth columnists, were long familiar with traditions of patriotic loyalty, service, and responsibility. For two centuries the practice of urban life and the study and practice of Roman law had, throughout central and northern Italy, habituated men to a committed public existence. Civic humanism reinforced this tradition and shaped it in new and more beautiful forms but it was not a great creative innovative force. Justinian was an ancient, too, and from the twelfth and thirteenth centuries the administrators, notaries, legists, and businessmen who read and reckoned with his works were fully aware of the demands and theories of ancient active citizenship and shaped their lives and institutions with these in mind.

NOTES

* This paper was read in substantially this form at a meeting of the Mid-west Conference of Medievalists held in Bloomington, Indiana, in October, 1966. It is neither a chapter nor a summary of a book in progress on "Citizen-ship and the Civic Spirit in Late Medieval Italy"; it is rather a slice or cross-section of some of my conclusions and evidence. The larger part of my work was done in Florence in 1964–65 when I benefited from a grant from the John Simon Guggenheim Memorial Foundation, and the hospitality of Harvard's Villa I Tatti. The Graduate School of Washington University and The American Philosophical Society have also aided my work (by financing a summer of research and writing in Florence.)

1. On matters of definition, see: Baldus, *Prima . . . quinta pars consil-iorum* (Lyons, 1550), vol. IV, cons. 401, 410; Bartolus, *Consilia* (Venice, 1576), vol. I, cons. 196; Lucas de Penna, *Commentaria* (Lyons, 1583), to C. 10.40.7; Bartolus, *Opera omnia* (Venice, 1602), to C. 10.40.7 and C. 10.39.2; Accursius, *Glossa ordinaria* (Venice, 1591), to C. 10.40.3; C. 10.40.7; D. 50.1.29. References to the *Corpus Iuris Civilis* and *Corpus Iuris Canonici* are to the modern editions of Mommsen and Krueger, and Friedberg re-spectively. These citations by no means exhaust the literature. Indeed, throughout, references will be suggestive rather than "complete." My state-ment on the percentage of the population that citizens constituted is a sub-jective generalization, that is, a hunch, which will need documentation in my larger study. The situation varied widely, and it may well be that no general estimate is possible.

2. Archivio di Stato di Perugia, Catasto, Catastini, 30.

3. Archivio di Stato di Firenze, (ASF) Manoscritti, 419.

4. ASF, Provvisioni 39, ff. 120–120v; 163–163v; 186v–187; 40, ff. 30, 38v–39.

5. For example, ASF, Prov. 40 (Dec. 17, 1352) f. 39; the four sons of the deceased Count Guido Alberti de Mutigliano are to be *veri cives*; they are not required to buy a house, nor are office-holding restrictions to be ob-served. A century later, Prov. 152 (Oct. 27, 1461) ff. 185v–186v reveals similar privileges in a grant of citizenship to a knight, two doctors of law, and one of medicine.

6. Comparison of several redactions of Bolognese and Florentine statutes is possible. For Bologna, see Luigi Frati, *Statuti di Bologna dall' anno 1245 all' anno 1267* (3 vols., Bologna, 1869–1877), Augusto Gaudenzi, *Statuti della società del popolo* (2 vols., Rome, 1889–1896), Gina Fasoli and Pietro Sella, *Statuti di Bologna dell' anno 1288* in *Studi e Testi*, 73 and 85 (2 vols, Vatican City, 1937–1939). For Florence, see Alessandro Gherardi, *Le consulte della Repubblica Fiorentina dall' anno MCCLXXX al MCCXCVIII* (2 vols.; Florence, 1896–1898), Roberto Caggese, *Statuti della Repubblica Fiorentina* (2 vols., Florence, 1910–1921), *Statuta Florentie 1355*, ASF, Statuti 16, *Statuti populi et communis Florentie . . . anno Salutis MCCCCXV* (3 vols., Friburg, 1778–1783). The only satisfactory attempt to trace out a city's citizenship policy is that of Dina Bizzari, "Ricerche sul diritto di cittadinanza nella costituzione comunale" (Turin, 1916), extr. from *Studi Senesi* XXXII fasc. 1–2. Sections 1–11 of her work constitute a more or less formal analysis of the law of citizenship; the final

section (13) of some 25 pages is an attempt to relate changes in Sienese citizenship policy to changing social, economic and political conditions.

7. Luigi Frati, *Statuti di Bologna*, I, p. 475.

8. H. Baron neglects the importance of the legists' discussion of wealth and enjoyment throughout the fourteenth century in his now famous article, "Franciscan Poverty and Civic Wealth as Factors in the Rise of Humanistic Thought," in *Speculum* XIII (1938), pp. 1–38. Here as elsewhere Baron too strongly characterizes an age in terms of too few ideas or directions of thought. For discussions of these and related issues, see, for example: Petrus de Ancharano, *Consilia . . .* (Venice, 1585), cons. 298; Angelus de Ubaldis, *Consilia seu responsa* (Lyons, 1532), cons. 68; Lucas de Penna, *Commentaria* (Lyons, 1583), Proemium to his comment on Book 10 of the Code, and to C. 10.32.26; Baldus, *Opera* (Venice, 1586), to C. 10.32.26, and C. 4.12.3.

9. The idea is found in a variety of places. For example, Paul de Castro, *Consiliorum sive responsum volumen primum . . . tertium* (Venice, 1580–81), vol. I, cons. 397; Jason de Mayno, *Consiliorum sive responsorum volumen primum . . . quartum* (Venice, 1581), vol. III, cons. 116; Lucas de Penna, *Commentaria* (Lyons, 1583), to C. 10.32.26; Baldus, *Opera* (Venice, 1586), to C. 4.43.1; Bartolus, *Opera* (Venice, 1602), to D. 50.1.4, D. 50.1.6; and St. Thomas Aquinas, *Summa Theologica*, ed. A. G. Pegis (2 vols., New York, 1945), II-I, q. 105 art. 2 and 3.

10. L. Frati, *Statuti di Bologna* (1259), Book XI, rubric 80, in vol. III; F. Bonaini, *Statuti inediti della città di Pisa dal XII al XIV secolo* (3 vols., Florence, 1854–70), Breve Pisani communis (1286), Lib. I, cap. 48; G. Sandri, "Gli statuti veronesi del 1276 colle correzioni e le aggiunte fino al 1323" (2 vols., Venice, 1940–59) in *Monumenti storici pubblicati dalla deputazione di storia patria per le Venezie, nuova serie*, vols., III and XIII, Bk. I, cap. 227 in vol. I; ASF Prov. 20, ff. 31v–32; S. Gaddoni, "Statuti di Imola del secolo XIV. 1. Statuti della città (1334)" in *Corpus statutorum italicorum* n. 13 (Milan, 1932), Book I, rubr. 51, Book II, rubr. 46; and G. degli Azzi, *Statuti di Perugia dell'anno MCCCXLII* (2 vols., Rome, 1913–16), Bk. I, cap. 92, in vol. I.

11. Nicolai Rubinstein, "The Beginnings of Political Thought in Florence," in *Journal of the Warburg and Courtauld Institutes*, V (1942), 198–227. Bartolus, *Opera* (Venice, 1602), to D. 33.9.4,ss4, and to D. 50.16.2. See, too, Jason de Mayno, *Consiliorum* (Venice, 1581), vol. IV, cons. 371.

12. G. Fasoli and P. Sella, *Statuti di Bologna dell'anno 1288*, I, p. 341. The words are "illi de lingua forasteria". The vote on the issue was 217 to 122.

13. The crucial verses, in the translation of the text of the *Società Dantesca Italiana* by J. D. Sinclair (London, 1948), are as follows: "All who were there at that time between Mars and the Baptist able to bear arms were a fifth of the number now living, but the citizenship, which is now mixed with Campi and Certaldo and Figline, was seen pure in the humblest artisan. Ah, how much better would it be to have these people I name for neighbors, with your bounds at Galluzzo and Trespiano, than to have them inside and to endure the stench of the boor from Aguglion and of him from Signa who already has a sharp eye for jobbery!. . . . The mixture of peoples was ever the beginning of the city's ills, as food in excess is of the body's . . . "

14. *Comedia di Dante degli Allagherii col commento di Jacopo della Lana*, ed. L. Scarabelli (3 vols., Bologna, 1866–67), vol. III, pp. 255–57.

15. *L'Ottimo commento della Divina Commedia*, ed. A. Torri (3 vols., Pisa, 1827–29), vol. III, pp. 368–72.

16. *Petri Allegherii, super Dantis ipsius genitoris comoediam commentarium*, ed. V. Nannucci (Florence, 1845), pp. 657–58.

17. *Benvenuti de Rambaldis de Imola comentum super Dantis Aldigherii comoediam*, ed. J. Lacaita (5 vols., Florence, 1887), vol. V, pp. 163, 167.

18. If one is to judge from the great number of city and guild offices with terms of three, four, or six months, there must have been an expectation of rather frequent service, despite legislation that specified intervals between occupancy of a given office.

19. P. O. Kristeller, "Studies on Renaissance Humanism During the Last Twenty Years," in *Studies in the Renaissance* IX (1962), 14.

20. For the importance of bearing responsibility as a defining condition of citizen status, see, for example Azo [Pileus], *Summa* (Venice, 1610), to C. 10.39; and Baldus, *Opera* (Venice, 1586), to C. 4.12.3. On fulfilling the obligations of office, see my *Inalienability of Sovereignty in Medieval Political Thought* (New York, 1956), pp. 22–47 and the literature cited therein.

21. See my "The *consilia* literature: a Prospectus", in *Manuscripta* VI (1962), 3–22.

22. Bartolus, *Consilia* (Venice, 1576), vol. II, cons. 29.

23. Baldus, *Consiliorum* (Lyons, 1550), vol V, cons. 409.

24. Angelus de Ubaldis, *Consilia* (Lyons, 1532), cons. 351.

25. On these concepts, see especially the studies of Gaines Post now collected in his *Studies in Medieval Legal Thought* (Princeton, 1964).

26. Paul de Castro, *Consiliorum* (Venice, 1580), vol. II, cons. 234.

27. Jason de Mayno, *Consiliorum* (Venice, 1581), vol. III, cons. 316.

28. Paul de Castro, *Consiliorum* (Venice, 1580), vol. I, cons. 21.

29. Alexander de Imola, *Liber primus . . . septimus consiliorum* (Lyons, 1549), vol. VI, cons. 99.

30. See above, n. 20.

31. Lucas de Penna, *Commentaria* (Lyons, 1583), to C. 10.39.1, and C. 10.40.7.

32. Baldus, *Opera* (Venice, 1586), to C. 6.42.31; C. 6.23.9; D. 1.1.2; *In decretales subtilissima commentaria* (Venice, 1571), to X. 1.3.36.

33. Bartolus, *Opera* (Venice, 1602), to D. 50.16.2, D. 48.5.16, D. 33.9.4.ss4, C. 10.40.4, C. 10.40.7, C. 10.39.2, and C. 10.39.4.

34. G. Almond and S. Verba, *The Civic Culture: Political Attitudes and Democracy in Five Nations* (Princeton, 1963). This is a brilliant comparative study of political attitudes, faiths, and practices in Mexico, Italy, W. Germany, the U.S.A., and Great Britain. About 1000 persons in each country were asked probing questions on the basis of the answers to which the authors have attempted to describe current political practices and relate these and attitudes to past history. In its suggestiveness and for its methodology, the book has already become a classic of modern research. Despite the queries recently raised with respect to validity of the data reported from some of the subject countries, the book remains extremely valuable given the quality of its conceptual approach.

35. *Cronica Aquilana rimata di Buccio di Ranallo di Poppolito di Aquila*, ed. V. de Bartholomaeis (Rome, 1907), pp. 3, 18–19, 25, 47.

36. Bonvicinus de Rippa, "De magnalibus urbis Mediolani", ed. F. Novati in *Bullettino dell'Istituto Storico Italiano*, XX (Rome, 1898), especially the prologue, ch. 3 and 6. Hans Baron finds here only what he is looking for, a "medieval work" and does not do it justice. See the new edition of his *The Crisis of the Early Italian Renaissance* (Princeton, 1966), pp. 196–98.

37. Antonio Pucci, *Poesie*, ed. F. Ildefonso di San Luigi (4 vols., Florence, 1772–75; vols. 3–6 of the *Delizie degli eruditi toscani*), vol. IV, pp. 210, 264–65. For Florence in the thirteenth century, see above, n. 11.

38. *Ibid.*, pp. 233–34. On public funerals, see Lauro Martines, *The Social World of the Florentine Humanists* (Princeton, 1963), pp. 239–45.

39. J. K. Hyde, *Padua in the Age of Dante* (Manchester, 1966), especially ch. 7, "The Commune and the Pars Marchionis," pp. 193–219.

40. For the distinction that came with public office, see L. Martines, *The Social World*, especially ch. 4, "Public Office in the Humanist Circle," pp. 145–98.

41. Almond and Verba, *The Civic Culture*, ch. 1, "An Approach to Political Culture," pp. 3–42.

42. Jerrold Seigel, " 'Civic Humanism' or Ciceronian Rhetoric? The Culture of Petrarch and Bruni," *Past and Present*, XXXIV (July, 1966), pp. 3–48. See, too Peter Herde, "Politik und Rhetorik in Florenz am Vorabend der Renaissance," in *Archiv für Kulturgeschichte* Band 47, heft 2 (1965), pp. 141–220.

43. This is one burden of Baron's life work, re-emphasized strongly in the revised one-volume edition of his *Crisis* published in 1966. Sympathetic to Baron's stress upon civic humanism is Eugenio Garin, for example in his *L'umanesimo italiano* (Bari, 1958; first Italian ed. 1951.)

44. ASF, Consulte e practiche, 34, ff. 145–147v. Revealed here are discussions held from January 6, 1400 (1401) to January 11, during which time the details of a conspiracy to aid Milan were uncovered.

INDEX